COMMON INTERESTS IN INTERNATIONAL LITIGATION

COMMON INTERESTS IN INTERNATIONAL LITIGATION

A Case Study on Natural Resource Exploitation Disputes

Claire Buggenhoudt

intersentia
Cambridge – Antwerp – Portland

Intersentia Ltd
Sheraton House | Castle Park
Cambridge | CB3 0AX | United Kingdom
Tel.: +44 1223 370 170 | Fax: +44 1223 370 169
Email: mail@intersentia.co.uk
www.intersentia.com | www.intersentia.co.uk

Distribution for the UK and Ireland:
NBN International
Airport Business Centre, 10 Thornbury Road
Plymouth, PL6 7 PP
United Kingdom
Tel.: +44 1752 202 301 | Fax: +44 1752 202 331
Email: orders@nbninternational.com

Distribution for Europe and all other countries:
Intersentia Publishing nv
Groenstraat 31
2640 Mortsel
Belgium
Tel.: +32 3 680 15 50 | Fax: +32 3 658 71 21
Email: mail@intersentia.be

Distribution for the USA and Canada:
International Specialized Book Services
920 NE 58th Ave. Suite 300
Portland, OR 97213
USA
Tel.: +1 800 944 6190 (toll free) | Fax: +1 503 280 8832
Email: info@isbs.com

Common Interests in International Litigation. A Case Study on Natural Resource Exploitation Disputes

ISBN 978-1-78068-446-8
D/2017/7849/4
NUR 828

British Library Cataloguing in Publication Data. A catalogue record for this book is available from the British Library.

ACKNOWLEDGEMENTS

This book concerns issues of common interests in international law. It was written as a thesis for the degree of doctor of law between 2009 and 2015. A common interest, to me, is an interest that reflects a shared value and requires collective action. In other words, a common interest is an interest that no one can reach alone and an interest of which no one person can reap all the benefits. In the same vein, one could describe academic research as a shared value within the academic community. However, it is the element of collective action that makes the process of writing a dissertation a true common interest (within a limited community). I could not have finished this work alone and I hope I am not the only one who will enjoy the finished result. Therefore, I would like to express my gratitude to all of you who have contributed to this collective effort.

First and foremost I would like to thank my supervisor, Prof. Dr Koen De Feyter, for believing in me, challenging me and giving me the freedom to find my own path while providing exactly the right amount of guidance. Furthermore, I am deeply indebted to the members of my individual doctoral committee. Prof. Dr Alexia Herwig, Prof. Dr Frank Maes and Prof. Dr Wouter Vandenhole, thank you for the detailed feedback after each meeting, the numerous academic opportunities you provided and the encouragement throughout.

I would also like to thank my colleagues at the University of Antwerp for creating a workplace where both the highs and lows of thesis writing can be shared. Special thanks go to the members of the Law and Development research group, who have enriched both my research and my life in many ways.

Last but not least, I would like to thank my family and friends for their sustained efforts in understanding my work and the support they have given me in every area of life. My special thanks go to my son Wannes, who kept me calm, happy and tired during the final months of this process, and Pieter, who taught me that 'the taste of love is sweet'.

CONTENTS

TABLE OF CASES

AFRICAN COMMISSION ON HUMAN AND PEOPLES' RIGHTS

EUROPEAN COURT OF HUMAN RIGHTS

INTER-AMERICAN COMMISSION AND COURT OF HUMAN RIGHTS

INTERNATIONAL CENTRE FOR SETTLEMENT OF INVESTMENT DISPUTES

INTERNATIONAL COURT OF JUSTICE

INTERNATIONAL CRIMINAL TRIBUNAL FOR THE FORMER YUGOSLAVIA

INTERNATIONAL TRIBUNAL FOR THE LAW OF THE SEA

PERMANENT COURT OF INTERNATIONAL JUSTICE

UNCITRAL

WORLD TRADE ORGANIZATION

LIST OF ABBREVIATIONS

AB	Appellate Body of the World Trade Organization
ACHPR	African Commission on Human and Peoples' Rights
ACtHPR	African Court on Human and Peoples' Rights
BIT	Bilateral Investment Treaty
CITES	Convention on International Trade in Endangered Species
DSM	Dispute Settlement Mechanism
DSU	Dispute Settlement Understanding
ECHR	European Convention on Human Rights
ECtHR	European Court of Human Rights
EEZ	exclusive economic zone
EIA	environmental impact assessment
FET	Fair and Equitable Treatment
GATS	WTO General Agreement on Trade in Services
GATT	WTO General Agreement on Tariffs and Trade
IACtHR	Inter-American Court of Human Rights
ICJ	International Court of Justice
ICRW	International Convention for the Regulation of Whaling
ICSID	International Centre for Settlement of Investment Disputes
ICTY	International Criminal Tribunal for the Former Yugoslavia
IEL	International Environmental Law
IIA	International Investment Agreement
ILC	International Law Commission
ITLOS	International Tribunal for the Law of the Sea
IUU	illegal, unregulated and unreported
MFN	Most Favoured Nation
NAFTA	North American Free Trade Agreement
NGO	non-governmental organisation
NT	National Treatment
PPM	Process and Production Method
SPS	WTO Agreement on the Application of Sanitary and Phytosanitary Measures
TBT	Technical Barriers to Trade (WTO Agreement)

TRIPS	Trade Related Aspects of Intellectual Property Rights (WTO Agreement)
UNCLOS	United Nations Convention on the Law of the Sea
UNEP	United Nations Environment Programme
VCLT	Vienna Convention on the Law of Treaties
WTO	World Trade Organization

CHAPTER 1
INTRODUCTION AND RESEARCH DESIGN

International law is finally overcoming the legal as well as moral deficiencies of bilateralism and maturing into a much more socially conscious legal order. Thus, a rising awareness of the common interests of the international community, a community that comprises not only States, but in the last instance all human beings, has begun to change the nature of international law profoundly.

B. Simma[1]

The emergence of different concepts of common interest in international law has sparked an increasing interest in the use of this concept among international lawyers, both inside and outside of academia.[2] International law has always been a balancing act. It continuously reconciles the national interests of different States with the shared interests that those States have identified at the international level, for example in international Treaties. However, it is not clear how, legally speaking, the new dimension of common interests, or interests of the international community as a whole, fits into this existing balance. This is especially true in the context of the international judicial system, which lacks the 'constitutional world court' that may seem necessary to enforce common interests at the international level. The proliferation of international law has created an international judiciary that consists of different courts each living on their separate island and focusing on the values that are being enforced by their island's regime.

In the present study, the practice of various international courts and tribunals will be analysed to identify whether and how these bodies reconcile the existence of common interests of the global community with the rules of their specific regime. At the same time, the study will examine how the different

1 B. Simma, 'From Bilateralism to Community Interest in International Law' (1994) 250 *Recueil des Cours (Collected Courses of the Hague Academy of International Law)* 217, 234.

2 See, for example, in the academic community: the edited volume of U. Fastenrath, R. Geiger, D.-E. Khan, A. Paulus, S. von Schorlemer and C. Vedder, *From Bilateralism to Community Interest – Essays in Honour of Judge Bruno Simma*, Oxford University Press, Oxford 2011. Outside of academia: the Universal Declaration for the Common Good of Humanity Project, an international collaboration of jurists and social leaders that formally presented this declaration at the 2013 World Social Forum in Tunisia (see <www.forumdesalternatives.org/en/universal-declaration-for-the-common-good-of-humanity-project>, last accessed June 2015).

judicial bodies balance their Treaty regime with the national interests of the litigating States. A similar tension exists, and a parallel can be drawn, between the consideration of domestic national interests and that of common interests by international dispute settlement bodies: first, because both the global common interest and the national interest may conflict with interests explicitly protected in an international Treaty regime; and secondly, because the national interests defended by individual States before the international judicial bodies often overlap with interests shared by the international community. The practice of the selected judicial bodies will be studied on the basis of the bodies' case law on natural resource exploitation, which will function as a case study for the approach to public and common interests in general.

The aim of this introductory chapter is twofold. First, it will introduce the background of the research and explain the link between the analytical, case study, research and the final part, which will explain why judicial bodies approach common interests in a certain way and will attempt to offer a framework to mitigate some of the negative effects of the fragmentation of international law. Secondly, the definitions and methodology used in the research as well as the structure of the book will be explained.

1.1. BACKGROUND

By way of introduction, the history and nature of international law will briefly be described. This description will introduce two, fairly recent, developments in international law that will serve as the background to this study; the emergence of the common interest in international law and the proliferation of international judicial bodies. The two discussed evolutions will subsequently be linked to the question of how different international judicial bodies approach common interests.

1.1.1. HISTORY AND NATURE OF INTERNATIONAL LAW

After the Peace of Westphalia, the modern nation State emerged in Europe as an entity with absolute sovereignty within its territorial boundaries. In this context, scholars from two different European legal schools, the 16th-century naturalist and the more modern positivist school, laid the foundations of modern international law.[3] Positivism emphasised the State as the main actor

[3] For a discussion on the role of European colonialism in the formation of international law see A. Anghie, *Imperialism, Sovereignty and the Making of International Law*, Cambridge University Press, Cambridge 2007, p 361.

in international law. In essence, the positivist school considered international law to be nothing more than the reality of what happened between States on the international level.[4] In the 17th and 18th centuries, this reality was limited to agreements and customs recognised by States. Instances of continued cooperation between States did not exist.[5] Naturalists, on the other hand, argued that a social contract exists between the individual and the State that justifies the power of the State – the foundation of modern democracy.[6]

Due to both the development of more complex domestic law and the growth of State powers during the 19th century, the State was more and more seen as a sovereign 'body' with its own 'will' whose laws did not need to be legitimised by others. The theory of positivism flourished and on the international level the State was considered to be the sovereign and supreme.[7] Because international law was defined as a law of contract, a law that governs the relations between States, the State was only considered bound by laws to which it consented itself. The well-known *Lotus* judgment of the Permanent Court of International Justice established that '[r]estrictions on the independence of States cannot ... be presumed'.[8]

Until the Second World War, the main aim of international law was to preserve each State's sovereign rights and to resolve disputes in the exercise of territorial jurisdictions on the basis of those rights.[9] This was confirmed in the *Island of Palmas* case.

> The development of the national organisation of States during the last few centuries and, as a corollary, the development of international law, has established [the] principle of the exclusive competence of the State in regard to its own territory in such a way as to make it the point of departure in settling most questions that concern international relations.[10]

---

4 Positivism has prevailed since the 19th century until today and determines that a State can only be bound by the rules to which it has consented.

5 For a concise overview of the history of international law see M. Shaw, *International Law*, Cambridge University Press, Cambridge 2003, pp 24–26.

6 The natural law theory prevailed from the 16th century to the end of the 18th century and assigns a central role to the individual in international law. It believed that 'the natural law' could be found through the employment of reason and assumed that the agreements and customs recognised by the State evolved from the social contract and therefore *ought* to be. Ibid, 26.

7 Ibid, 26–29. On positivism and naturalism in the 19th century see S. Neff, *A Short History of International Law*, Pre-publication Draft, 2003, available at <www.oup.com>, 14–21 (later published in *International Law*, Oxford University Press, Oxford 2003, pp 31–58).

8 PCIJ, *The Case of the S.S. Lotus (France v Turkey)*, Judgment of 1927, p 18. This quote became known as the 'Lotus principle'.

9 S. Villalpando, 'The Legal Dimension of the International Community: How Community Interests Are Protected in International Law' (2010) 21 *European Journal of International Law* 387, 390.

10 Arbitral award, *Case of Island of Palmas (Netherlands v United States of America)*, Judgment of 1928.

However, the scope of international law has been gradually expanding since the beginning of the 20th century. Globalisation and technical developments led to an increasingly interdependent world. In light of this growing interdependence, Treaties were agreed upon to establish friendship and cooperation between different States. Although international law was historically limited to regulations on the preservation of peace and rules of war, it now encompasses a wide variety of issues, such as regulations on space, the international financial system, world trade and environmental protection. While ultimately these rules also aim to preserve the interests of the sovereign nations, the net of obligations and rights that exists between States now embraces 'all the interests of contemporary international life'.[11] As a result, the expansion of international law also led to a multiplication of actors and more sophisticated follow-up machineries.[12]

In the following sections, two developments will be discussed that have been brought about by the expansion of international law. The first section will discuss the emergence of the common interest. In the course of establishing more intense international cooperation, States encountered common interests, interests that could only be satisfied fully if all States engaged in their protection.[13] As a consequence, a shift is taking place in international law from a purely bilateral understanding to a model that also considers common interests. Secondly, the proliferation of international judicial bodies and the issue of fragmentation will be discussed. The development of new legal regimes in international law led to the establishment of new (quasi) judicial bodies to help with the implementation and interpretation of the relevant Treaties. Because of the lack of hierarchy between these bodies, the concern was raised that the proliferation of judicial bodies would threaten the unity of international law.

1.1.2. EMERGENCE OF THE COMMON INTEREST IN INTERNATIONAL LAW

As stated above, the expansion of international law led to a gradual introduction of common interests in positive international law. International law traditionally served to protect the State's absolute sovereign right to pursue the public interest as defined by the State itself.[14] During the previous century, international law gradually transformed to a regime that no longer accepts the public interest of a State as absolute but subjects State measures taken 'in the national interest' to the scrutiny of the international judiciary. Examples of this type of judicial review

---

11 Shaw, above n 5, p 43; Villalpando, above n 9, 390.

12 P.-M. Dupuy, 'The Danger of Fragmentation or Unification of the International Legal System and the International Court of Justice' (1999) 31 *International Law and Politics* 791, 795.

13 For a definition of common interest, as used in this study, see pp 17ff.

14 For a definition of public interest, as used in this study, see pp 17ff.

include the interpretation of the public interest exception to the right to property by the European Court of Human Rights (ECtHR) and the interpretation of the general exceptions clauses in Article XX of the General Agreement on Tariffs and Trade (GATT) by the World Trade Organization's (WTO) panels and Appellate Body (AB).[15]

Furthermore, a new form of interests, namely common interests, was introduced in international law.[16] The recognition of common interests was described by Wolfgang Friedmann as one of the features of the transition in international law from a law of coexistence to a law of cooperation.[17] It seems that in the process of a more intensified cooperation, States became aware of the importance of protecting certain common interests, such as peace, humanity and the environment. The ambivalence towards these interests in earlier times may be explained by the lack of interchange at the level of products, capital, people and knowledge.[18] When there is only limited interaction between States, it is, for example, unlikely that States in one continent would be aware of an environmental disaster occurring in another continent and its consequences for the global environment.[19] However, when there is higher level of interchange between States, States will come more easily to the realisation that the interests of all States are harmed by one State's failure to protect the environment. As a consequence, the incentive to agree on a global obligation to protect the environment is much higher.

Besides solving disputes between sovereign interests, the aim of international law has now expanded to the preservation and protection of common interests. In the following pages, the introduction of common interests in international law will be explored. Four examples will be given of common interests that have been explicitly recognised in positive international law. The examples will show that international law has developed a number of concepts to indicate the common interest in upholding certain values or protecting certain goods, such as the 'common heritage of mankind' or the 'common concern of mankind'.[20]

The issues that will be discussed are peace and security, environmental concerns, spaces beyond national territorial jurisdiction, and human rights. Before examining the selected examples of recognised common interests, it must be stressed that this list is not exhaustive. The selection was made on the

15 See p 89 (WTO) and p 117 (ECtHR).

16 See examples on pp 6ff.

17 See W. Friedmann, *The Changing Structure of International Law*, Columbia University Press, New York 1964, p 367.

18 Villalpando, above n 9, 393.

19 Environmental disaster should here be understood as a disaster due to human activity, in contrast to a natural disaster.

20 The definition of common interests used to delineate this study is elaborated in detail in the next section. See pp 17ff.

basis of the common interests that are likely to be affected in disputes on natural resource exploitation. Other interests, such as the protection of the world's cultural heritage, could also be included.[21] Trade liberalisation will, however, not be considered a common interest in this study. Although the WTO's purpose is to raise standards of living, which could be considered a common interest, the WTO agreements do not impose any obligations on States to redistribute the benefits of trade liberalisation in such a way that standards of living are raised.[22] Therefore, the protection and preservation of free trade that is pursued by the WTO agreements is not considered a common interest.

1.1.2.1. Peace and Security

One of the first issues that was recognised by States as an interest of the international community as a whole, rather than that of individual States, is international peace and security. In the preamble to the Charter of the United Nations, it is stated that one of the goals for the establishment of the UN is 'to unite our strength to maintain international peace and security'.[23] Therefore, Article 24 of the UN Charter, read together with the first paragraph of the preamble, Article 1 and Chapter VII, provide that recourse to military force by individual States is, in principle, forbidden, and that the use of force may only be authorised by the Security Council in the interest of maintaining or restoring international peace and security.

While the mandate of the Security Council to protect international peace and security was traditionally considered to be limited to preventing and ending violent conflict between States, a broader interpretation imposes itself. Although the Security Council's activities in the past were focused on the use of force in inter-State conflicts, it now also acts in instances of internal conflict. The UN Charter concept of international peace and security is now also used to protect groups and individuals against gross and systematic human rights violations internally.[24] This change in the Security Council's approach gives weight to the idea that the maintenance of peace and security is an interest of the international community, regardless of the inter-State context.[25] The same idea is raised by

---

21 A more complete list, including an analysis of how common interests are protected in international law, can be found in K. De Feyter, *Globalization and Shared Responsibilities of States*, Ashgate, London 2012.

22 Preamble Marrakesh Agreement Establishing the World Trade Organization of 15 April 1994, United Nations Treaty Series, vol. 1867, 154.

23 Preamble Charter of the United Nations of 26 June 1945, Treaty Series, 993.

24 For example, in the recent conflict in Libya, the binding Security Council resolutions 1970 and 1973, identified the existence of a threat to international peace and security and drew a number of legal consequences.

25 R. Wolfrum, 'Enforcing Community Interests through International Dispute Settlement: Reality or Utopia?' in U. Fastenrath, R. Geiger, D.-E. Khan, A. Paulus, S. von Schorlemer

the responsibility to protect, which attributes to the international community the responsibility to intervene if the State fails to protect its citizens from mass atrocities.[26] In a similar vein, the International Criminal Court was set up on the basis of complementary jurisdiction because 'grave crimes threaten the peace, security and well-being of the world'.[27] From these practices it can be concluded that the protection of peace and security, which is broader than inter-State peace and security, is considered a common interest in international law.

1.1.2.2. Environmental Concerns

Environmental protection was first linked to the common interest in the 1972 Stockholm Declaration on the Human Environment, which stated that 'to defend and improve the human environment for present and future generations has become an imperative goal for mankind'.[28] This link was confirmed in the 1973 CITES Treaty on the protection of endangered species.[29] The 'common concern of mankind' was first introduced in 1988 by General Assembly Resolution 43/53, which defined climate change as a common concern of mankind, a statement that was later confirmed in the preamble to the UN Framework Convention on Climate Change.[30] The same concept was included in the preamble to the Convention on Biological Diversity to confirm that the purpose of the Convention was a common concern of humankind.[31]

The shift to an approach focused on the common interest of humankind, rather than that of States, was endorsed in subsequent environmental instruments,[32] especially in the Rio Declaration of 1992, which introduced the principle

and C. Vedder (eds), *From Bilateralism to Community Interest – Essays in Honour of Judge Bruno Simma*, Oxford University Press, Oxford 2011, p 1134.

26 World Summit Outcome, UN General Assembly Resolution of 2005 UN Doc. A/RES/60/1.

27 Preamble Rome Statute of the International Criminal Court of 17 July 1998, UN Treaty Series, vol. 2187, 90.

28 Declaration of the United Nations Conference on the Human Environment of 1973 UN Doc. A/Conf.48/14/Rev. 1.

29 Convention on International Trade in Endangered Species of Wild Fauna and Flora of 3 March 1973, UN Treaty Series, vol. 993, 243.

30 Protection of Global Climate for Present and Future Generations of Mankind, UN General Assembly Resolution of 1988 UN Doc. A/RES/43/53; United Nations Framework Convention on Climate Change of 9 May 1992, UN Treaty Series, vol. 1771, 107.

31 Preamble Convention on Biological Diversity of 5 July 1992, UN Treaty Series, vol. 1760, 79. UNEP equally chose to incorporate the concept of common concern in its preamble. It is said that UNEP chose this concept because it had no specific legal connotations at the time. M. Fitzmaurice, 'International Protection of the Environment' (2001) 293 *Recueil des Cours (Collected Courses of the Hague Academy of International Law)* 9, 163.

32 S. Stec, 'Humanitarian Limits to Sovereignty: Common Concern and Common Heritage Approaches to Natural Resources and Environment' (2010) 12 *International Community Law Review* 361, 368.

of sustainable development.[33] Sustainable development linked the issue of environmental concerns with social and economic considerations. The common interest character of sustainable development was further reflected in its goal of preserving natural resources for future generations.[34] Through the concept of sustainable development, the common interest in environmental protection has been recognised to go well beyond the settlement of conflicts over acute industrial pollution.[35]

1.1.2.3. *Areas beyond National Territorial Jurisdiction*

In a discussion on issues of common interest, the protection of the so-called common areas (such as the high seas and outer space) and the resources located in those areas (such as the resources under the deep seabed) automatically springs to mind. While concepts such as 'common concern' and 'common heritage of mankind' should not be treated as equivalents to the common interest concept, they are closely interlinked.[36] The term 'common interest' already appeared in the 1946 International Convention for the Regulation of Whaling. This Convention confirmed the 'interest of the nations of the world in safeguarding for future generations the great natural resources represented by the whale stocks'.[37] In the context of outer space, the 1967 Outer Space Treaty established the 'common interest of all mankind in the progress of the exploration and use of outer space for peaceful purposes'.[38] These examples clarify that, in the context of goods beyond national jurisdiction, the common interest refers to security as well as environmental interests.[39]

In contrast to the common interest concept, the 'common heritage of mankind' has a more specific meaning and seems to generate specific legal consequences. The concept of the common heritage of mankind was developed in the context of the law of the sea. It was first used as a legal concept in the 1970 UN Resolution on the use of the seabed, the ocean floors and its resources 'in the interest of

33 Rio Declaration on Environment and Development of 1992 UN Doc. A/CONF. 151/26.

34 Wolfrum, above n 25, p 1136.

35 Stec, above n 32, 371.

36 The concept of common concern leaves existing legal regimes intact. E. Hey, 'Global Environmental Law: Common Interests and the (Re)Constitution of Public Space' (2009) 1 *Iustum Aequum Salutare* 41, 43.

37 Preamble International Convention for the Regulation of Whaling of 2 December 1946, UN Treaty Series, vol. 155, 349.

38 Preamble Treaty on Principles Governing the Activities of States in the Exploration and Use of Outer Space, Including the Moon and Other Celestial Bodies of 27 January 1967, UN Treaty Series, vol. 610, 205.

39 Stec, above n 32, 365–366.

mankind'.[40] This resolution would later become the basis of Part XI of the 1982 UN Convention on the Law of the Sea.[41] The concept was also included in the 1979 Moon Treaty.[42] In these two Treaties four qualities were attached to the common heritage of mankind: non-appropriation, international management, sharing of benefits and use for peaceful purposes.[43] However, there does not seem to be agreement on the exact definition of the term and whether it has consequences besides those explicitly provided for in each regime.[44]

1.1.2.4. Protection of Human Rights

In contrast to the issues of common interest discussed above, which all address the interest of the community of States as such, the implementation and enforcement of human rights benefits individuals. The question therefore arises why human rights are of common interest. It is not obvious that the international community, especially the community of States, has an interest in the protection of human rights. Traditionally, human rights protection was based on reciprocity in the protection of foreign nationals. Therefore, it was considered an individual interest of each State. However, this focus on the protection of foreign nationals was later abandoned and human rights protection broadened to the protection of all humans with the establishment of the UN and the enactment of international human rights Conventions. The Universal Declaration of Human Rights recognises that the 'recognition of the ... rights of all members of the human family is the foundation of freedom, justice and peace in the world'.[45] As

---

40 Declaration of Principles Governing the Sea-Bed and the Ocean Floor, and the Subsoil Thereof, Beyond the Limits of National Jurisdiction, UN General Assembly Resolution of 1970 UN Doc. A/RES/25/2749 (XXV).

41 United Nations Convention on the Law of the Sea of 10 December 1982, UN Treaty Series, vol. 1833, 3; Agreement relating to the Implementation of Part XI of the United Nations Convention on the Law of the Sea of 10 December 1982 of 28 July 1994, UN Treaty Series, vol. 1836, 42.

42 Agreement Governing the Activities of States on the Moon and Other Celestial Bodies of 5 December 1979, UN Treaty Series, vol. 1363, 3.

43 FITZMAURICE, above n 31, 153.

44 The 'heritage of mankind' concept is most often cited in the context of the protection of the world's cultural heritage (it is used in the preamble to the UNESCO Convention Concerning the Protection of the World Cultural and Natural Heritage of 23 November 1972, UN Treaty Series, vol. 1037, 151). However, it remains unclear what consequences are attached to it in this context. On this topic see J.P. FISHMAN, 'Locating the International Interest in Intranational Cultural Property Disputes' (2009) 35 *Yale Journal of International Law* 347, 374–404; F. FRANCIONI, 'Beyond State Sovereignty: The Protection of Cultural Heritage as a Shared Interest of Humanity' (2004) 25 *Michigan Journal of International Law* 1209, 1209–28.

45 Preamble Universal Declaration of Human Rights, UN General Assembly Resolution of 1948 UN Doc. A/810 at 71.

a consequence, human rights protection is no longer a purely national interest, it is a common interest.[46]

After the Second World War, States aimed to maintain international peace and security by the creation of a universal political organisation based on the fundamental values of humanity. The recognition of human rights of all humans independent of their nationality was a first step in that process.[47] As stated by the UN Charter, one of the purposes of the UN is to 'achieve international co-operation in … promoting and encouraging respect for human rights and for fundamental freedoms for all'.[48] Furthermore, the Member States 'pledge themselves to take joint and separate action in cooperation with the Organization for the achievement of … universal respect for, and observance of, human rights and fundamental freedoms for all'.[49] Thus, the international community placed the duty to cooperate at the heart of human rights protection and implicitly recognised the protection of human rights as a common interest of States because, in the long term, the realisation of human rights is in the interest of all States and their inhabitants.[50]

1.1.3. PROLIFERATION OF INTERNATIONAL JUDICIAL BODIES

The general expansion of international law not only led to the emergence of common interests in international law, it also led to a significant expansion of international litigation.[51] Since the early 1990s, both the number of judicial bodies and the number of litigated cases have multiplied. On the one hand, the establishment of new courts and tribunals attracted new topics and disputes to the international level. On the other hand, the dockets of the more traditional judicial bodies, such as the International Court of Justice (ICJ) and the ECtHR, have never been as loaded as in the last couple of years.

In the last three decades, a number of new (quasi) judicial bodies have been established, including the African Court on Human and Peoples' Rights, the

46 Wolfrum, above n 25, p 1137.

47 D. Shelton, 'Common Concern of Humanity' (2009) 1 *Iustum Aequum Salutare* 33, 35. This evolution was inspired by humanitarian law, which provides for the protection of humans as such and not because of their nationality.

48 Preamble Charter of the United Nations of 26 June 1945, Treaty Series, 993.

49 Ibid, Articles 55–56.

50 See A. Paulus, 'Reciprocity Revisited' in U. Fastenrath, R. Geiger, D.-E. Khan, A. Paulus, S. von Schorlemer and C. Vedder (eds), *From Bilateralism to Community Interest – Essays in Honour of Judge Bruno Simma*, Oxford University Press, Oxford 2011, pp 125–26; Wolfrum, above n 25, p 1136.

51 For an introduction to this topic see M. Rask Madsen, 'Judicial Globalization: The Proliferation of International Courts' in S. Cassese (ed), *Research Handbook on Global Administrative Law*, Edward Elgar, Cheltenham 2016.

International Tribunal for the Law of the Sea, the WTO panels and AB, the International Criminal Court and the World Bank Inspection Panel.[52] This proliferation of international judicial mechanisms is caused, inter alia, by the establishment of new international organisations with a specific or regional focus in addition to the more universal and general organisations.[53] One of the reasons for the creation of these more specialised organisations is that States have become more interdependent as a consequence of economic globalisation. The increasing interdependence between States resulted in more complex problems and disputes at the international level, which States preferred to deal with in the context of specialised regimes. Moreover, the existing general court, the ICJ, seemed to operate too slowly to deal with this growing number of 'specialised' disputes. Thus, a number of (quasi) judicial bodies were created to answer the needs of different legal regimes, such as international investment law and the law of the sea.[54]

At the same time, the caseload of the international judicial bodies has increased significantly. Two prominent examples of the 'boom' in judicial dispute settlement at the transnational level are the ECtHR and the WTO Dispute Settlement Body. The ECtHR, which mainly receives individual claims, has witnessed a ten-fold multiplication of its pending applications in the 21st century, reaching a total of 151,600 pending applications allocated to a judicial formation in 2011.[55] The WTO Dispute Settlement Body, a purely inter-State dispute settlement mechanism, was equally successful. It recorded circa 500 requests for consultations following its establishment in 1995, a number that completely overshadows the total of 131 cases that were dealt with by its predecessor in the period 1948–94.[56]

The increase in international litigation shows that both State and non-State actors have grown more willing to submit their disputes to adjudication. Three reasons may be cited for this growing dependence on judicial decisions. First, since the end of the Cold War there has been a general shift towards relying on the rule of law at the international level.[57] Secondly, the positive experiences with international adjudication have probably led State and non-State actors to be more open to this kind of dispute settlement. Because of their more

52 Some of these institutions will be examined in the case study. Other examples are the ad hoc Tribunals for Rwanda and Yugoslavia.

53 C. Brown, *A Common Law of International Adjudication*, Oxford University Press, Oxford 2007, p 16.

54 Ibid, 23.

55 In 2012, for the first time since 1998, this number decreased to 128,100. Statistics available at <www.echr.coe.int> under Statistics (last accessed June 2015).

56 Both pre- and post-GATT numbers available at <www.wto.org> under Disputes (last accessed June 2015).

57 Brown, above n 53, p 22.

limited issue area, specialised judicial bodies have been able to develop a more efficient and sophisticated jurisprudence.[58] Thirdly, the more complex and evolved international law becomes, the more States need the help of judicial bodies to determine their rights and obligations.[59] Therefore the proliferation of international courts and tribunals should not be seen as a negative evolution. In general, it has expanded the scope of international disputes that are justiciable and has made international law less dependent on its subjects, thus more objective.[60]

However, parallel to the proliferation of international courts and tribunals, concern has risen over the so-called fragmentation of the international legal system, or at least the interpretation of its norms. In this context, the International Law Commission (ILC) has made a distinction between the substantive and the institutional fragmentation of international law.[61] From a substantive perspective, law itself is fragmented into special regimes that may not be coherent or even conflicting.[62] From an institutional perspective, there may be a lack of practical coordination and institutional hierarchy. Therefore, fragmentation implies that international courts and tribunals need to 'pay attention to each other's jurisprudence'.[63]

In most States, a two-tiered system exists for the judiciary to deal with conflicts of interests. In the first place, the judicial bodies will be guided by a set of substantive values that have been identified as superior. These values are often protected in the constitution. Secondly, an institutional structure will exist, a list of instances that will successively decide on the balance of interests. So, in the end, even when it is impossible to determine with certainty which substantive interest should prevail, there will be only one institution to make that decision.[64]

---

58 A. Paulus, *From Territoriality to Functionality? Towards a Legal Methodology of Globalization*, Pre-publication Draft, 2004, available at <www.cpogg.org> (published in *Governance and International Legal Theory*, Martinus Nijhoff, Leiden 2004, pp 59–95), 15; G. Hafner, 'Pros and Cons Ensuing from Fragmentation of International Law' (2004) 25 *Michigan Journal of International Law* 849, 859.

59 Dupuy, above n 12, 806.

60 Ibid, 796.

61 Difficulties arising from the Diversification and Expansion of International Law, International Law Commission Report of the Study Group on Fragmentation of International Law of 2003, UN Doc. A/CN.4/L.644, paras. 6–7. The ILC chose to focus on the substantive fragmentation of international law in its reports.

62 Not all commentators agree on this topic. Cassese suggested that fragmentation on the substantive level is countered by the 'cross-fertilization' of different regimes and international law is becoming more integrated, not fragmented. A. Cassese, *International Law*, Oxford University Press, Oxford 2001, p 45.

63 Difficulties arising from the Diversification and Expansion of International Law, International Law Commission Report of the Study Group on Fragmentation of International Law of 2003 UN Doc. A/CN.4/L.644, para. 6. This was also explicitly recognised in Article 61 of the African Charter on Human and Peoples' Rights of 21 October 1986, OAU Doc. CAB/LEG/67/3 rev. 5.

64 Paulus, above n 58, 4.

In international law, there are no rules of hierarchy. No formal links exist between the different courts and tribunals and there is no final arbiter to decide on conflicting interests. The International Criminal Tribunal for the Former Yugoslavia (ICTY) Appeals Chamber aptly described this situation in its *Tadić* decision:

> International law, because it lacks a centralized structure, does not provide for an integrated judicial system operating an orderly division of labour among a number of tribunals, where certain aspects or components of jurisdiction as a power could be centralized or vested in one of them but not the others. In international law, every tribunal is a self-contained system (unless otherwise provided).[65]

There have been attempts at introducing substantive as well as institutional hierarchy at the international level.[66] In the substantive category, the concept of *jus cogens* obligations should be mentioned. This concept establishes superior rules that could give guidance to international courts and tribunals in the case of conflicting interests.[67] However, only a few values have been recognised as *jus cogens* obligations.[68] As a consequence, the concept does not solve more ordinary value conflicts between, for example, free trade and environmental protection.[69] On the institutional level, the UN Charter established the ICJ as the 'principal judicial organ of the UN'.[70] Nevertheless, the ICJ may only exercise its jurisdiction if each party consents to it.[71] Moreover, it does not act as an appellate structure to other judicial bodies, nor does it have a procedure to answer questions referred to it by other international judicial bodies.

This combination of a lack of hierarchy, on the one hand, and a growing number of international judicial bodies, on the other, is seen as a threat to the unity of international law because it increases the risk of inconsistent decisions. As the proliferation of international courts and tribunals increases, States are confronted with judicial decisions from more and more unconnected Treaty regimes and the risk of fragmentation grows. One of the causes of fragmentation has been identified as the 'topic autonomy' of international judicial bodies. Topic autonomy is the assumption that each body adjudicates cases on a different, independent subject of international law.[72] What Dupuy describes as the

---

65 ICTY, *Case of Prosecutor v Tadić, Decision on the Defence Motion for Interlocutory Appeal on Jurisdiction*, Judgment of 1995, para. 11.

66 An overview of the different approaches (in academia as well as practice) can be found in Chapter 4.

67 Paulus, above n 58, 10.

68 On this issue, see the ICJ's use of *jus cogens* obligations on p 231.

69 Paulus, above n 58, 14.

70 Article 92 Charter of the United Nations of 26 June 1945, Treaty Series, 993.

71 See International Court of Justice, section on jurisdiction, pp 33ff.

72 Brown, above n 53, p 25.

'illusion of completely autonomous sub-systems' could easily lead to a biased perspective.[73] *If* specialised judicial bodies consider themselves to operate in isolation from each other and general international law, the concern that the proliferation of international courts and tribunals will lead to inconsistent decisions, incoherence in international law and forum shopping is well founded.

The concern over topic autonomy is closely related to the issue of conflicting jurisdiction. In spite of the theory of topic autonomy, the jurisdictions of international judicial bodies overlap in reality. In recent years, a small number of disputes have been referred to multiple judicial bodies. For example, in 2000, Chile submitted a dispute concerning the sustainable exploitation of swordfish to a Special Chamber of the International Tribunal for the Law of the Sea (ITLOS).[74] Chile had prohibited the importation of swordfish that violated the Chilean measures to protect swordfish stocks. The EC found this measure to be in violation of the GATT 1994 and instituted proceedings before the WTO on the same issue. In the end, the parties themselves agreed on a provisional accord through negotiation. Nevertheless, the case provides an interesting example of how two disputes on the same facts may be brought before two different international fora.

1.1.4. THE COMMON INTEREST IN INTERNATIONAL LITIGATION

So far, this chapter has highlighted two important trends in international law. The first section of the chapter described the introduction of the common interest concept in international law that took place in the context of a general shift 'from bilateralism to community interest'.[75]As globalisation shifted territorial borders to functional boundaries, common interest issues such as the protection of the environment transcended territorial boundaries, leaving the State unable to strike the balance between conflicting national and common interests in isolation.[76] What is more, the role of the State in balancing different interests has not been replaced on the international level; there exists no international body with a 'final' legal competence to decide on conflicting interests.[77] As the second section of the chapter established, the international judicial system has

73 Dupuy, above n 12, 796–97.

74 For a complete discussion, see M.A. Orellana, 'The Swordfish Dispute between the EU and Chile at the ITLOS and the WTO' (2002) 71 *Nordic Journal of International Law* 55, 55–81.

75 Simma, above n 1, 217–384.

76 Paulus, above n 58, 59.

77 Difficulties arising from the Diversification and Expansion of International Law, International Law Commission Report of the Study Group on Fragmentation of International Law of 2003 UN Doc. A/CN.4/L.644.

proliferated. International litigation is governed by separate instances pursuing different goals such as the promotion of free trade and the law of the sea.[78]

Now that it has been established that certain issues of common interest are recognised and explicitly protected in international law, the question remains how respect for these interests is enforced in a judicial system that has proliferated.[79] In this context, it is important to note that the institutionalisation of international law is, for the moment, incomplete. In particular in the field of common interests, States are generally reluctant to provide for strong global judicial dispute settlement.[80] There exists, for example, no specialised global judicial body to enforce environmental protection or human rights law.[81] As a consequence, the existing mechanisms are being used to enforce common interests.[82] Taking into account that most of these instances are associated with one issue area rather than another, an element of bias is likely to appear in deciding conflicts of interests. It has, for example, been argued that investment arbitrations of the International Centre for Settlement of Investment Disputes (ICSID) – in an attempt to protect investor rights – take little account of common interests.[83] Besides the fact that these bodies may be biased, the procedural as well as the substantive rules of the existing judicial mechanisms are, in general, not designed to deal with the enforcement of common interests.[84] As a consequence, judicial bodies of different regimes are faced with the same, politically sensitive, demand of (re)interpreting their procedural and substantive rules in light of the same common interest issues.

---

78 Paulus, above n 58, 60.

79 This study will focus on the judicial enforcement of common interests concerns, which is traditionally considered a 'friendly' way of enforcement. 'International adjudication is a small, but not irrelevant, component in the complex international governance structure through which states and other actors seek to deliver global public goods' (A. Nollkaemper, *International Adjudication of Global Public Goods: The Intersection of Substance and Procedure*, SHARES Research Paper 09 (2012), ACIL 2012-08, Amsterdam Center for International Law, 2012, available at sharesproject.nl, 33).

80 C. Tams, 'Individual States as Guardians of Community Interests' in U. Fastenrath, R. Geiger, D.-E. Khan, A. Paulus, S. von Schorlemer and C. Vedder (eds), *From Bilateralism to Community Interest – Essays in Honour of Judge Bruno Simma*, Oxford University Press, Oxford 2011, p 383.

81 At the international level, the ICC is an example of a judicial body that expressly does protect a common interest. At the regional level States seem to reach consensus much more easily. In Europe, for example, there is the ECtHR and the 1998 Aarhus Convention, which provides access to justice in environmental matters.

82 Paulus, above n 50, p 128.

83 B. Choudhury, 'Recapturing Public Power: Is Investment Arbitration's Engagement of the Public Interest Contributing to the Democratic Deficit' (2008) 41 *Vanderbilt Journal of Transnational Law* 775, 775.

84 The traditional bilateral judicial mechanisms are based on consent and inter-state litigation. Therefore, the enforcement of most common interest rules on the international level depends on the initiative of individual States. M. Benzing, 'Community Interests in the Procedure of International Courts and Tribunals' (2006) 5 *The Law and Practice of International Courts and Tribunals* 369, 373–74.

The proliferation of judicial bodies adds another layer of interest to this demand because it forces the judicial bodies to decide whether or not to follow the example of their peers in answering these questions. Therefore, this research will not only examine how judicial bodies approach common interests in their case law, it will also focus on the commonalities and conflicts in their decision-making process. If this initial research reveals that a similar approach is followed, this would counter some of the concerns raised in the context of the fragmentation of international law. It would suggest that the international judicial bodies look beyond their legal island and consider themselves part of a 'community of courts'.[85] If, on the other hand, the study shows major inconsistencies or a lack of consideration, an attempt will be made to define how common interests could be considered in a more coherent manner within the existing framework of international litigation.[86]

In light of the foregoing, the following research questions will be addressed. To what extent do international judicial bodies engage with common interests when interpreting their procedural and substantive rules? What differences or similarities can be found in the decision making of the different judicial bodies? What reasons can be found for these differences or similarities? And, if relevant, what options exist to reach a higher level of coherence when addressing common interests?

1.2. DEFINITIONS, METHODOLOGY AND STRUCTURE

Now that the general picture of international litigation and the emergence of common interests has been painted, it is time to dig into the details. In the following chapters, the case law of a number of international judicial bodies will be analysed in order to answer the key research questions set out in the previous section. However, before presenting the results of this analysis, it is necessary to clarify what the limits of the study are. This will be done in two steps. First, the different concepts used in this study are defined. The difference between public interest and common interest is elaborated and some background is provided on the courts and tribunals that are examined. The first section further

85 See A.-M. Slaughter, 'A Global Community of Courts' (2003) 44 *Harvard International Law Journal* 191, 191–220. For a similar reasoning with a focus on procedural issues see Brown, above n 53, p 303.

86 As Paulus points out, 'It is the task of international lawyers to further develop a methodology which allows for the respect for the values of other issue areas within institutional settings such as WTO dispute settlement'. Paulus, above n 58, 94.

clarifies what is and what is not considered natural resource exploitation for the purpose of this research. Secondly, the research methodology and the limits that are inherent in this methodology are briefly described. In conclusion, the logic behind the structure of the book is explained.

1.2.1. DEFINITIONS

1.2.1.1. Public and Common Interests

The 'public interest' and related concepts, such as the 'common interest' and the 'common good', can be traced back to traditional political philosophy.[87] Aristotle uses 'the common interest' to make a distinction between different methods of ordering society. He declares that 'those constitutions which seek the common advantage are correct and accord with simple right, while those which seek only the advantage of the rulers are all mistaken and perversions of the correct constitutions'.[88] Aquinas argued that the common good (*bonum commune*), a universal final cause, should be the end of law and government.[89] In a similar vein, Locke argued that the power of the legislator should be directed to 'no other end but the peace, safety and public good of the people'.[90] Drawing from these philosophical texts, it may be concluded that attaining the public or common interest should be the ultimate aspiration of the State.

As a benchmark for political action, the public interest has also been the subject of voluminous political science literature that, particularly in the 1950–60s, focused on defining the concept.[91] The point of departure for most of these writings is the work of Walter Lippmann, the American journalist who first defined the concept in 1955. Lippmann states that, whereas living adults share the same public interest, the public interest is mixed with and may be at odds with their private interests. Therefore, the public interest should be 'what men would choose if they saw clearly, thought rationally, acted disinterestedly and benevolently', rather than the sum of individual interests.[92]

At the beginning of the 1970s, several Anglo-American political scientists attempted to categorise the various public interest theories created in earlier

---

87 B. Diggs, 'The Common Good as Reason for Political Action' (1973) 83 *Ethics* 283, 283.

88 Aristotle with W. Newman, *The Politics of Aristotle*, Arno, New York 1973, p. III.6, 1279a.

89 T. Aquinas with T. Gilby, *Summa theologiae – Law and Political Theory*, Cambridge University Press, Cambridge 2006, p 90, 2.

90 J. Locke with T. Peardon, *The Second Treatise of Government*, Liberal Arts Press, New York 1952, para. 131.

91 For a concise overview see B. Bozeman, *Public Values and Public Interest: Counterbalancing Economic Individualism*, Georgetown University Press, Washington 2007, pp 83–95.

92 W. Lippmann, *The Public Philosophy*, Transaction Publisher, New Brunswick 2006, pp 41–42.

decades.[93] One of the most familiar categorisations is that of Cochran,[94] who identifies three theories that recognise the public interest concept: normative theories, consensualist theories and process theories.[95] In short, normative theories consider the public interest to be an interest of the whole community, and advance the concept as an ethical standard for evaluating rights, procedures and State policies.[96] Consensualist theories also emphasise that the public interest is an important element of political decision making but they do not require the public interest to be an interest of the whole community.[97] Instead, it can be found by 'reasoned discourse which attempts to relate the anticipated effects of a policy to community values and to test that relation by formal principles'.[98] In contrast, process theories state that there are many publics and many interests, rather than one public that holds one interest and several techniques exist to reconcile these interests.[99]

Despite these different interpretations of what the public interest is and how it can be found, all theories agree that, in the end, it is defined by politics and stands as a measure for State policies. This interpretation is confirmed by the use of the term 'public interest' in international law. In many international Treaties, so-called public interest exceptions are included that allow the State to pursue certain interests even if the necessary measures to pursue those interests are inconsistent with their international commitments. One example, which will be elaborated later, is Article 1 of the European Convention on Human Rights' (ECHR) First Protocol, which provides that '[n]o one shall be deprived of his possessions except *in the public interest* and subject to the conditions provided for by law and by the general principles of international law' (emphasis added).[100]

---

93 No significant literature on the subject was found outside of the Anglo-American sphere.

94 Other important categorisations include that of Virginia Held, who distinguished three general categories: preponderance or aggregative theories, unitary theories and common interest theories (V. Held, *The Public Interest and Individual Interests*, Basic Books, New York 1970; cited in A. McHarg, 'Reconciling Human Rights and the Public Interest: Conceptual Problems and Doctrinal Uncertainty in the Jurisprudence of the European Court of Human Rights' (1999) 62 *Modern Law Review* 671, 674.) and that of Frank Sorauf, who identified five ways to define the public interest: as a commonly held value, as the wise or superior interest, as a moral imperative, as a balance of interest or as an undefined concept (F. Sorauf, 'The Public Interest Reconsidered' (1957) 19 *The Journal of Politics* 616, 616–39).

95 C. Cochran, 'Political Science and "The Public Interest"' (1974) 36 *The Journal of Politics* 327, 330–31. Cochran also identifies a fourth type of theories that do not support the public interest concept, known as abolitionist theories.

96 Bozeman, above n 91, 292.

97 Cochran, above n 95, 347.

98 Ibid.

99 The process theories are generally divided into three subcategories, theories that consider the public interest to be (1) the sum of individual interest (aggregation theories), (2) the outcome of a particular political process (pluralistic conception) or (3) the reconciliation of interests taking account of the standards of due process (proceduralists). Ibid, 339–47.

100 First Protocol to the Convention for the Protection of Human Rights and Fundamental Freedoms of 4 November 1950, ETS, no. 5.

In the interpretation of the ECtHR, the concept refers to what the State considers to be of public interest.[101]

At this point it seems advantageous to draw a distinction between what is referred to as the *public* interest and what is described as the *common* interest in this book. From the discussion in the previous chapter, on the emergence of the common interest, it can be deduced that 'the common interest' may be interpreted as an interest that transcends the interests of individual States and that, in the research presented here, common interests have a global dimension, they are global interests and not interests of a group of States. What further distinguishes common interests from other transnational interests is, first, the importance of the values at stake and, secondly, the requirement of collective action. The first element, the status of the underlying value, is reflected in the use of the common interest concept in the preambles to many international Treaties to stress the importance of the issue and is also implicit in the ICJ definition of *erga omnes* obligations as obligations that arise 'by their very nature' 'in view of the importance of the rights involved'.[102] The second element, collective action, according to Shelton, implies that common interests 'require collective action in response; no single state can resolve the problems they pose or receive all the benefits they provide'.[103]

As a final note on the common interest concept used in this study the difference with other frequently used concepts should be briefly addressed, in particular the common concern and the general interest.[104] There is little difference between the common concern and the common interest and these terms can often be used as interchangeable terms. Nevertheless, the common concern more often refers to the problem that may arise, for example climate change, while the common interest reflects how a potential problem should be addressed, for example by safeguarding whale stocks.[105] A second concept that

---

101 See pp 120ff for an overview of case law on this provision.

102 For examples see the previous section, pp 4ff. The element of the value at stake and the link with the ICJ's definition of *erga omnes* obligations is identified in Shelton, above n 47, 34. For a further discussion on *erga omnes* obligations in the case law of the ICJ see pp 173ff.

103 Ibid. Although Shelton uses this definition in the context of common concerns rather than interests, both terms are used as interchangeable terms in her paper.

104 A third term that is not frequently used but may refer to similar issues is the global interest, see for example J. d'Aspremont, *Contemporary International Rulemaking and the Public Character of International Law*, International Law and Justice Working Papers, no. 2006/12, New York University School of Law 2006, available at <www.iilj.org>.

105 Compare 'climate change is a common concern of mankind, since climate is an essential condition which sustains life on earth' (Protection of Global Climate for Present and Future Generations of Mankind, UN General Assembly Resolution of 1988 UN Doc. A/RES/43/53) and 'it is in the common interest to achieve the optimum level of whale stocks as rapidly as possible without causing widespread economic and nutritional distress' (Preamble International Convention for the Regulation of Whaling of 2 December 1946, UN Treaty Series, vol. 155, 349).

is often used as a synonym for common interest is general interest. This term has been linked to the interest of the international community of States as a whole in the Commentaries on the Draft Articles on State Responsibility but it is often also used to identify the domestic public interest (as a translation of *l'intérêt général*).[106] Thus, to avoid conceptual confusion, this term will not be used unless it is explicitly referred to by other sources and its meaning is clarified by the context in which it is used.

The terms public and common interest are used interchangeably in international law writings, which may result in confusion. Therefore, based on the considerations above, this study will use the concept of 'public interest' to reflect what is considered by the State as the standard for its policies and it will use the 'common interest' only to refer to an interest that transcends the interests of individual States. This strict divide between the two concepts of course does not imply that a public interest of the State may not coincide with a common interest. Furthermore, it is important to note here that by limiting the research to public and common interests as defined above, interests of specific groups or 'peoples' are not dealt with explicitly.[107]

1.2.1.2. International Litigation

The aim of this study is to show how international law is interpreted by jurisdictional bodies to accommodate common interest concerns. This topic falls within the field of study that is most commonly referred to as public international law and, more specifically, the peaceful settlement of disputes. While the peaceful settlement of international disputes is an old objective, most techniques and institutions to reach this objective are relatively new.[108] It was only after the First World War, with the establishment of the Permanent Court of International Justice, that States started establishing innovative and flexible mechanisms to settle international disputes in peace.

A comprehensive list of dispute settlement mechanisms can be found in the 1982 Manila Declaration on the Peaceful Settlement of International Disputes,[109]

---

106 In the commentaries the ILC links general interests to interests of the international community as a whole and, in contrast to the definition used here, defines common interests as interests shared by a group of States. Commentaries on Article 48 Draft Articles on Responsibility of States for Internationally Wrongful Acts, International Law Commission of 2001 UN Doc. A/56/10.

107 The same interpretations of procedural law that can be used to pursue common interest can, however, often also be applied in favour of peoples' interests. For example, third party interventions by non-state actors may also serve to present the interest of a people.

108 International disputes are not confined to inter-State disputes. Disagreement between a state and an individual or cooperation can equally have international consequences.

109 Declaration on the Peaceful Settlement of International Disputes, UN General Assembly Resolution of 1982 UN Doc. A/RES/37/10.

which reaffirms the 1970 UN Declaration on Friendly Relations[110] and Articles 2.3 and 33 of the Charter of the United Nations. The Manila Declaration establishes that

> States shall seek in good faith and in a spirit of co-operation an early and equitable settlement of their international disputes by any of the following means: negotiation, inquiry, mediation, conciliation, arbitration, judicial settlement, resort to regional arrangements or agencies or other peaceful means of their own choice, including good offices.[111]

Generally, the means of peaceful dispute settlement are divided into two categories: diplomatic methods (negotiation, mediation, conciliation, good offices, etc.) and legal or jurisdictional methods (arbitration, judicial settlement and resort to regional arrangements or agencies).[112] Since it is only by the latter means that adjudication is carried out in accordance with legal principles, the focus of this book will be on the jurisdictional methods of dispute settlement. In general, two types of jurisdictional or legal methods are distinguished: arbitration and adjudication.[113] The oldest and most commonly used legal method of dispute settlement, arbitration, is a procedure for the settlement of disputes on the basis of law in which the parties set up a tribunal themselves to settle their dispute. It is undertaken voluntarily and the parties have to agree that they will treat the decision as a binding award. Adjudication, on the other hand, encompasses the traditional judicial process. In other words, adjudication is a procedure for the settlement of disputes between two or more parties concerning the interpretation or application of the law that results in a binding award by an existing court.

Although this book will focus on adjudication, one arbitration system will be studied in detail, namely the ICSID.[114] ICSID is an institution which facilitates

---

110 Declaration on Principles of International Law concerning Friendly Relations and Co-operation among States in accordance with the Charter of the United Nations, UN General Assembly Resolution of 1970 UN Doc. A/RES/25/2625.

111 Sect. I, para. 5 Declaration on the Peaceful Settlement of International Disputes, UN General Assembly Resolution of 1982 UN Doc. A/RES/37/10. The enumerated means do not have a compulsory order, States can freely agree on the appropriate means to peacefully settle their disputes.

112 The most important difference between these two categories is the binding authority of the settlement. Whereas parties accept the binding authority of the decision beforehand when turning to jurisdictional methods, they are free to disagree with the settlement when using diplomatic means of dispute settlement. J. Merrills, 'The Means of Dispute Settlement' in M. Evans (ed), *International Law*, Oxford University Press, Oxford 2006, pp 535–55; Shaw, above n 5, p 914; R. Wallace and O. Martin-Ortega, *International Law*, Sweet & Maxwell, London 2009, p 331.

113 A. Cassese, *International Law*, Oxford University Press, Oxford 2005, p 285; Merrills, above n 112, pp 542–47; Wallace and Martin-Ortega, above n 112, p 331.

114 Public ICSID arbitration orders and awards are available at <icsid.worldbank.org>. Interesting recent literature on the ICSID includes G. Van Harten, *Investment Treaty Arbitration and Public Law*, Oxford University Press, Oxford 2007; O.K. Fauchald, 'The

arbitration between foreign investors and host States on alleged violations of investment agreements.[115] International investment arbitration is included in this study on judicial mechanisms because the decision-making process is very similar. While arbitral investment tribunals are ad hoc and have no appellate jurisdiction, there are some clear elements of judicialisation.[116] From a structural perspective, the tribunals are the judges of their own competence and decide freely on non-regulated procedural issues.[117] Furthermore, like courts, the tribunals are obliged to justify their decisions.[118] Thus, like judges, international investment arbitrators establish the relevant facts and the applicable law to come to an impartial and independent judgment.[119] What is more, on the substantive level a practice of precedence has taken shape. Although the tribunals enforce thousands of different international investment agreements, they 'contribute to the harmonious development of investment law and thereby meet the legitimate expectations of the community of States and investors towards certainty of the rule of law'.[120]

Two more traditional, or old-style, international courts that will be discussed are the International Court of Justice and the International Tribunal for the Law of the Sea. The ICJ was established in 1945 as the principal judicial organ of

---

Legal Reasoning of ICSID Tribunals – An Empirical Analysis' (2008) 19 *European Journal of International Law* 301, 301–64; C. Schreuer, F. Ortino and P. Muchlinski, *The Oxford Handbook of International Investment Law*, Oxford University Press, Oxford 2008; U. Kriebaum, A. Reinisch, C. Schreuer and C. Binder, *International Investment Law for the 21st Century: Essays in Honour of Christoph Schreuer*, Oxford University Press, Oxford 2009; A. Lowenfeld, 'The ICSID Convention: Origins and Transformation' (2009) 38 *Georgia Journal of International and Comparative Law* 47, 47–61; C. Schreuer, *The ICSID Convention: A Commentary*, Cambridge University Press, Cambridge 2009; R. Mackenzie, C.P. Romano, Y. Shany and P. Sands, *Manual on International Courts and Tribunals*, Oxford University Press, Oxford 2010; C. Schreuer, 'From ICSID Annulment to Appeal Half Way Down the Slippery Slope' (2011) 10 *The Law and Practice of International Courts and Tribunals* 211, 211–25; R. Dolzer and C. Schreuer, *Principles of International Investment Law*, Oxford University Press, Oxford 2012.

115 See <icsid.worldbank.org>.

116 A. Stone Sweet, 'Investor-State Arbitration: Proportionality's New Frontier' (2010) 4 *Law & Ethics of Human Rights* 46, 59.

117 Articles 41–44 Convention on the Settlement of Investment Disputes Between States and Nationals of Other States of 14 October 1966, UN Treaty Series, vol. 575, 159.

118 Article 52(1)(e) ICSID Rules of Procedure for Arbitration Proceedings of 10 April 2006, available at <icsid.worldbank.org>. Stone Sweet, above n 116, 60. Moreover, a number of ICSID decisions are publicly available and, consequently, may be subjected to scrutiny. ICSID records the existence of arbitrations publicly. Other tribunals do not do this, unless the parties agree to do so. Therefore, the number of non-ICSID investment arbitrations is impossible to verify.

119 C. Brower and S. Schill, 'Is Arbitration a Threat or a Boon to the Legitimacy of International Investment Law' (2008–09) 9 *Chicago Journal of International Law* 471, 492. This is very different from private-law arbitration in which the parties determine the applicable law and can control the way the decision is made.

120 ICSID, *Saipem S.P.A. Claimant v the People's Republic of Bangladesh*, Award, 30.06.2009, para. 80.

the United Nations.[121] It adjudicates disputes between States and issues advisory opinions on legal questions submitted by the authorised entities. The ITLOS is a much more recent but similar dispute settlement mechanism that was primarily established to adjudicate inter-State disputes concerning the UN Convention on the Law of the Sea (UNCLOS).[122] In addition, the ITLOS has jurisdiction to receive claims by non-State entities on specific issues and the Tribunal's Seabed Disputes Chamber may render advisory opinions on questions that relate to the activities of the International Seabed Authority. A third inter-State mechanism that will be examined is the dispute settlement system of the WTO.[123] This

121 Judgments, orders and advisory opinions of the ICJ are available at <www.icj-cij.org>. Interesting recent literature on the ICJ includes S.A. Alexandrov, 'The Compulsory Jurisdiction of the International Court of Justice: How Compulsory Is It?' (2006) 5 *Chinese Journal of International Law* 29, 29–38; P.-M. Dupuy, 'Competition among International Tribunals and the Authority of the International Court of Justice' in U. Fastenrath, R. Geiger, D.-E. Khan, A. Paulus, S. von Schorlemer and C. Vedder (eds), *From Bilateralism to Community Interest – Essays in Honour of Judge Bruno Simma*, Oxford University Press, Oxford 2011; G. Hernandez, *The International Court of Justice and the Judicial Function*, Oxford University Press, Oxford 2013; R. Kolb, *The International Court of Justice*, Hart Publishing, Oxford 2013; Mackenzie et al., above n 114; E. Posner and M. De Figueiredo, *Is the International Court of Justice Biased?*, John M. Olin Program in Law and Economics Working Paper, no. 234, University of Chicago Law School, 2004, available at <chicagounbound.uchicago.edu/law_and_economics_wp>, 43; A. Riddell and B. Plant, *Evidence before the International Court of Justice*, British Institute of International and Comparative Law, London 2009; S. Rosenne and Y. Ronen, *The Law and Practice of the International Court, 1920–2005*, Brill/Nijhoff, Leiden 2006; C. Schulte, *Compliance with Decisions of the International Court of Justice*, Oxford University Press, Oxford 2004; C.J. Tams and J. Sloan, *The Development of International Law by the International Court of Justice*, Oxford University Press, Oxford 2013; H. Thirlway, 'The International Court of Justice' in M. Evans (ed), *International Law*, Oxford University Press, Oxford 2006; A. Zimmermann, K. Oellers-Frahm, C. Tomuschat and C. Tams, *The Statute of the International Court of Justice: A Commentary*, Oxford University Press, Oxford 2012.

122 Judgments, orders and advisory opinions of the ITLOS are available at <www.itlos.org>. Interesting recent literature on the ITLOS includes A. Boyle, 'The Environmental Jurisprudence of the International Tribunal for the Law of the Sea' (2007) 22 *The International Journal of Marine and Coastal Law* 369, 369–81; Mackenzie et al., above n 114; J.-G. Mahinga, *Le Tribunal du droit de la mer: Organisation, compétence et procédure*, Larcier, Brussels 2013; T. Mensah, 'The Tribunal and the Prompt Release of Vessels' (2007) 22 *The International Journal of Marine and Coastal Law* 425, 425–49; L. Nelson, 'The Jurisprudence of the International Tribunal for the Law of the Sea: Some Observations' in T.A. Mensah, T.M. Ndiaye, R. Wolfrum and C. Kojima (eds), *Law of the Sea, Environmental Law and Settlement of Disputes: Liber Amicorum Judge Thomas A. Mensah*, Martinus Nijhoff Publishers, Leiden 2007; P.C. Rao and P. Gautier, *The Rules of the International Tribunal for the Law of the Sea: A Commentary*, Nijhoff, Leiden 2006; H. Tuerk, 'The Contribution of the International Tribunal for the Law of the Sea to International Law' (2007) 26 *Penn State International Law Review* 289, 289–316; F. Orrego Vicuna, 'The International Tribunal for the Law of the Sea and Provisional Measures: Settled Issues and Pending Problems' (2007) 22 *The International Journal of Marine and Coastal Law* 451, 451–62; M. Wood, 'The International Tribunal for the Law of the Sea and General International Law' (2007) 22 *International Journal of Marine and Coastal Law* 351, 351–67.

123 Decisions of WTO panels and the Appellate Body are available at <www.wto.org>. Interesting recent literature on the WTO dispute settlement system includes C.P. Bown, *Self-Enforcing Trade: Developing Countries and WTO Dispute Settlement*, Brookings Institution Press,

compulsory mechanism renders decisions on disputes, which could not be settled through consultations, between WTO Member States on issues arising under the covered agreements. Considering the lack of a worldwide court on human rights issues and given the importance that is attached to the case law of the regional human rights courts in the case law of other international courts and tribunals, this study will also discuss the case law of the ECtHR,[124] the Inter-American Court of Human Rights (IACtHR)[125] and the African Court and Commission on Human and Peoples' Rights (ACHPR and ACtHPR).[126]

Washington, DC 2009; Mackenzie et al., above n 114; M. Martin, *WTO Dispute Settlement Understanding and Development*, Martinus Nijhoff Publishers, Leiden 2013; M. Matsushita, T. Schoenbaum and P. Mavroidis, *The World Trade Organization: Law, Practice and Policy*, Oxford University Press, Oxford 2006; A. Mitchell, *Legal Principles in WTO Disputes*, Cambridge University Press, Cambridge, New York 2008; A. Narlikar, M. Daunton and R.M. Stern, *The Oxford Handbook on the World Trade Organization*, Oxford University Press, Oxford 2012; J. Pauwelyn, *Conflict of Norms in Public International Law: How WTO Law Relates to Other Rules of International Law*, Cambridge University Press, Cambridge 2008; I. Van Damme, *Treaty Interpretation by the WTO Appellate Body*, Oxford Scholarship Online, 2009, available at <www.oxfordscholarship.com>; A. Alvarez-Jimenez, 'The WTO Appellate Body's Decision-Making Process: A Perfect Model For International Adjudication?' (2009) 12 *Journal of International Economic Law* 289, 289–331; I. Van Damme, 'Treaty Interpretation by the WTO Appellate Body' (2010) 21 *European Journal of International Law* 605, 605–48; B. Wilson, 'Compliance by WTO Members with Adverse WTO Dispute Settlement Rulings: The Record to Date' (2007) 10 *Journal of International Economic Law* 397, 397–403.

124 Judgments, orders and advisory opinions of the ECtHR are available at <hudoc.echr.coe.int>. Interesting recent literature on the ECtHR includes P. Van Dijk, F. van Hoof, A. van Rijn and L. Zwaak, *Theory and Practice of the European Convention on Human Rights*, Intersentia, Antwerp 2006; S. Greer, *The European Convention on Human Rights: Achievements, Problems and Prospects*, Cambridge University Press, Cambridge 2008; D.J. Harris, C. Warbrick and M. O'Boyle, *Law of the European Convention on Human Rights*, Oxford University Press, Oxford 2009; P. Leach, *Taking a Case to the European Court of Human Rights*, Oxford University Press, Oxford 2012; Mackenzie et al., above n 114; A. Mowbray, *Cases, Materials, and Commentary on the European Convention on Human Rights*, Oxford University Press, Oxford 2012; R. White, F. Jacobs and C. Ovey, *The European Convention on Human Rights*, Oxford University Press, Oxford 2010; E. Voeten, 'The Impartiality of International Judges: Evidence from the European Court of Human Rights' (2008) 102 *American Political Science Review* 417, 417–32.

125 Judgments, orders and advisory opinions of the IACtHR are available at <www.corteidh.or.cr>. Interesting recent literature on the IACtHR includes C. Burbano Herrera, *Provisional Measures in the Case Law of the Inter-American Court of Human Rights*, Intersentia, Antwerp 2010; L. Burgorgue-Larsen and A. Úbeda de Torres, *The Inter-American Court of Human Rights Case Law and Commentary*, Oxford University Press, Oxford 2011; Mackenzie et al., above n 114; J. Pasqualucci, *The Practice and Procedure of the Inter-American Court of Human Rights*, Cambridge University Press, Cambridge 2013; T. Buergenthal, 'Remembering the Early Years of the Inter-American Court of Human Rights' (2004) 37 *New York University Journal of International Law and Politics* 259, 259–80; C. Grossman, 'The Inter-American System of Human Rights: Challenges for the Future' (2008) 83 *Indiana Law Journal* 1267, 1267–82; M. Tan, 'Upholding Human Rights in the Hemisphere: Casting Down Impunity Through the Inter-American Court of Human Rights' (2008) 43 *Texas International Law Journal* 243, 243–86; J. Cavallaro and S. Brewer, *Reevaluating Regional Human Rights Litigation in the Twenty-First Century: The Case of the Inter-American Court*, Public Law & Legal Theory Working Paper Series, no. 09-31, Harvard Law School, 2008, available at <ssrn.com>, 768–827.

126 Judgments, orders and advisory opinions of the ACHPR and the ACtHPR are available at <caselaw.ihrda.org>. Interesting recent literature on the system includes M. Evans and

For the purpose of this book, international litigation will be limited to contentious cases. In other words, the advisory opinions of the selected judicial bodies will not be studied in detail.[127] The reason for this limitation is that the dynamics of reaching a decision in such cases are very different, first, because the court is not bound by the same procedural rules in giving advisory opinions, and secondly, and more importantly, because the court fulfils a different role. Instead of focusing on the settlement of a dispute between two parties in specific circumstances, it is asked to give a more general interpretation of a legal rule, as if it were a constitutional court. However, this does not mean to imply that the advisory proceedings do not touch upon issues of common interest. On the contrary, advisory opinions often touch upon common interest issues. Well-known examples include the ICJ's advisory opinions on Reservations to the Genocide Convention and on Nuclear Weapons.[128] Therefore, the study will discuss the advisory opinions of the examined judicial bodies in cursory terms. Rather than exploring the specificities of the relevant advisory opinions, the study will refer to the advisory opinions when they complement or give context to the contentious case law of the court.

1.2.1.3. Natural Resource Exploitation

At first glance, defining 'natural resource exploitation' seems rather straightforward. According to the *Encyclopedia Americana* and the *Oxford English Dictionary*, natural resource exploitation could be described as the 'profitable management'[129] of 'naturally occurring materials that are useful to

---

R. Murray, *The African Charter on Human and Peoples' Rights: The System in Practice, 1986–2006*, Cambridge University Press, Cambridge, New York 2008; Mackenzie et al., above n 114; M. Ssenyonjo, *The African Regional Human Rights System: 30 Years After the African Charter on Human and Peoples' Rights*, Martinus Nijhoff Publishers, 2011; F. Viljoen, *International Human Rights Law in Africa*, Oxford University Press, Oxford 2012; S. Ebobrah, 'The Admissibility of Cases before the African Court on Human and Peoples' Rights: Who Should Do What?' (2009) 3 *Malawi Law Journal* 87, 87–113; C. Heyns, 'The African Regional Human Rights System: The African Charter' (2004) 108, *Penn State Law Review* 679–702; D. Juma, 'Provisional Measures under the African Human Rights System: The African Court's Order against Libya' (2012) 30 *Wisconsin International Law Journal* 344, 344–73; M.P. Pedersen, 'Standing and the African Commission on Human and Peoples' Rights' (2006) 6 *African Human Rights Law Journal* 407, 407–22; F. Viljoen, 'State Compliance with the Recommendations of the African Commission on Human and Peoples' Rights, 1994–2004' (2007) 101 *The American Journal of International Law* 1, 1–34.

127 Selected judicial bodies that enjoy advisory jurisdiction are the ICJ, the ITLOS, the ECtHR and the IACtHR.

128 ICJ, *Case of Reservations to the Convention on Genocide, Advisory Opinion*, Judgment of 1951; ICJ, *Case of Legality of the Threat or Use of Nuclear Weapons, Advisory Opinion*, Judgment of 1996.

129 *Oxford English Dictionary Online*, available at <www.oed.com> (last accessed June 2015).

man or could be useful under certain conceivable technological, economic or social circumstances'.[130] However, when reviewing diverse sources on natural resources, a more complex picture arises. Being the object of study of a wide variety of sciences, natural resources are often defined from a specific angle. Whereas a geographical reference book stresses the importance of the ecosystem in which natural resources are embedded, economical literature places special importance on the scarcity and supply of resources.[131]

The same angle-specific approach exists in international law. The few international Treaties that provide a definition of natural resources all stress different elements of the concept. While the 1968 African Convention on the Conservation of Nature and Natural Resources refers to natural resources as 'renewable resources, that is soil, water, flora and fauna',[132] the 1972 Stockholm Declaration establishes that the natural resources of the Earth include 'the air, water, land, flora and fauna and … natural ecosystems'[133] and the 1992 Biodiversity Convention contends that 'biological' resources are 'genetic resources, organisms or parts thereof, populations, or any other biotic component of ecosystems with actual or potential use or value for humanity'.[134]

Most international law literature equally fails to provide a (coherent) legal definition of natural resources.[135] A welcome exception is the definition given by Schrijver in the context of sovereignty over natural resources. Schrijver describes natural resources as 'supplies drawn from natural wealth which may be either renewable or non-renewable and which can be used to satisfy the needs of human beings and other living species'.[136] In order to broadly, yet clearly, demarcate the research field, an identical definition of natural resources will be adopted here with the restriction that natural resources do not include agricultural products.[137] Thus, for the purpose of this study, natural resource exploitation will be defined as the management of supplies drawn from natural wealth which may be either renewable or non-renewable, which are not the

130 *The Encyclopedia Americana: International Edition*, Grolier, Danbury 1986, p 792, v. 19.

131 See, for instance, R. Johnston, *The Dictionary of Human Geography*, Blackwell Publishers, Oxford 2000, p 535; M. Parkin, *Economics*, Pearson, Boston, MA 2008, pp 395–97.

132 Article III.1 African Convention on the Conservation of Nature and Natural Resources of 15 September 1968, UN Treaty Series, vol. 1001, 4.

133 Principle 2 Declaration of the United Nations Conference on the Human Environment of 1973 UN Doc. A/Conf.48/14/Rev. 1.

134 Article 2 Convention on Biological Diversity of 5 July 1992, UN Treaty Series, vol. 1760, 79.

135 For a short overview of legal literature's attempts to define the concept see N. Schrijver, *Sovereignty over Natural Resources: Balancing Rights and Duties*, Cambridge University Press, Cambridge 2008, p 15.

136 Ibid, 19.

137 Agricultural labour is to be understood as raising crops and feeding, breeding and raising livestock. Under this definition, goods such as trees, fish and rubber are not considered a crop if they are taken from areas in which humans do not systematically intervene to produce them.

fruit of agricultural labour and which can be used to satisfy the needs of human beings and other living species.

1.2.2. METHODOLOGY

To answer the question of how different international judicial bodies approach common interests, the case law of the selected bodies will be studied in detail. This case law study is based on a desk study of the materials that are made available by the judicial bodies.[138] The study will focus on case law of a limited number of judicial bodies concerning one specific type of disputes, namely cases on natural resource exploitation, to delimit the examined case law and make a more in-depth survey possible. The selection of cases was done by searching the databases of the selected bodies for all cases of the past two decades that are related to natural resource exploitation, followed by hand picking those cases with a common interest angle.[139] While it can be argued that such a selection also limits the number of topics or interests that are examined, case law research is inherently limited because it depends on the claims that have been brought before the relevant bodies. In addition, the natural resource cases will be complemented with landmark cases to show the relevance of those specific cases in the full body of case law of each regime.

The topic of natural resource exploitation was chosen for three reasons. The first reason is that cases concerning this issue have frequently been addressed by a large variety of international judicial bodies in the last decades. Examining that young and relatively large body of case law ensures that the conclusions drawn in this study reflect the current positions of the judicial bodies. The second reason for focusing on natural resource exploitation is that litigation on this topic is bound to become increasingly important in the coming years as the disputes and conflicts over the ownership and use of natural resources become more acute.[140] Furthermore, the significant overlap in the types of facts presented in these cases makes the possibility and risk of inconsistent decisions more tangible. The last, but certainly not least, reason for looking at disputes

---

138 Typically through their websites. See the Project on International Courts and Tribunals' website (<www.pict-pcti.org>) for an overview of the existing judicial bodies and where their case law can be found. See also the references on pp 20ff.

139 For judicial bodies that provide a searchable database, a variety of search terms were used to include natural resource cases, including 'mining', 'fishing', 'gas', etc. In the other databases, the selection was made by reading the summaries of the available cases.

140 On the one hand, because of the growing importance of natural resources in the global economy and, on the other hand, because the environmental degradation and human rights violations that often go hand in hand with this exploitation create local and transnational contestation.

on natural resource exploitation in the context of a study on common interest is that, by their very nature, these disputes often have a close link with conflicts between individual interests, such a property and livelihood, State interests, for example economic development, and more general common interests such as environmental protection.

The selection of judicial bodies in this study was inspired by the focus on natural resource cases that highlight the existing tensions between different individual and shared interests. The case law of seven (quasi) judicial regimes will be discussed: the International Court of Justice, the WTO Dispute Settlement Mechanism (DSM), the International Tribunal for the Law of the Sea, the European Court of Human Rights, the Inter-American Court of Human Rights, the African Commission on Human and Peoples' Rights, and the tribunals of the International Centre for Settlement of Investment Disputes. Because the previous section offered a more detailed discussion on what is considered as international litigation in this study,[141] it suffices to add that all of these bodies have dealt with disputes on natural resource exploitation on multiple occasions and, in addition, represent different forms of judicial dispute settlement at the international level.

In comparing the decision making of the different judicial systems, the basic principles of comparative law, as described by Reitz, will be followed. The first of these principles determines that it does not suffice to describe the relevant regimes and leave the act of comparison to the reader. Only by explicitly drawing the comparison between legal regimes will the intellectual benefit of studying a variety of judicial bodies become clear.[142] An added advantage of this approach that is particularly relevant in international law is that it clearly indicates why the law of international legal regimes that are less familiar to the reader (in analogy with comparative law: 'foreign law') can be relevant for the legal regime that he or she is most interested in ('the domestic legal system').

Secondly, comparative law takes a functional approach. In other words, it considers how different legal regimes deal with the same problem even though they use different terminologies, rules and procedures. Therefore, it is necessary to look at the regime as a whole when addressing differences or similarities. In this study, sufficient attention will therefore go to the context in which the judicial bodies operate as well as the substantive and procedural law that they apply. When looking at the latter elements it may seem that comparing the case law of different international judicial bodies is comparing apples with oranges. Nevertheless, comparison is possible and useful in this specific case because of the common problem that has been identified, in comparative law terms the

---

141 See pp 20ff.

142 J. Reitz, 'How To Do Comparative Law' (1998) 46 *American Journal of Comparative Law* 617, 618–20.

tertium comparationis.[143] In this context, it is important to note that in this study the problem of protecting common interest in international litigation is used as an analytical tool to compare how each legal system aims to solve this problem or does not address it at all. It should, however, not be seen as a normative argument in favour of protecting these interests by way of litigation. A third principle of comparative law states that, although comparison can stop with the identification of similarities and differences, it becomes more interesting when reasons are found for those commonalities or differences.[144] By looking at the broader system behind a specific judicial body, this study will try to identify at least some of 'the reasons why'. And lastly, to avoid the combination of a detailed description of each regime with an inevitably short and simplistic comparison at the end, the comparative law approach requires that each section of this study is comparative.[145]

1.2.3. STRUCTURE

The comparative approach strongly dictates the structure of this book. To make each section comparative, the overall problem of protecting common interests will be dealt with in different chapters that focus on the different steps of the judicial decision in which it manifests itself. Chapters 2 and 3 will clarify and compare how different international judicial bodies approach issues of common interest, when considering both procedural and substantive issues, by analysing their case law. These chapters will answer the questions of the extent to which international judicial bodies engage with common interests and what differences or similarities can be found between the different judicial bodies. Chapter 4 will identify some of the reasons that explain the differences or similarities in the decision making of the studied bodies. And, in conclusion, the analytical work done in the first chapters of the study will serve to address some of the concerns raised in the context of the fragmentation of international law. How can it be avoided that the adjudication of common interests on the international level leads to conflicting decisions? What options exist to come to more consistent decision making in common interest cases? These questions will be answered by identifying the positive and problematic aspects of the approaches in light of, on the one hand, the unity of international law and, on the other hand, the pursuit of common interests.

143 Ibid, 622–23.
144 Ibid, 626–27.
145 Ibid, 634.

CHAPTER 2
PROCEDURAL CONSIDERATIONS AND COMMON INTERESTS

2.1. INTRODUCTION

The procedure of an international court or tribunal is stipulated in its constitutive Treaty and elaborated in the relevant Statute or rules of procedure. At the procedural stage, the role of the judicial body therefore seems limited to applying those rules to which the parties consented (as a mere *bouche de la loi*) and it may be questioned whether the discussed 'emergence of the common interest' could be reflected in the decision-making process at this stage of the proceedings. However, closer examination shows that, in general, the procedural rules of international courts and tribunals often (purposely) leave gaps or only include minimal provisions that leave much room for interpretation. Furthermore, most statutes expressly provide that the relevant international court or tribunal has the power to determine its own rules of procedure[146] and to make procedural orders.[147] Thus, in most instances, the State parties have little to no impact on the specific content of the procedural decisions made by international courts and tribunals.[148]

When interpreting the broad procedural rules provided by the State parties, judicial bodies use different techniques that often have a 'harmonizing effect'

---

146 See, for example, Article 30 Statute of the International Court of Justice of 26 June 1945, Treaty Series, 993; Article 16 Annex VI United Nations Convention on the Law of the Sea of 10 December 1982, UN Treaty Series, vol. 1833, 3; Article 26(d) Convention for the Protection of Human Rights and Fundamental Freedoms of 4 November 1950, ETS, no. 5; Article 60 American Convention on Human Rights of 18 July 1978, OAS Treaty Series, no. 36; Article 17(9) Understanding on Rules and Procedures Governing the Settlement of Disputes, Marrakesh Agreement Establishing the World Trade Organization, Annex 2 of 15 April 1994, UN Treaty Series, vol. 1869, 401.

147 For example, Article 44 Convention on the Settlement of Investment Disputes Between States and Nationals of Other States of 14 October 1966, UN Treaty Series, vol. 575, 159.

148 In some instances, the Statute expressly provides that the parties may propose modifications or change the rules for one specific dispute. See Article 101 ICJ Rules of the Court of 14 April 1978, available at <www.icj-cij.org>; Article 48 ITLOS Rules of the Tribunal of 17 March 2009 (amended), available at <www.itlos.org>; Article 44 Convention on the Settlement of Investment Disputes Between States and Nationals of Other States of 14 October 1966, UN Treaty Series, vol. 575, 159.

on the procedures of the different courts and tribunals.[149] Thus, although the impact of the emerging common interest concept on the procedure of the international courts and tribunals has not sparked much interest, there is a large margin of discretion at this stage and a clear cross-fertilisation of jurisprudence, making the interpretation of procedural rules even more interesting in the context of the proliferation of international courts and tribunals.[150] This chapter will examine whether the selected judicial bodies provide openings to common interests in their procedure. It will focus on five types of procedural decisions, in order of appearance: decisions on jurisdiction, standing, evidence, third party interventions and provisional measures. Only a selection of judicial bodies will be studied for each procedural issue. This selection was made on the basis of the availability of case law that shows a link with both natural resource exploitation and common interests.

2.2. JURISDICTION

The first hurdle to overcome in bringing a case before an international court or tribunal is establishing that the judicial body approached has jurisdiction, that it has the right to interpret and apply the law. The jurisdiction of the examined judicial bodies is very different. In most of the examined cases, the bodies discussed enjoy compulsory jurisdiction over their members (and constituents). For example, the WTO DSM has compulsory jurisdiction over any dispute between WTO members arising under any of the covered agreements.[151] Under the Law of the Sea Convention, the ITLOS is only one of the options offered to the States to settle their disputes, nevertheless, it has compulsory jurisdiction in most of its case law because of specific provisions in the UNCLOS that, for example, give the Tribunal special jurisdiction in provisional measures.[152] The ECtHR enjoys compulsory contentious jurisdiction over alleged violations of the ECHR.[153] And a similar relationship exists between the IACtHR and the

---

149 Brown, above n 53, p 41.

150 One notable exception is an article by Benzing, who claims to be the first to study this topic in full. Benzing, above n 84, 369–408.

151 Article 1.1 Understanding on Rules and Procedures Governing the Settlement of Disputes, Marrakesh Agreement Establishing the World Trade Organization, Annex 2 of 15 April 1994, UN Treaty Series, vol. 1869, 401.

152 Article 287 United Nations Convention on the Law of the Sea of 10 December 1982, UN Treaty Series, vol. 1833, 3. State parties may also choose to bring their dispute before the ICJ or an Annex VII or Annex VIII arbitral tribunal. Arbitration falls under the provisions of Annex VII of the Convention or Annex VIII (for certain categories of disputes: fisheries, protection and preservation of the marine environment and marine scientific research or navigation); aside from the UNCLOS, State parties may also confer jurisdiction on the Tribunal in a multilateral agreement.

153 Article 32 Convention for the Protection of Human Rights and Fundamental Freedoms of 4 November 1950, ETS, no. 5.

American Convention and the ACHPR and the African Convention on Human and Peoples' Rights.[154] In these instances of compulsory jurisdiction, the consent of the parties has typically been given before the dispute arises by the ratification of the relevant Treaty and whether or not the procedure is (primarily) aimed at the enforcement of a common interest is of little relevance for the establishment of jurisdiction. Therefore, the discussion on jurisdiction will focus on the case law of the ICJ and will, only briefly, mention the case law of the ICSID tribunals.

2.2.1. INTERNATIONAL COURT OF JUSTICE

The ICJ's jurisdiction in contentious cases is based on Article 36 of the ICJ Statute.[155] Article 36 provides that the Court has jurisdiction (a) if the parties refer a dispute to it by special agreement, (b) if the ICJ's jurisdiction is provided for in a Treaty or Convention or (c) if the parties recognised the Court's compulsory jurisdiction a *proprio motu*. This Article reflects the principle of consent of the litigating parties, a principle that is applied strictly by the Court.[156] Unlike the bodies discussed above, the ICJ's jurisdiction is, in essence, always based on the consent of the parties; it only enjoys compulsory jurisdiction if the parties consented to recognise such jurisdiction. Because of this strict focus on consent, the Court's approach to matters of jurisdiction seems unlikely to be influenced by the involvement of common interest concerns.

At first glance, the ICJ's case law on natural resource exploitation confirms this assumption. Even in cases that concern *jus cogens* norms, norms from which no derogation is permitted because they are fundamental to the international community, the requirement of consensual jurisdiction prevails.[157] An example of the ICJ approach on *jus cogens* cases at the stage of jurisdiction can be found in *Armed Activities on the Territory of the Congo (DRC v Rwanda)*.[158] In this case,

---

154 Article 62 American Convention on Human Rights of 18 July 1978, OAS Treaty Series, no. 36; Article 45 African Charter on Human and Peoples' Rights of 21 October 1986, OAU Doc. CAB/LEG/67/3 rev. 5.

155 Article 36 Statute of the International Court of Justice of 26 June 1945, Treaty Series, 993.

156 A. von Bogdandy and I. Venzke, *On the Functions of International Courts: An Appraisal in Light of Their Burgeoning Public Authority*, ACIL Research Paper, no. 2012-10, Amsterdam Center for International Law, 2012, available at <ssrn.com>, 16 (later published in (2013) 26 *Leiden Journal of International Law* 49–72). An early example of this strict application can be found in the *Corfu Channel* case between the United Kingdom and Albania. In this case the Court refused to rely on a Security Council Resolution as a basis for jurisdiction. It stated that only the individual consent of the parties could establish its jurisdiction (ICJ, *Corfu Channel case (United Kingdom v Republic of Albania), Judgment*, Judgment of 1949).

157 The definition of peremptory norms can be found in Article 53 Vienna Convention on the Law of Treaties of 23 May 1969, UN Treaty Series, vol. 1155, 331.

158 ICJ, *Case of Armed Activities on the Territory of the Congo (New Application: 2002) (Democratic Republic of the Congo v Rwanda), Jurisdiction and Admissibility, Judgment*, Judgment of 2006.

the DRC requested that the Court establish the responsibility of Rwanda for the actions of Rwandese military units that had massacred civilians, destroyed property and plundered natural resources in the DRC.

In contrast to the similar case of *Armed Activities on the Territory of the Congo (DRC v Uganda)*,[159] jurisdiction in the Rwanda case could not be based on the optional declaration on compulsory jurisdiction made under Article 36 of the ICJ Statute.[160] Therefore, the DRC tried to establish jurisdiction on various bases, including the Genocide Convention. Its plea for jurisdiction based on *jus cogens* is of special relevance here because Rwanda had made a reservation to the Court's jurisdiction under the Genocide Convention. The DRC therefore claimed that the violation of a *jus cogens* norm confers jurisdiction on the ICJ that cannot be defeated by a reservation to the relevant Convention. It argued that Rwanda's reservation to the Article of the Genocide Convention that confers jurisdiction to the ICJ was invalid because the reservation is incompatible with the object and purpose of the Treaty.[161]

While the Court did recognise the existence of a *jus cogens* norm in its decision, it emphasised the consensual nature of its jurisdiction under Article 36 of its Statute and rejected the DRC's claim on the basis of admissibility.[162] According to the Court, a procedural reservation that only eliminates one method of adjudication does not contravene the object and purpose of the Treaty.[163] In other words, the Court confirmed that an application is inadmissible if the parties have not consented to its jurisdiction, even if *jus cogens* norms are invoked.[164] The Court did not limit this reasoning to peremptory norms.

---

159 ICJ, *Case of Armed Activities on the Territory of the Congo (Democratic Republic of the Congo v Uganda), Judgment*, Judgment of 2005.

160 Rwanda never made such a declaration. For a current list of countries that accepted the compulsory jurisdiction of the Court, see <www.icj-cij.org>, under contentious jurisdiction.

161 ICJ, *Case of Armed Activities on the Territory of the Congo (New Application: 2002) (Democratic Republic of the Congo v Rwanda), Jurisdiction and Admissibility, Judgment*, Judgment of 2006, para. 57.

162 Ibid, para. 64.

163 Ibid, para. 85. This decision was met by criticism. Judge Koroma criticises the Court's reasoning because there was no other method of adjudication. (ICJ, *Case of Armed Activities on the Territory of the Congo (New Application: 2002) (Democratic Republic of the Congo v Rwanda), Jurisdiction and Admissibility, Dissenting Opinion of Judge Koroma*, Judgment of 2006. Orakhelashvili regrets that the Court made this decision without examining the object and purpose of the Genocide Convention. A. Orakhelashvili, 'Case concerning Armed Activities on the Territory of the Congo (Democratic Republic of the Congo v. Rwanda), Jurisdiction and Admissibility, Judgment of 3 February 2006' (2006) 55 *International & Comparative Law Quarterly* 753, 759.

164 ICJ, *Case of Armed Activities on the Territory of the Congo (New Application: 2002) (Democratic Republic of the Congo v Rwanda), Jurisdiction and Admissibility, Judgment*, Judgment of 2006, para. 64.

It stated that the Court's jurisdiction always depends on the parties' consent, regardless of the substance of the dispute.[165]

In the context of its contentious case law, the fact that common interests are at risk does not lead the Court to abandon its strict application of consensual jurisdiction. The reason behind this approach may well be the reflex of the Court to protect its own continued authority. If the Court were to allow certain norms to defy the well-established principle of consensual jurisdiction, it would undermine its own legitimacy by opening the door to a number of cases involving non-consenting parties that would likely not comply with the Court's decision.[166] Nevertheless, several judges expressed their concern with the Court's differentiation between substance and jurisdiction in the *DRC v Rwanda* case. Their joint separate opinion indicates that the strict interpretation should in the future, in specific circumstances, be more flexible when establishing jurisdiction. In particular, they feel that it is not self-evident that a reservation made to the jurisdiction of the Court under the Genocide Convention is not incompatible with that Convention, which appoints the States as monitors of each other's compliance with the help of the ICJ.[167]

While the Court has not broadened its jurisdiction in favour of common interest concerns, it could be argued that it indirectly allowed Canada to enforce such concerns by rejecting jurisdiction in the 1998 *Fisheries Jurisdiction (Spain v Canada)* case.[168] This case concerned Canada's right to forcefully enforce its domestic legislation on the protection of fish stock in the high seas, outside its exclusive economic zone (EEZ), on Spanish vessels. Canada argued that the Court could not exercise its jurisdiction in this case because it had made a reservation to the ICJ's compulsory jurisdiction with regard to disputes on 'conservation and management measures for the purpose of fisheries conservation'. The Court included Canada's seizure by force of a Spanish vessel in the high seas in its broad interpretation of 'conservation and management measures' and rejected jurisdiction.[169]

An issue related to consensual jurisdiction that may hinder the Court in accepting jurisdiction in common interest cases is the ICJ's indispensable or

165 Ibid, para. 125. The Court's recognition of *jus cogens* norms may, however, in the future lead to jurisdiction based on Article 66 of the VCLT in cases where a dispute exists between a treaty (which came into force after the VCLT) and a peremptory norm of international law. M. Stephen, 'The 2006 Judicial Activity of the International Court of Justice' (2007) 101 *American Journal of International Law* 602, 604–05.

166 Nollkaemper, above n 79, 21; D. Hammer, 'Allowing Genocide?: An Analysis of Armed Activities on the Territory of the Congo, Jurisdictional Reservations, and the Legitimacy of the International Court of Justice' (2007) 16 *Minnesota Journal of International Law* 495, 508.

167 ICJ, *Case of Armed Activities on the Territory of the Congo (New Application: 2002) (Democratic Republic of the Congo v Rwanda), Joint Separate Opinion of Judges Higgins, Kooijmans, Elaraby, Owada and Simma*, Judgment of 2006, paras. 24–29.

168 ICJ, *Case of Fisheries Jurisdiction (Spain v Canada), Jurisdiction, Judgment*, Judgment of 1998.

169 Ibid, 87.

necessary third party doctrine. This doctrine or 'procedural straightjacket' was first defined in the *Monetary Gold* case and requires that each third party in the dispute accepts the Court's jurisdiction if its 'legal interests would not only be affected by the decision, but would form the very subject matter of the decision'.[170] The Court applied the necessary third party doctrine in the context of *erga omnes* obligations, obligations towards the international community as a whole, in the case concerning *East Timor (Portugal v Australia)*.[171]

In the 1995 *East Timor* case, Portugal asked the ICJ to establish, inter alia, that Australia did not respect the right of the people of East Timor to self-determination. However, in examining this issue the Court would inevitably rule on the lawfulness of the actions of a third party, namely Indonesia. Thus, the ICJ recognised the *erga omnes* character of the right to self-determination but rejected jurisdiction on the basis of the *Monetary Gold* principle because Indonesia did not consent to its jurisdiction. As stated by the Court, 'the *erga omnes* character of a norm and the rule of consent to jurisdiction are two different things'.[172] While this decision does not detract from the Court's recognition of *erga omnes* rules, it does not help their enforcement either.

Interestingly, the Court's interpretation of the indispensable third party doctrine was more liberal in the 2005 case of *Armed Activities on the Territory of the Congo (DRC v Uganda)*.[173] In essence, this case addressed the same factual situation as the discussed case of the *DRC v Rwanda* and similar violations were claimed, i.e. violation of the principle of non-intervention, violations of human rights and international humanitarian law (*jus cogens*) and the illegal exploitation of natural resources. However, despite the lack of consent from the third party Rwanda, the Court found it had jurisdiction in this case because the legal interests of Rwanda did not form the subject matter of its decision and

---

170 ICJ, *Case of the monetary gold removed from Rome in 1943 (Preliminary Question), Judgment*, Judgment of 1954, 17; Simma, above n 1, 298.

171 ICJ, *Case of East Timor (Portugal v Australia), Judgment*, Judgment of 1995. *Erga omnes* rules were first recognised in the *Barcelona Traction* case (ICJ, *Case of Barcelona Traction, Light and Power Company, Limited, Judgment*, Judgment of 1970), see p 40.

172 ICJ, *Case of East Timor (Portugal v Australia), Judgment*, Judgment of 1995, para. 29. The concepts of both *erga omnes* and *jus cogens* refer to rules which are of common interest. While an *erga omnes* rule refers to a norm that is owed to the international community, the concept of *jus cogens* endows such a norm with specific legal effects. Simma, above n 1, 300.

173 ICJ, *Case of Armed Activities on the Territory of the Congo (Democratic Republic of the Congo v Uganda), Judgment*, Judgment of 2005. This is in line with the Court's decision in *Nauru v Australia* and not the more restrictive precedent of the *Monetary Gold* case. In *Nauru v Australia*, the ICJ established that it cannot decline jurisdiction in cases in which a third State 'has an interest of a legal nature which may be affected by the decision in the case', provided that 'the legal interests of the third State which may possibly be affected do not form the very subject-matter of the decision that is applied for'. ICJ, *Case of Certain Phosphate Lands in Nauru (Nauru v Australia), Preliminary Objections, Judgment*, Judgment of 1992, para. 54.

Rwanda's responsibility did not need to be determined to come to a judgment on the alleged violations by Uganda.[174]

It can therefore be concluded that the Court's strict interpretation of the principle of consensual jurisdiction seems to be broadened in comparison to its earlier decision in the *East Timor* case. Thus, common interest considerations have affected at least one step of the ICJ's decision-making process, namely its identification of the indispensable third parties. This was confirmed by ad hoc Judge Dugard (in his *separate opinion* to the Rwanda case) in relation to the *DRC v Uganda* case: 'Although the Court did not indicate that its choice was influenced by the fact that norms of jus cogens were involved in this case, it may safely be assumed that the gravity of the issues raised influenced the Court's choice.'[175]

A more relaxed interpretation of the indispensable third party doctrine may prove especially relevant in common interest cases, where it is often not possible to determine the contribution of each party involved and to find a judicial body that has jurisdiction on each of them.

2.2.2. INTERNATIONAL CENTRE FOR SETTLEMENT OF INVESTMENT DISPUTES

In determining its jurisdiction, an ICSID tribunal has to take account of both the relevant investment agreement (IIA) and the ICSID Convention. Article 25 of the ICSID Convention provides that

> [t]he jurisdiction of the Centre shall extend to any legal dispute arising directly out of an investment, between a Contracting State (or any constituent subdivision or agency of a Contracting State designated to the Centre by that State) and a national of another Contracting State, which the parties to the dispute consent in writing to submit to the Centre. When the parties have given their consent, no party may withdraw its consent unilaterally.[176]

Of special importance for common interest disputes is the Convention's limitation to conflicts that arise directly from investments. In the case of *Suez, Sociedad General de Aguas de Barcelona S.A. and Vivendi Universal S.A. v Argentine Republic*, Argentina held that the Tribunal did not enjoy jurisdiction

174 ICJ, *Case of Armed Activities on the Territory of the Congo (Democratic Republic of the Congo v Uganda), Judgment*, Judgment of 2005, para. 204.

175 ICJ, *Case of Armed Activities on the Territory of the Congo (New Application: 2002) (Democratic Republic of the Congo v Rwanda), Jurisdiction and Admissibility, Separate Opinion Judge Ad Hoc Dugard*, Judgment of 2006, para. 11.

176 Article 25 Convention on the Settlement of Investment Disputes Between States and Nationals of Other States of 14 October 1966, UN Treaty Series, vol. 575, 159.

because, in essence, the dispute concerned the appropriateness of public interest measures and did not arise directly out of the investments affected by these measures.[177] However, the claimants argued that the disputed measures 'specifically, concretely, and directly' violated the provisions of the concession granted to them by Argentina.[178] The ICSID Tribunal endorsed the latter argument and held that 'the disagreement arises directly out of the investment impacted by governmental measures, not out of the measures themselves'.[179]

The ICSID Convention is not the only source of procedural provisions that has to be applied by ICSID tribunals. International investment agreements often prescribe specific obligations (such as waiting periods before the start of an arbitration) and specific limitations to the jurisdiction of the ICSID Tribunal (for example jurisdiction limited to the amount of compensation in expropriation disputes). To escape these requirements and limitations, claimants have argued that investment tribunals should apply the more favourable provisions of other IIAs on the basis of the Most Favoured Nation (MFN) clause in the applicable IIA. In international investment law, an MFN clause is a non-discrimination clause that guarantees that a covered foreign investor is given a treatment that is no less favourable than the treatment given to a third foreign investor. By including this clause in an international investment agreement, the agreement allows the parties to invoke more favourable provisions of IIAs that have been concluded between the host State and third States. In other words, it multilateralises bilateral and regional investment agreements.[180]

There has been some discussion on whether MFN treatment is also applicable in procedural matters. The *ejusdem generis* principle determines that an MFN clause only applies to issues belonging to the same subject matter or the same category of subjects to which the clause relates. However, in the case of *Maffezini v Spain*, an ICSID tribunal determined that procedural and substantive rights are inextricably linked in modern IIAs.[181] Therefore, it found that the *ejusdem generis* rule was not violated by invoking the relevant MFN clause in the context of procedural rules. The *Maffezini* case did not concern the jurisdiction of the Tribunal but the length of the waiting period required by the BIT before the party could bring a claim before an investment tribunal. In deciding on the jurisdiction of the Tribunal, most tribunals have decided against the use of MFN clauses because a

---

177 ICSID, *Suez, Sociedad General de Aguas de Barcelona S.A., and Vivendi Universal S.A. v the Argentine Republic, Decision on Jurisdiction*, ICSID case no. ARB/03/19, 03.08.2006, para. 27.

178 Ibid, para. 28.

179 Ibid, para. 29.

180 S. Schill, *The Multilateralization of International Investment Law*, Cambridge University Press, Cambridge 2009, pp 151ff.

181 ICSID, *Maffezini v Spain, Decision on Objections to Jurisdiction* ICSID case no. ARB/97/7, 25.01.2000, paras. 54–55.

fundamental requirement for arbitration is the clear and unambiguous consent of the parties.[182] Thus, the majority of ICSID tribunals are not willing to extend their jurisdiction on the basis of an MFN clause that does not explicitly include procedural matters.

2.2.3. SUMMARY: JURISDICTION AND COMMON INTEREST

As stated in the introduction, it is not easy to see how the consideration and enforcement of common interests fits into the existing international judicial system. This is especially true for institutions that were explicitly established to preserve the 'individual' interests of States in the international arena. Institutions such as the ICJ have a strictly bilateral character and their jurisdiction is based on consent. As shown above, the principle of consensual jurisdiction presents a major obstacle in the enforcement of common interest concerns before the ICJ. In its contentious case law, the substance of the dispute does not affect the Court's strict application of consensual jurisdiction. This strict approach is likely inspired by a fear that non-consenting parties would not comply with the Court's decisions and thus affect its authority. Nevertheless, it has been observed that the Court is no model of consistency when it comes to matters of jurisdiction. In the margins of its decisions on jurisdiction, it is adopting a more lenient approach to the doctrine of necessary third parties in cases that involve common interests. In spite of the discussed difficulties in establishing jurisdiction for the sole purpose of enforcing common interests, disputes that, inter alia, focus on common interests are brought to the ICJ with the consent of the parties or under its compulsory jurisdiction. Furthermore, compulsory jurisdiction has been established in different areas of international law. Thus, the traditional bilateral character of dispute settlement at the international level does not prevent common interest cases from being brought before international judicial bodies.

2.3. STANDING

For a claim to be admissible, the judicial body must not only confirm that it has jurisdiction to hear the dispute, but it must also find that the claimant has standing, the right to initiate a suit. When discussing the requirement of

---

182 See, among others, ICSID, *Salini v Jordan, Decision on Jurisdiction*, ICSID case no. ARB/02/13, 15.11.2004, para. 198; ICSID, *Plama v Bulgaria, Decision on Jurisdiction*, ICSID case no. ARB/03/24, 08.02.2005. Schill prefers a broad application of the MFN clause, but provides a good overview of the majority line of reasoning that applies a strict interpretation in cases on jurisdiction. SCHILL, above n 180, pp 165–71.

standing, two elements should be examined that affect the probability that the judicial body will be faced with issues of common interest. First, it is important to determine which entities can acquire standing: is standing limited to States or victims or can groups, NGOs or non-victimised individuals, who may have easier access to knowledge and resources than the victims, also obtain standing? A second element that may affect the consideration of common interests is the qualification of standing, in other words whether the claimant must establish a legal interest to obtain the right of standing or whether the common interest of enforcing the relevant legal regime *an sich* suffices.

2.3.1. INTERNATIONAL COURT OF JUSTICE

Article 34§1 of the ICJ Statute provides that '[o]nly states may be parties in cases before the Court'. As a consequence, both non-governmental and governmental public interest organisations are excluded from bringing a claim before the Court. Thus, only an individual State can bring a claim before the ICJ to enforce a common or public interest.[183] Whether the bilateral ICJ procedure allows for such a case to be brought forward by a State that has no direct, individual, legal interest in the issue is disputed.

In the 1966 *South West Africa Case (Ethiopia and Liberia v South Africa)* the Court had to decide whether Ethiopia and Liberia could file a claim against South Africa for not fulfilling its duties as a mandate holder over South West Africa (now Namibia).[184] The ICJ rejected the claim, holding that international law does not include a right for each State to take legal action in the common interest.[185] However, the Court seemed to distance itself from this decision with the recognition of *erga omnes* rules in the 1970 *Barcelona Traction Case (Belgium v Spain)*.[186]

In *Barcelona Traction*, Belgium filed a claim against Spain for restricting a Canadian business operating in Spain that was largely owned by Belgian stockholders. The Court found that Belgium did not have standing because only Canada could exercise diplomatic protection over the company. The Court made a distinction between two types of obligations.

> [A]n essential distinction should be drawn between the obligations of a State towards the international community as a whole, and those arising vis-à-vis another State in the

183 Fitzmaurice suggests granting standing to international public interest organisations with consultative status at the UN, in particular in *erga omnes* cases that relate to the common interest. Fitzmaurice, above n 31, 398.

184 ICJ, *Case of South West Africa, Second Phase, Judgment*, Judgment of 1966.

185 Ibid, para. 88.

186 ICJ, *Case of Barcelona Traction, Light and Power Company, Limited, Judgment*, Judgment of 1970.

> field of diplomatic protection. By their very nature, the former are the concern of all States. In view of the importance of the rights involved, all States can be held to have a legal interest in their protection; they are obligations erga omnes.[187]

By adopting the *erga omnes* concept, the Court recognised that fundamental community interests warrant judicial protection by the ICJ. Nevertheless, the question whether all States have standing in cases when *erga omnes* obligations are at risk remained completely unanswered until 2012 because the *erga omnes* concept was never used by States to obtain standing before the ICJ.

In the context of Uganda's counterclaim in *Armed Activities on the Territory of the Congo (DRC v Uganda)*, the Court could have established standing on the ground of the alleged violation of obligations of a general nature, but it neglected to do so. As part of its counterclaim, Uganda stated that the Congolese Forces Armées Congolaises (FAC) had subjected Ugandan nationals to inhumane treatment at Ndjili International Airport and argued that this treatment was in breach of the international minimum standards on the treatment of foreign nationals.[188] The Court assumed that, with this claim, Uganda wished to exercise its right to diplomatic protection of its nationals. The Court, however, found this claim to be inadmissible because it could not be proven that the persons concerned were Ugandan nationals.[189] Therefore, Uganda did not enjoy standing.

In this case, the ICJ preferred to stay within the framework of diplomatic protection despite the human rights and humanitarian issues at stake. The ICJ did not give Uganda standing to claim the breach of *erga omnes* obligations with respect to persons that may not have been its nationals. While it could be argued that Uganda did not intend to protect non-nationals, Judge Simma accuses the Court of 'unnecessary caution' in this matter:[190] 'A reminder by the Court of the applicability of international humanitarian and human rights law standards and of Uganda's standing to raise violations of the obligations deriving from these standards by the DRC would, in my view, not have gone ultra petita partium.'[191]

Whether all States have standing in cases where *erga omnes partes* obligations are at risk was answered in the 2012 case of *Questions concerning the Obligation to Prosecute or Extradite (Belgium v Senegal)*, at least to the extent that the relevant obligation is included in a Treaty. In this case, Belgium asserted that

---

187 Ibid, para. 32.

188 ICJ, *Case of Armed Activities on the Territory of the Congo (Democratic Republic of the Congo v Uganda), Judgment*, Judgment of 2005, para. 313.

189 Ibid, para. 333.

190 ICJ, *Case of Armed Activities on the Territory of the Congo (Democratic Republic of the Congo v Uganda), Separate Opinion Judge Simma*, Judgment of 2005, paras. 17–18. On the issue of standing, Simma recognises that Uganda did not ask for standing on the basis of humanitarian or human rights law, but argues that it would have standing in these circumstances. Ibid, paras. 32–36.

191 Ibid, para. 37.

Senegal was obliged, under the Convention against Torture, to prosecute or extradite Hissène Habré, the former president of Chad. Belgium argued that it had standing because of its specific interest as a home State of former victims of the regime and because of the *erga omnes* nature of the relevant obligations. The Court focused only on the latter argument: '[t]he common interest in compliance with the relevant obligations under the Convention against Torture implies the entitlement of each State party to the Convention to make a claim concerning the cessation of an alleged breach by another State party.'[192]

2.3.2. INTERNATIONAL TRIBUNAL FOR THE LAW OF THE SEA

Like the ICJ Statute, Article 291 of the UNCLOS determines that in principle only States have access to the Tribunal. The fact that non-State entities do not enjoy the right to bring a case before the ITLOS automatically limits the number of common interest cases. However, in comparison with other international judicial mechanisms, the UNCLOS and the ITLOS Rules have a lot to offer to non-State actors. According to Article 20 of the ITLOS Statute 'entities other than States' (corporations and citizens of State parties) have access to the Seabed Dispute Chamber in disputes concerning the seabed, ocean floor and subsoil and to the Tribunal in cases based on an agreement that confers jurisdiction on the ITLOS.[193] Nevertheless, it is disputed whether NGOs could be granted standing under this provision and whether an 'agreement conferring jurisdiction' includes agreements between States and non-State actors.[194] To date, no disputes have, however, been brought to the Seabed Disputes Chamber or the Tribunal by non-State entities and therefore it remains uncertain whether this exception will have an impact on the enforcement of common interest obligations.

Another issue that has yet to be raised in the Tribunal's case law is whether the ITLOS requires a claimant State to have a direct legal interest in the dispute. Such a demand would limit the possibilities for States to enforce obligations *erga omnes*, owed to the international community as a whole. In the context of the Tribunal's procedure for the prompt release of vessels, the UNCLOS does state that 'the application for release may be made only by or on behalf of the flag

---

192 ICJ, *Case of Questions relating to the Obligation to Prosecute or Extradite (Belgium v Senegal), Judgment*, Judgment of 2012, para. 69.

193 Article 291(2), 187 United Nations Convention on the Law of the Sea of 10 December 1982, UN Treaty Series, vol. 1833, 3; Article 20(2), 37 Annex VI United Nations Convention on the Law of the Sea of 10 December 1982, UN Treaty Series, vol. 1833, 3.

194 Gautier argues that NGOs that are considered to have international legal personality may have standing before the ITLOS. P. Gautier, 'NGOs and Law of the Sea Disputes' in T. Treves (ed), *Civil Society, International Courts and Compliance Bodies*, Cambridge University Press, Cambridge 2005, pp 235–36.

State of the vessel'.[195] Nevertheless, the ITLOS case law shows that the Tribunal interprets this provision rather broadly to ensure that the common values of the international community are respected.

In its first judgment on the merits, the *M/V 'Saiga' (No. 2) Case (Saint Vincent and the Grenadines v Guinea)*, the Tribunal had to pronounce on the legitimacy of the use of force in arresting a vessel.[196] The conflict between Saint Vincent and the Grenadines and Guinea arose after Guinean patrol boats violently arrested the *M/V Saiga*, a tanker supplying gas oil to vessels fishing in the Guinean EEZ. During the arrest, two members of the *M/V Saiga*'s crew suffered gunshot wounds. In response, Saint Vincent sought an order for prompt release of the vessel and its crew at the ITLOS, which was granted shortly afterwards.[197] Guinea did not comply with this order, but agreed to submit the dispute to the Tribunal for a judgment on the merits.

One of the first issues addressed by the Tribunal was the capacity of Saint Vincent as the flag State of the *M/V Saiga*. Guinea argued that the ship did not have a nationality at the time of the arrest. Despite inconclusive evidence to the contrary,[198] the Tribunal found that '[i]n the particular circumstances of this case, it would not be consistent with justice if the Tribunal were to decline to deal with the merits of the dispute'.[199] The Tribunal took a similar stance in examining whether it could decide on issues that concerned crew members who did not have the nationality of Saint Vincent and the Grenadines. In this regard, the ITLOS found that the ship and everyone involved in its operations constituted one entity that was linked to the flag State.[200] The Tribunal based its finding on the fact that 'undue hardship would ensue' if it obliged each person to seek the protection of its own State.[201]

2.3.3. WTO DISPUTE SETTLEMENT MECHANISM

Because the WTO's dispute settlement system is strictly intergovernmental, the actor denouncing the inconsistency of a Member State's measure(s) with

---

195 Article 292(2) United Nations Convention on the Law of the Sea of 10 December 1982, UN Treaty Series, vol. 1833, 3.

196 ITLOS, *The M/V 'Saiga' (No. 2) Case, Judgment*, Judgment of 1999.

197 ITLOS, *The M/V 'Saiga' Case, Prompt Release*, Judgment of 1997.

198 ITLOS, *The M/V 'Saiga' (No. 2) Case, Dissenting opinion of Judge Warioba*, Judgment of 1999, paras. 22–29.

199 ITLOS, *The M/V 'Saiga' (No. 2) Case, Judgment*, Judgment of 1999, para. 73. For a commentary on the ITLOS' interpretation of 'flag state' and 'genuine link', see B. Oxman and V. Bantz, 'The M/V "Saiga" (No. 2) (Saint Vincent and the Grenadines v. Guinea), Judgment (ITLOS Case No. 2)' (2000) 94, *American Journal of International Law* 140, 140–50.

200 ITLOS, *The M/V 'Saiga' (No. 2) Case, Judgment*, Judgment of 1999, para. 106.

201 Ibid, para. 107.

WTO trade rules has to be a WTO Member State.[202] Therefore, private parties, including those that pursue common interest goals, may not bring claims before the WTO DSM. Despite the inter-State nature of the mechanism, it is generally accepted that private firms and industry sectors indirectly participate in the WTO dispute settlement procedure through ad hoc networks with public authorities. The panel in the case of *US – Sections 301–310 of the Trade Act* explicitly recognised that the WTO ultimately protects the economic activities of individuals.[203] Although the private interests behind a WTO claim are often hidden, it may be assumed that partnerships between governments and private partners are common in the costly WTO system.[204] Because the private partners pursue their individual trade interests, it seems unlikely that these partnerships influence the advancement of common interest arguments.

A second element that may affect the consideration of common interests is the qualification of standing, in other words whether the claimant must establish a legal interest to obtain the right of standing or whether the common interest of enforcing the WTO system, in the interest of sustainable development, suffices. In the case of *European Communities – Regime for the Importation, Sale and Distribution of Bananas*, the AB held that neither the Dispute Settlement Understanding (DSU) nor the GATT require a legal interest to obtain standing.[205] Nevertheless, the AB did confirm the panel's reasoning that 'with the increased interdependence of the global economy … any deviation from the negotiated balance of rights and obligations is more likely than ever to affect [other Members], directly or indirectly'.[206]

It may therefore be concluded that the WTO's judicial bodies interpret standing very broadly. A mere potential impact on the interest of the complainant was considered sufficient to establish standing in the case of *EC – Bananas*. Furthermore, a member may challenge a domestic provision that it considers inconsistent with international trade law before it is even applied.[207] However, it is uncertain whether the WTO DSM considers WTO obligations as obligations owed to all WTO members, *erga omnes partes*. At least an indirect

202 Article 3 Understanding on Rules and Procedures Governing the Settlement of Disputes, Marrakesh Agreement Establishing the World Trade Organization, Annex 2 of 15 April 1994, UN Treaty Series, vol. 1869, 401.

203 WTO Panel Report, *United States – Sections 301–310 of the Trade Act of 1974*, WT/DS152/R, adopted 22.12.1999, paras. 7.71ff.

204 An older book by Shaffer provides insight into the dynamics of these public–private partnerships. G.C. Shaffer, *Defending Interests: Public-private Partnerships in WTO Litigation*, Brookings Institution Press, Washington, DC 2003.

205 WTO Appellate Body Report, *European Communities – Regime for the Importation, Sale and Distribution of Bananas*, WT/DS27/AB/R, adopted 09.09.1997, para. 132.

206 Ibid, para. 136.

207 Ibid, paras. 132–35.

nexus between the interests of the complainant and the alleged violation seems to be required.[208]

2.3.4. REGIONAL HUMAN RIGHTS MECHANISMS

2.3.4.1. *European Court of Human Rights*

Whether the ECtHR may allow applicants to bring common or public interest cases before it is answered partially by the Convention's requirements on standing. With the entry into force of Protocol 11 in 1998, the number of entities that may bring cases before the ECtHR was significantly expanded. Article 34 of the ECHR now provides that

> [t]he Court may receive [individual] applications from any person, nongovernmental organisation or group of individuals claiming to be the victim of a violation by one of the High Contracting Parties of the rights set forth in the Convention or the protocols thereto.

While the European Convention allows NGOs and groups to submit a complaint, all non-State entities must fulfil the same requirements as individual claimants. One of these requirements is that the claimant has to be the direct victim of a violation of the human rights protected by the Convention. This limits the consideration of common interest cases because an *actio popularis*, a claim justified by the common interest of observing the Convention, may only be instituted by a State under Article 33 ECHR.[209] Thus, the enforcement of common interests often depends on the willingness of States to bring cases before the Court.[210] Because of the requirement of 'victimhood', NGOs mainly operate as representatives of victims in the context of the European Court.[211] An example of an exploitation case in which an NGO served as one of the victims' legal counsel is the case of *Tătar v Romania*.[212] This case concerned a massive spill of cyanide-contaminated water from a goldmine in Baia Mare. The Association for the Defence of Human Rights in Romania/Helsinki Committee (APADOR-CH) represented the applicants, who claimed that Romania had failed to fulfil its

---

208 Benzing, above n 84, 398.

209 Unlike Article 33, Article 34 does not allow complaints *in abstracto* of a violation of the Convention. The Court has always rejected cases designed to ascertain the compatibility of a law with the ECHR and *actio popularis* (ECtHR 27.03.1962, *De Becker v Belgium*, no. 214/5, para. 14; ECtHR 06.09.1978, *Klass and Others v Germany*, no. 5029/71, para. 33.

210 Looking at the number of inter-State cases this is low (not even a dozen cases can be found in the HUDOC database available at <hudoc.echr.coe.int>).

211 Serving as a representative has become the primary way NGOs come before the ECtHR.

212 ECtHR 27.01.2009, *Tătar c. Roumanie* (only available in French), no. 67021/01.

positive obligation to protect their private and family life by not taking sufficient steps to prevent (future) accidents. After the Court's decision, the NGO stressed the broader importance of the case, which served to stop the use of sodium cyanide not only at Baia Mare, but also at other exploitation sites.[213]

2.3.4.2. Inter-American Court of Human Rights

The requirement of standing before the IACtHR is different from that of the ECtHR. The Court does not grant direct access to individual petitioners but only deals with contentious cases that have been processed by the Inter-American Commission on Human Rights (IACHR) and only the Commission itself or a State that is a party in the dispute can refer such a case to the Court.[214] The Commission thus functions as a gatekeeper for the Court, which limits standing *ratione personae*.[215] The Commission will refer the case if the Commission's recommendations have not been followed by the State unless an absolute majority of Commission members decides otherwise.[216]

The requirement of standing at the level of the Commission is, in principle, extremely lenient. According to the Convention, a right to petition is granted to any person or group or NGO and there is no requirement of victimhood.[217] However, at the level of the Court a concrete violation of a human right of a specific individual is required. This introduction of the requirement of victimhood is heavily inspired by the case law of the European Court.[218] In line with the Court, the Commission now also requires that there are specific, individual and identifiable victims, although the claimant does not have to be a victim.[219] Thus, similar to the European human rights regime, an *actio popularis*

---

213 APADOR-CH, The European Court of Human Rights Judgement in the case Tatar & Tatar v. Romania, Press Release 27.01.2009.

214 Article 61 American Convention on Human Rights of 18 July 1978, OAS Treaty Series, no. 36.

215 The Commission's role is, however, different with regard to the OAS members that did not ratify the Convention. For those members, the Commission promotes and monitors compliance with the Declaration's provisions in a quasi-judicial manner. L. Hennebel, 'The Inter-American System for Human Rights: Operation and Achievements' in F. Gómez Isa and K. De Feyter (eds), *International Human Rights Law in a Global Context*, University of Deusto, Bilbao 2009, pp 807–10.

216 Article 45(1) Rules of Procedure of the Inter-American Commission on Human Rights of 1 August 2013, available at <www.oas.org>.

217 Article 44 American Convention on Human Rights of 18 July 1978, OAS Treaty Series, no. 36.

218 See multiple references to ECtHR cases in Inter-American Court of Human Rights, *Case of International Responsibility for the Promulgation and Enforcement of Laws in Violation of the Convention (Arts. 1 and 2 of the American Convention on Human Rights), Advisory Opinion* Judgment of 9 December 1994, para. 47.

219 See for example Inter-American Commission of Human Rights, *Case of Metropolitan Nature Reserve v Panama*, Judgment of 22.10.2003, para. 28.

with the sole purpose of enforcing a common interest will not be accepted in the inter-American system.[220]

2.3.4.3. *African Commission on Human and Peoples' Rights*

Unlike the European and Inter-American Court, the African Commission has received complaints of both (groups of) victims and those complaining on behalf of such victims from its inception.[221] This wide acceptance of complainants has contributed significantly to the (relative) success of the Commission, as NGOs have been shown to be its main litigants.[222] As a consequence of the Commission's acceptance of *actio popularis*, its case law includes various cases that concern interests much wider than those of the typical individual petitioner. One example thereof is the landmark decision of *The Social and Economic Rights Action Center and the Center for Economic and Social Rights v Nigeria*.[223] This case was brought to the Commission by the Social and Economic Rights Action Center and the Center for Economic and Social Rights, two NGOs that accused the State-owned oil-extracting company of causing large-scale environmental and health problems in the territory of the indigenous Ogoni Community. In its decision, the Commission thanks the NGOs for bringing the complaints under its purview: 'Such is a demonstration of the usefulness to the Commission and individuals of actio popularis, which is wisely allowed under the African Charter'.[224]

2.3.5. SUMMARY: STANDING AND COMMON INTEREST

The examination of standing in the selected judicial bodies has shown that an *actio popularis*, or a claim in the public interest, is accepted in certain circumstances. The ICJ has recently and rather unexpectedly accepted that

220 See also C. Schall, 'Public Interest Litigation concerning Environmental Matters before Human Rights Courts: A Promising Future Concept' (2008) 20 *Journal of Environmental Law* 417, 422–23.

221 Article 55 African Charter on Human and Peoples' Rights of 21 October 1986, OAU Doc. CAB/LEG/67/3 rev. 5. This Article does not pose any limitations on who can lodge a complaint with the Commission.

222 N. Mbelle, 'The Role of Non-governmental Organisations and National Human Rights Institutions at the African Commission' in M.D. Evans and R. Murray (eds), *The African Charter on Human and Peoples' Rights: The System in Practice, 1986–2000*, Cambridge University Press, Cambridge 2008, p 308.

223 African Commission on Human and Peoples' Rights October 2001, *The Social and Economic Rights Action Center and the Center for Economic and Social Rights v Nigeria*, no. 155/96.

224 Ibid, para. 49.

each State party to a specific Treaty has standing to demand the cessation of a violation of an *erga omnes partes* obligation included in the said Treaty. The WTO would most likely follow a similar interpretation when an important obligation in one of the covered agreements is breached. However, despite the AB's broad interpretation of the requirements for obtaining standing, it seems unlikely that States would bring violations of WTO law before the WTO DSM without having an economic or other interest in the dispute. The ITLOS has gone one step further by applying a broad interpretation of standing where a common interest is at stake that is not explicitly protected by the Law of the Sea Convention, namely the protection of the human rights of seamen. The regional human rights courts use a more strict definition of standing for individuals that requires (at least) an identifiable violation and victim. The interpretation of standing by the IACtHR in this matter was clearly influenced by the ECtHR's approach, which is expected to become increasingly strict as the number of cases brought before the Court keeps increasing and the Court struggles to fulfil its primary purpose (in individual complaints) of remedying specific and direct human rights violations. The African Commission does not follow this interpretation, which is limited to individual victims and allows public interest litigation. This different approach reflects the substantive law of the African Charter, which includes peoples' rights besides individual human rights.

2.4. EVIDENCE

A third procedural issue that may be influenced by considerations of common interest is the Court's rules on evidence. Aside from the ICC and tribunals, most of the international judicial bodies have an adversarial procedure. This implies that the court relies strictly on the submissions of the parties when establishing the facts of the case and only in exceptional circumstances uses the fact-finding powers that it might have or that are considered to be inherent in its function. While this adversarial procedure and hesitant use of fact-finding powers serves its purpose in disputes that only concern the parties, a more active fact-finding role may be necessary for the court to obtain a clear picture of the complex circumstances when common interests are at stake that are not, or not extensively, presented by the parties.[225] In studying the effect of common interests on procedural decisions, it is therefore useful to determine whether judicial bodies are more likely to use their fact-finding tools in such situations. In addition, the allocation of the burden of proof and the determination of the standard of proof, or the quality of evidence required, may also be affected by the

[225] Benzing, above n 84, 383–84.

common interests that are involved, especially in situations where provisional measures are requested.

2.4.1. INTERNATIONAL COURT OF JUSTICE

In spite of its adversarial nature, the ICJ has some procedural mechanisms at its disposal to complement the facts put forward by the litigating States. The ICJ has always adopted a liberal approach to the procedural issue of evidence and found that it has a certain 'freedom in estimating the value of the various elements of evidence'.[226] Thus, although the provisions on evidence are no different in cases where public or common interests are involved, the Court may consider the context of the case and choose to interpret them accordingly.

The provisions in the ICJ Statute with regard to evidence and procedure empower the Court to request the production of evidence from the parties, order an expert opinion and ask 'relevant questions' during the hearing and make site visits.[227] In general, the Court is rather reluctant to apply its fact-finding mechanisms. It is therefore all the more noticeable that those cases in which the Court did take a more active stance involve interests of common concern.[228] For example, the first and currently only case in which the ICJ has made a site visit is the dispute on the *Gabčíkovo-Nagymaros Project (Hungary/Slovakia)*.[229]

The *Gabčíkovo-Nagymaros* case concerned a conflict between Hungary and Slovakia on a joint project for the construction of a system of dams on the Danube. The dispute arose when Hungary refused to further implement the project in 1989 (as had been agreed in a Treaty of 1977) for environmental reasons and Slovakia in response constructed an alternative system on its own territory. During the proceedings, the Court was invited by both parties to visit the disputed project and collect evidence *in situ*.[230] To say that the ICJ's decision to accept this invitation was influenced by the presence of important environmental issues is pure speculation. Nevertheless, the relation between a more active Court and the involvement of common interests seemed noteworthy.[231]

---

226 ICJ, *Case of Military and Paramilitary Activities in and against Nicaragua (Nicaragua v United States of America), Judgment on the merits*, Judgment of 1986, para. 60.

227 Articles 44, 49–51 Statute of the International Court of Justice of 26 June 1945, Treaty Series, 993.

228 For an overview of cases involving 'community interests' see Benzing, above n 84, 385–86.

229 ICJ, *Case of Gabčíkovo-Nagymaros Project (Hungary/Slovakia), Judgment*, Judgment of 1997.

230 Ibid, para. 10. See for a description of the procedure and the visit itself P. Tomka and S. Wordsworth, 'The First Site Visit of the International Court of Justice' (1998) 92 *American Journal of International Law* 133, 133–40.

231 Benzing remarks that this site visit might be linked to the 'community interest involved'. Benzing, above n 84, 386.

In the more recent dispute on the *Pulp Mills on the River Uruguay (Argentina/Uruguay)*[232] the Court chose not to use its fact-finding powers to complement or verify the evidence presented by the parties. The *Pulp Mills* dispute concerned the construction of two pulp mills on the banks of the River Uruguay in violation of the 1975 bilateral Statute between Argentina and Uruguay on the river's use. The evidence included a vast number of technical reports and the Court's decision not to involve experts was heavily criticised, both from within and outside the Palace walls.[233] In their joint dissenting opinion, Judges Al-Khasawneh and Simma stated that the ICJ had interpreted its role too restrictively in this case and that the decision not to involve experts to evaluate the evidence was regrettable.[234]

Another interesting discussion in the *Pulp Mills* case concerned the burden of proof. While the Court mostly avoids considering the question of the allocation of the burden of proof directly, the ICJ has always followed the rule that it is the litigant seeking to establish a fact who bears the burden of proving it.[235] In light of the application of the precautionary principle, a corollary of the public interest goal of sustainable development, Argentina asked for a reversal of the burden of proof. The Court, however, found that this principle does not reverse the burden of proof, although it could affect the interpretation and application of the disputed Statute.[236] Thus, a prudent conclusion would be that common interest considerations might affect the Court's use of its evidentiary rules, but not in such a way as to reverse them.

2.4.2. INTERNATIONAL TRIBUNAL FOR THE LAW OF THE SEA

The procedure before the ITLOS is, like that of the ICJ, party driven or adversarial in nature. In other words, the Court applies the law to the facts provided by the litigating parties. Nevertheless, the ITLOS equally has procedural mechanisms

---

232 ICJ, *Case of Pulp Mills on the River Uruguay (Argentina v Uruguay), Judgment*, Judgment of 2010.

233 See on this issue J. Guillermo, S. Coustasse and E. Sweeney, 'Adjudicating Conflicts Over Resources: The ICJ's Treatment of Technical Evidence in the Pulp Mills Case' (2011) 3 *Goettingen Journal of International Law* 447, 447–71.

234 ICJ, *Case of Pulp Mills on the River Uruguay (Argentina v Uruguay), Joint dissenting opinion of Judges Al-Khasawneh and Simma*, Judgment of 2010.

235 Overview of case law of the Court on this issue in Brown, above n 53, pp 94–95.

236 ICJ, *Case of Pulp Mills on the River Uruguay (Argentina v Uruguay), Judgment*, Judgment of 2010, paras. 163–64. Cf. *Southern Bluefin Tuna* (p 51) and *EC – Hormones* (p 54) where the standard of proof was not reversed but relaxed in favour of the petitioner. The finding of the ICJ limits the possibility of States to challenge economic developments on the basis of environmental risks. See ICJ, *Case of Pulp Mills on the River Uruguay (Argentina v Uruguay), Separate opinion of Judge Greenwood*, Judgment of 2010, para. 26.

at its disposal by which it can complement or verify the provided factual basis. For example, the ITLOS may seek evidence itself, appoint experts *proprio motu* and make site visits.[237] Despite the availability of these mechanisms, the ITLOS has not made use of its extensive fact-finding powers. This is largely due to the prompt nature of the Tribunal's decisions, including mostly orders of provisional measures and proceedings on the prompt release of vessels.

Another reason may be found in the fact that the ITLOS seems to lower the standard of proof in common interest cases with inconclusive evidence. In the *Southern Bluefin Tuna Cases (New Zealand and Australia v Japan)* on provisional measures, Australia and New Zealand asked the Tribunal to stop Japan from overfishing southern bluefin tuna.[238] Japan allegedly initiated a unilateral experimental fishing programme in violation of the 1993 Convention for the Conservation of Southern Bluefin Tuna, which all parties ratified. As a provisional measure, the ITLOS ordered the limitation of experimental fishing programmes by all parties to the dispute.[239] The Tribunal came to this conclusion while admitting that the evidence concerning the impact of the experimental fishing on the fish stock was inconclusive.[240]

The Tribunal justifies its extremely prudent stance by referring to the common interest in the conservation of the southern bluefin tuna stock.[241] Thus, the involvement of a common interest in this case seemed to relax the standard of proof used by the Tribunal.[242] While the Tribunal lessened the standard of proof, it did not reverse the burden of proof.[243] It did not require Japan to prove that its activities would cause no harm. The ITLOS balances the exploitation rights of the State with environmental protection; it does not give priority to the latter.[244] While the Tribunal's decision in this case to lower the standard of proof may be

---

237 Articles 77 and 81 ITLOS Rules of the Tribunal of 17 March 2009, available at <www.itlos.org>. Most of these mechanisms are provided in the ITLOS Rules. The UNCLOS only contains a few Articles on evidence, which allow the ITLOS to appoint scientific or technical experts and establish its own rules on evidence and procedure. (Articles 16 and 27 United Nations Convention on the Law of the Sea of 10 December 1982, UN Treaty Series, vol. 1833, 3.) On this issue, see Brown, above n 53, pp 83ff.

238 ITLOS, *Southern Bluefin Tuna Case (New Zealand v Japan; Australia v Japan), Provisional Measures*, Judgment of 1999.

239 Ibid, para. 90(d).

240 Ibid, para. 79.

241 Ibid, para. 77.

242 Boyle, above n 122, 375–76.

243 Orellana states that the burden of proof is shifted to the fishing State (M. Orellana, 'The Law on Highly Migratory Fish Stocks: ITLOS Jurisprudence in Context' (2004) 34 *Golden Gate University Law Review* 459, 490); in my opinion the burden is lessened in favour of the claiming State. (Cf. J.E. Vinuales, *Foreign Investment and the Environment in International Law: An Ambiguous Relationship*, Research Paper, no. 02, Centre for International Environmental Studies, 2010, available at <ssrn.com> (published in (2009) 80 *British Yearbook of International Law* 244–332), 34).

244 Boyle, above n 122, 376.

seen as a consequence of the urgency of instituting provisional measures, it may also be interpreted as an application of the precautionary principle, which will be discussed in detail below.[245]

In the *MOX Plant Case (Ireland v United Kingdom)* on provisional measures, Ireland expressly asked the Tribunal to rely on the precautionary principle when establishing the burden of proof.[246] The MOX Plant dispute between Ireland and the UK concerned the risk of pollution of the Irish Sea by a MOX (mixed oxide fuel) plant in the north-west of England. The disputed plant reprocesses nuclear waste into MOX, a substance that is not used in the UK but is exported by sea. Ireland asked the Tribunal to order the UK to suspend the authorisation of the plant and stop the transport of radioactive materials over sea while the case was pending.[247]

In its defence, the UK argued that no provisional measures were necessary because the risk of pollution was extremely small. It stated that no MOX fuel would be exported before the establishment of the arbitral tribunal.[248] Furthermore, the UK pointed out that Ireland had no scientific evidence to support its claim.[249] Ireland, on the other hand, argued that it was the duty of the UK 'to demonstrate that no harm would arise'.[250] In the end, the Tribunal did not order the suspension of the plant demanded by Ireland, but ordered the parties to cooperate in the monitoring and prevention of environmental risks.[251] Thus, while the *Southern Bluefin Tuna* case seems to deviate from the basic rules of the standard of proof in favour of establishing environmental risk, this approach was not confirmed in the *MOX Plant* case.[252]

---

245 Brown, above n 53, p 286; M. Gavouneli, 'From Uniformity to Fragmentation? The Ability of the UN Convention on the Law of the Sea to Accommodate New Uses and Challenges' in A. Strati, M. Gavouneli and N. Skourtos (eds), *Unresolved Issues and New Challenges to the Law of the Sea: Time Before and Time After*, Martinus Nijhoff Publishers, Leiden 2006, p 224; Tuerk, above n 122, 301. Judges Warioba and Laing expressed their concerns about this formulation because it does not follow the parties' arguments. (ITLOS, *Southern Bluefin Tuna Case (New Zealand v Japan; Australia v Japan), Separate Opinion of Judge Laing*, Judgment of 1999; ITLOS, *Southern Bluefin Tuna Case (New Zealand v Japan; Australia v Japan), Declaration of Judge Warioba*, Judgment of 1999).

246 The dispute triggered proceedings before several bodies, including the ECJ, but ultimately ended without substantive findings. See N. Lavranos, 'The Epilogue in the MOX Plant Dispute: An End Without Findings' [2009] *European Energy and Environmental Law Review* 180, 180–84.

247 For a detailed background to this dispute see C. Brown, 'Provisional Measures Before the ITLOS: The MOX Plant Case' (2002) 17 *International Journal of Marine and Coastal Law* 267, 267–88.

248 ITLOS, *The MOX Plant Case (Ireland v United Kingdom), Provisional Measures*, Judgment of 2001, para. 79.

249 Ibid, para. 75.

250 Ibid, para. 71.

251 Ibid, para. 89.

252 Compare ITLOS, *Southern Bluefin Tuna Case (New Zealand v Japan; Australia v Japan), Provisional Measures*, Judgment of 1999, paras. 79–80; ITLOS, *The MOX Plant Case (Ireland v*

2.4.3. INTERNATIONAL CENTRE FOR SETTLEMENT OF INVESTMENT DISPUTES

The ICSID Convention does not include many guidelines on the issue of evidence. It merely states that a tribunal may call upon the parties to produce evidence and it may conduct an on-site investigation, unless the parties agree otherwise.[253] Further questions of procedure are to be answered by each tribunal on an ad hoc basis.[254] The 'call' of the tribunal to produce evidence, is not as non-committal as it seems. In *Biwater Gauff (Tanzania) Ltd v Tanzania*, the Tribunal found that 'the only ground which might justify a refusal by the Republic to produce documents to this Tribunal is the protection of privileged or politically sensitive information'.[255] In other words, States are under an obligation to produce any evidence that is requested unless the tribunal agrees that the requested documents contain sensitive information.

The ICSID tribunals have confirmed the rule that the burden of proof is with the party asserting the fact. This general rule applies unless there is a presumption of correctness of the facts on the basis of prima facie evidence. In this case, the burden of proof may shift to the other party.[256] In the context of public interest exceptions, the allocation of the burden of proof and whether it shifts to the other party depends entirely on the margin of deference that is given to the State in determining whether a measure was in the public interest and suitable to attain that interest. Because the ICSID tribunals have not adopted a consistent approach on this issue, it will be discussed in depth in the chapter on public interest exceptions.[257]

2.4.4. WTO DISPUTE SETTLEMENT MECHANISM

The WTO Dispute Settlement Understanding is a prime example of a system based on bilateralism in that it establishes a party-driven procedure, which primarily depends on the litigating parties providing factual evidence to the WTO panel. In general, the WTO DSM applies the principle of *actori incumbit*

United Kingdom), Provisional Measures, Judgment of 2001, paras. 69–81. See also VINUALES, above n 243, 34. For a discussion on the difference between these two cases, see the section on provisional measures on p 77.

253 Article 43 ICSID Rules of Procedure for Arbitration Proceedings of 10 April 2006, available at <icsid.worldbank.org>.

254 Ibid, Article 44.

255 ICSID, *Biwater Gauff (Tanzania) Limited v United Republic of Tanzania, Procedural Order No. 2*, ICSID case no. ARB/05/22, 24.05.2006, 9.

256 SCHREUER, above n 114, p 669.

257 See pp 102ff.

probatio. From its inception, it has always held that 'the burden of proof rests upon the party, whether complaining or defending, who asserts the affirmative of a particular claim or defence'.[258] However, in its early case law, the WTO developed a specific application of the principle that the party that asserts a fact must prove it.

In the dispute on *EC Measures Concerning Meat and Meat Products (EC – Hormones)* the AB explained that, when the complaining party establishes a prima facie case of inconsistency with WTO law, 'the burden of proof *moves* to the defending party, which must in turn counter or refute the claimed inconsistency' (emphasis added).[259] This approach gave rise to controversy because it provides the panels with a nearly unlimited discretion to establish a prima facie inconsistency and significantly lower the burden of proof of the complaining party; an issue that is especially problematic for measures justified by scientific uncertainty, including public health and environmental concerns.[260] In such cases, it has been argued that the precautionary principle should apply. This principle will be discussed later, in the context of the Agreement on the Application of Sanitary and Phytosanitary Measures (SPS), which reflects the precautionary principle by allowing States to protect public health at a level higher than that of existing international standards.[261]

Despite the party-driven nature of the WTO's dispute settlement system, Article 13 of the DSU allocates significant fact-finding powers to the panels. It allows the panels 'to seek information and technical advice from any individual or body which it deems appropriate' and to consult 'any relevant source' and experts on the matter.[262] Furthermore, the AB established that such requests for information are binding and extend to all WTO members.[263] These strong fact-finding powers have been explained in the context of the constitutionalisation of the WTO as a legal regime that incorporates community interests.[264] In practice,

258 This principle was first established in WTO Appellate Body Report, *United States – Measure affecting Imports of Woven Wool Shirts and Blouses from India*, WT/DS33/AB/R, adopted 25.04.1997, IV.

259 WTO Appellate Body Report, *EC Measures Concerning Meat and Meat Products (Hormones)*, WT/DS26/AB/R; WT/DS48/AB/R, adopted 16.01.1998, para. 174.

260 Brown, above n 53, p 96.

261 See the chapter on substantive considerations on p 98.

262 Article 13 Understanding on Rules and Procedures Governing the Settlement of Disputes, Marrakesh Agreement Establishing the World Trade Organization, Annex 2 of 15 April 1994, UN Treaty Series, vol. 1869, 401.

263 It justified this interpretation by stating that concluding otherwise would negate the panels' right to seek information and, consequently, the member's right to dispute resolution under the DSU. WTO Appellate Body Report, *Canada – Measures Affecting the Export of Civilian Aircraft*, WT/DS70/AB/R, adopted 02.08.1999, 185–86.

264 See D.Z. Cass, *The Constitutionalization of the World Trade Organization: Legitimacy, Democracy, and Community in the International Trading System*, Oxford University Press, Oxford 2005, p 195.

the panels have primarily used Article 13 of the DSU to request expert advice in cases involving complex scientific evidence. Examples include the cases of *EC – Asbestos* and *US – Shrimp*, which will be discussed below.[265]

2.4.5. REGIONAL HUMAN RIGHTS MECHANISMS

2.4.5.1. European Court of Human Rights

The ECtHR has always adopted a broad approach to the collection of evidence. From the start, the Court established that it is not bound by strict rules of evidence and may rely on evidence presented by third parties or obtained on its own motion.[266] Furthermore, Rule A1(1) of the Rules of Court allows the Court to 'adopt any investigative measure which it considers capable of clarifying the facts of the case'.[267] The ECtHR may adopt such measures at the request of one of the parties, but also *proprio motu*.[268] In the last decade, the Court has only carried out such measures in a limited number of cases.[269] While those participating in the ECtHR agree that fact-finding missions or hearings are only carried out when the facts cannot be established, it is not clear which other considerations have affected the Court's decision to assume a fact-finding role.[270] The seriousness of the violation seems to influence the ECtHR's decision, as research shows that the majority of fact-finding missions concern cases involving Articles 2 or 3 of the Convention.[271] Thus, the substance of the case seems to affect the application of procedural rules by the Court.

Two other procedural elements that may be affected by the disputed interests are the burden and the standard of proof.[272] The former element, the burden of proof,

---

265 See, among others, p 86 (*EC – Asbestos*) and p 91 (*US – Shrimp*).

266 ECtHR 18.01.1978 *Ireland v the United Kingdom*, no. 5310/71, 160.

267 Rule A1(1) annex European Court of Human Rights, Rules of Court of 1 July 2014, available at <www.echr.coe.int>.

268 Ibid, Rule A1(1) annex.

269 From the entry into force of Protocol No. 11 in 1998 until the beginning of 2009, the Court has only carried out fact-finding missions in 18 cases. While this is partially due to the transition from a dual system in which the Commission carried out the fact-finding role, the number remains remarkably low compared to the number of applications. P. Leach, C. Paraskeva and G. Uzelac, *International Human Rights & Fact-Finding: An Analysis of the Fact-finding Missions Conducted by the European Commission and Court of Human Rights*, Report, Human Rights and Social Justice Research Institute, London Metropolitan University, 2009, available at <www.londonmet.ac.uk>, 30.

270 Ibid, 37–38.

271 Ibid, 38.

272 For example ECtHR 18.01.1978 *Ireland v the United Kingdom*, no. 5310/71, 161; J. Christoffersen, *Fair Balance – A Study of Proportionality, Subsidiarity and Primarity in the European Convention on Human Rights*, Dissertation, University of Copenhagen, Faculty of Law, 2008, available at <www.humanrights.dk>, 170.

is unlikely to be influenced by the facts of the case because the Court does not place the burden of producing evidence on either party. Most proceedings before the Court concern claims against State measures by individuals. In such cases, the State would have an advantage if the burden of proof were placed on the individual. Therefore, the Court has established that the general obligation of the Contracting Parties to cooperate with the Court (Article 38 ECHR) implies that 'neither party can passively await the other party's collection and submission of evidence'.[273] Furthermore, the Court shifts the burden of proof when the alleged violation happens in police custody and finds a 'procedural violation' of Articles 2 and 3 when the State fails to investigate the events or to submit convincing evidence to the contrary.[274] This shifting burden can also be found in non-discrimination cases, where the burden shifts to the State after the applicant has established prima facie discrimination.[275]

The standard of proof seems to be interpreted more or less strictly depending on the circumstances. For example, the Court has required proof 'beyond reasonable doubt' in cases concerning serious violations of Articles 2, 3 and 14, but does not apply this high standard in other cases.[276] In the context of justifying measures that pursue public or common interests, it is especially important to examine the Court's approach to the proof of future facts or effectiveness.[277] Because the requirements set by the Court in relation to the establishment of future facts is closely related to the Court's use of the proportionality test, this issue will be discussed further under the section on public interest exceptions.[278]

2.4.5.2. *Inter-American Court of Human Rights*

Like the European Court, the IACtHR is explicitly granted the power to supplement evidence supplied by the parties with evidence it obtained itself if that is 'helpful and necessary'.[279] Furthermore, the Court can request relevant information from anyone, including expert witnesses, at any time during the

---

273 Deduced from the Court's reasoning in ECtHR 18.01.1978 *Ireland v the United Kingdom*, no. 5310/71, 148. See Christoffersen, above n 272, 168.

274 P. Kinsch, 'On the Uncertainties Surrounding the Standard of Proof in Proceedings Before International Courts and Tribunals' [2009] *Individual Rights and International Justice* 427, 438.

275 For a more nuanced and detailed perspective see O.M. Arnardóttir, *Non-discrimination Under Article 14 ECHR: The Burden of Proof*, Scandinavian Studies in Law, 1999–2012, available at <ssrn.com>.

276 Although the Court has mitigated this standard in cases on Articles 2 and 3. Ibid, 37.

277 On proportionality and the law of information in the ECtHR see Christoffersen, above n 272, 172ff.

278 See pp 117ff.

279 Article 58(1) Rules of Procedure of the Inter-American Court of Human Rights of November 2009, available at <www.corteidh.or.cr>.

proceedings.[280] This allows for a broad collection of evidence from different sources. The flexible approach to evidence is also upheld in the determination of the standard and burden of proof. The Court explicitly followed the ICJ's lead in stating that international courts and tribunals can freely choose the standard of proof they apply in each individual case, while taking account of the circumstances of the case and the procedural balance between the parties.[281] The Court thus bases its evaluation of evidence on logic and experience rather than strict procedural rules.[282] The Court takes account of the seriousness of the allegations when determining the standard of proof but, in contrast to the European Court, never uses the strict standard of proof 'beyond reasonable doubt'.[283]

The burden of proof is traditionally placed on the party making the allegations by the Inter-American Court. This burden is, however, reversed when the party denying the allegations is in a better position to provide evidence. In other words, when the victim of a human rights violation cannot provide evidence without the cooperation of the State, the burden of proof will rest on the State.[284] Moreover, the Inter-American Court uses rebuttable presumptions in cases where the evidence is in the hands of, but not provided by, the State. For example, when persons that are in custody of the State are ill-treated, the IACtHR presumes the responsibility of the State.[285] Furthermore, in *Sawhoyamaxa Indigenous Community of the Enxet People v Paraguay*, the Court shifted the burden of proof to the State in the context of the right to life, once the causal connection between the victims' living conditions and their death was established.[286] It did not require that the victims of the human rights violations provide evidence of the State's failure to fulfil its positive obligations.[287] This shift in the burden of

280 Ibid, Article 58(1).

281 Inter-American Court of Human Rights, *Case of Kawas-Fernández v Honduras*, Judgment of 03.04.2009, 82. In this paragraph, the IACtHR refers back to parts of its previous case law that explicitly refer to the case law of the ICJ.

282 Pasqualucci, above n 125, p 174.

283 Kinsch, above n 274, 437–38.

284 Pasqualucci, above n 125, p 171.

285 Ibid, 170.

286 This was not always the case in previous decisions. See, for example, Inter-American Court of Human Rights, *Case of Yakye Axa Indigenous Community v Paraguay*, Judgment of 17.06.2005, paras. 177–78. The Sawhoyamaxa case law was followed in later decisions, see Inter-American Court of Human Rights, *Case of Xákmok Kásek Indigenous Community v Paraguay*, Judgment of 24.08.2010, para. 231.

287 This flexible approach to evidence in proving the lack of due diligence of the State is, according to Judge Cançado Trindade, based on the idea that the State is responsible for achieving the 'common good' and this implies that 'States guarantee all the individuals under their respective jurisdictions conditions allowing them to live with dignity'. Inter-American Court of Human Rights, *Case of Sawhoyamaxa Indigenous Community v Paraguay, Separate Opinion by Judge A.A. Cançado Trindade*, Judgment of 29.03.2006, para. 27.

proof makes it considerably easier to provide the necessary evidence of a State's failure to mitigate the negative effects of being displaced, as in the *Sawhoyamaxa* case.

2.4.5.3. African Commission on Human and Peoples' Rights

Like the other regional human rights Treaties, the African Charter gives the Commission permission to 'resort to any appropriate method of investigation' and to ask assistance of any person 'capable of enlightening it'.[288] This wide provision allows the participation of, inter alia, specialised institutions, experts and NGOs.[289] The African Commission actively uses its mandate to conduct country visits and, in addition to promotional activities, carries out on-site fact-finding missions. Although it is not communicated which missions are connected to pending communications and which missions are undertaken under the other protective mandates of the Commission, some of the missions are geared towards collecting evidence in the context of a communication. It is not clear on which basis the Commission decides when to carry out a fact-finding mission, but Evans suggest three important factors. Widespread and serious allegations, pressure by civil society and recent developments in the case all seem to affect the decision to carry out a fact-finding mission.[290] Despite the willingness of the Commission to make site visits, Evans questions the value of the missions in the context of the communications procedure because the Commission seems to prefer not to carry out rigorous fact finding.[291] The Commission only implicitly states the burden and standard of proof. Nevertheless, its case law shows that the victim has to provide prima facie evidence of the allegations. If the State fails to cooperate, in other words if it does not provide information in answer to the allegations, the burden on the victim to substantiate the claim is lessened.[292]

2.4.6. SUMMARY: EVIDENCE AND COMMON INTEREST

The procedural rules on evidence are of great importance when addressing common interests. The case law of the examined bodies does not show that common interests systematically affect their interpretation of the standard or burden of proof. While in inter-State disputes all of the judicial bodies require

---

288 Article 46 African Charter on Human and Peoples' Rights of 21 October 1986, OAU Doc. CAB/LEG/67/3 rev. 5.

289 Evans and Murray, above n 222, p 141.

290 Ibid, 146.

291 Ibid, 147–48.

292 Ibid, 158.

that the State that alleges a certain fact must prove it, the individual is protected from this burden in the regional human rights regimes that oblige the States to cooperate in providing evidence and shift the burden of proof to the State when necessary. In the context of the standard of proof, it can be concluded that international courts and tribunals apply a liberal approach to evidence, determining its value on an ad hoc basis and relying on both the evidence presented by the parties and that obtained by the judicial body. Concerning the latter, there does seem to be a link between the use of fact-finding powers by the court and the substance of the case. Although all of the selected bodies start from the evidence presented by the parties they all consider themselves entitled to procure evidence *proprio motu*. This has been shown to be especially true in cases that concern complex issues that are of interest to a larger community than that of the individual parties.

2.5. THIRD PARTY INTERVENTIONS

A procedure that has a high potential for bringing common interest issues to the attention of the court is the acceptance of third party interventions.[293] *Amicus curiae* briefs shed light on previously non-discussed domestic or international concerns involved in the dispute. This additional knowledge may not only affect the judicial body's decision on the balance between the different interests at stake; in the context of determining the standard of review, it may also change its understanding of the expertise of the host State. Although NGOs do not necessarily represent the common interest, the procedure *an sich* may help to legitimise the decisions in common interest cases.

2.5.1. INTERNATIONAL COURT OF JUSTICE

In contrast to some of the other judicial bodies that are examined, the ICJ's jurisdiction is strictly based on consent, which implies that access to the Court is necessarily restrictive.[294] As an adversarial and inter-State dispute settlement mechanism, the ICJ focuses almost exclusively on the contributions of the States that are parties to the ongoing dispute. Particularly in such a closed procedure, third party interventions would bring issues to the Court's attention that have

---

293 On the role of non-state actors in international legal dispute settlement mechanisms see E. De Brabandere, 'Non-State Actors and the Proliferation and Individualization of International Dispute Settlement' in B. Reinalda (ed), *The Ashgate Research Companion to Non-State Actors*, Routledge, Ebook 2016.

294 H. Ascensio, 'L'*amicus curiae* devant les juridictions internationales' (2001) 105 *Revue Générale de Droit International Public* 897, 907.

not been raised by the litigating parties. Especially in the context of public interest issues, additional materials could provide relevant information and 'multilateralise' a bilateral dispute.[295]

In the Court's contentious proceedings, third party interventions are reserved to States under the mechanisms of Articles 62 and 63 of the ICJ Statute.[296] The Statute allows third States to intervene if they have a legal interest in doing so. While some envision an important role for interventions in public interest matters, the ICJ allows interventions only exceptionally, when the individual interest of the State is at risk.[297] For example, the Court does not consider an interest 'regarding the applicable general principles and rules of international law' as an interest allowing intervention.[298] Moreover, intervention is the only way in which States can participate in contentious proceedings. States may not act as *amicus curiae* before the ICJ.[299] While States have attempted to inform the Court of their point of view by sending communications to the Court, it is not clear whether the Court uses this information.[300]

The only manner in which non-State actors can submit 'information' to the Court in contentious cases is through Article 34§2 of the ICJ Statute.[301] This Article allows the Court to request or receive relevant information of 'public international organizations'. However, the mechanism of Article 34§2 is rarely used because the Court has limited 'public international organizations' to intergovernmental organisations and rarely requests information from such organisations.[302] Furthermore, intergovernmental organisations themselves do

---

295 Benzing, above n 84, 298; D. Shelton, 'The Participation of Nongovernmental Organizations in International Judicial Proceedings' (1994) 88 *American Journal of International Law* 611, 625.

296 For an extensive commentary on Articles 62–63 see C. Chinkin, 'Arts. 62–63' in A. Zimmermann, C. Tomuschat and K. Oellers-Frahm (eds), *The Statute of the International Court of Justice: A Commentary*, Oxford University Press, Oxford 2006, pp 1331–92.

297 Chinkin, for example, is a proponent of public interest intervention. Ibid.

298 ICJ, *Case of Continental Shelf (Libyan Arab Jamahiriya/Malta), Application to Intervene, Judgment*, Judgment of 1984.

299 On why and how the Court should allow *amicus curiae* briefs of third States, in particular in cases on *erga omnes* obligations, see P. Palchetti, 'Opening the International Court of Justice to Third States: Intervention and Beyond' (2002) 6 *Max Planck Yearbook of UN Law* 139, 139–81.

300 Ibid, 166.

301 There is not enough practice to conclude whether or not 'information' includes legal arguments and policy submissions (B. Lance, 'The Amicus Curiae before International Courts and Tribunals' (2005) 5 *Non-State Actors and International Law* 209, 213). For an extensive commentary on Article 34 see P.-M. Dupuy, 'Article 34' in A. Zimmermann, C. Tomuschat and K. Oellers-Frahm (eds), *The Statute of the International Court of Justice: A Commentary*, Oxford University Press, Oxford 2006, pp 545–63.

302 Article 69(4) ICJ Rules of the Court of 14 April 1978, available at <www.icj-cij.org>. This issue was not settled at the drafting of the Statute. Lance, above n 301, 214; Shelton, above n 295, 620–21.

not take the initiative to make submissions to the ICJ in contentious cases.[303] For example, the United Nations Environment Programme (UNEP) could have provided the Court with specialised environmental information in the case of the *Gabčíkovo-Nagymaros* dam project, but neglected to do so.[304] Non-State actors other than intergovernmental organisations cannot intervene or submit *amicus curiae* briefs to the Court. Nevertheless, the ICJ did accept a limited amount of NGO involvement in the *Gabčíkovo-Nagymaros* case. In this case, Hungary claimed that its suspension and abandonment of a major joint project with Slovakia was justified by environmental reasons. To strengthen its defence, Hungary attached several Hungarian, Slovakian and international NGO reports to its submission in the form of 'scientific reports'.[305] The Court accepted Hungary's submission and (implicitly) the involvement of NGOs at the pre-trial stage.

However, true *amicus curiae* briefs, i.e. submissions that are not directly endorsed by one of the parties, continue to cause disagreement within the Bench.[306] To date, *amicus curiae* submissions have not been accepted in the ICJ's contentious case law and it is unlikely that they will be accepted in the Court's future case law without a change in the Statute's provisions.[307] It could therefore be concluded that the Court is reluctant to accept third party interventions that are purely based on common interest grounds. In principle, only intergovernmental public organisations could bring forward interests of common concern. However, as stated above, they are hesitant to do so.[308]

2.5.2. INTERNATIONAL TRIBUNAL FOR THE LAW OF THE SEA

The drafters of the ITLOS Statute (Annex VI UNCLOS) were inspired by the Statute of the ICJ. This is especially true for the Tribunal's procedural rules on third party interventions. Article 31 of the ITLOS Statute provides that State

303 Dupuy, above n 301, p 553.

304 Lance, above n 301, 214.

305 *Case of Oil Platforms (Islamic Republic of Iran v United States of America), Judgment, Separate Opinion Judge Simma.*

306 Former President of the Court Guillaume even argued that the ICJ should be protected against 'powerful pressure groups'. ICJ, *Case of Legality of the Threat or Use of Nuclear Weapons, Advisory Opinion, Separate Opinion Judge Guillaume,* Judgment of 1996.

307 Benzing, above n 84, 403.

308 See Ascensio, above n 294, 905–08. The Court does allow for *amicus curiae* briefs of third States and international organisations in its advisory proceedings in accordance with Article 66 of the Statute of the International Court of Justice of 26 June 1945, Treaty Series, 993. The only way for NGOs to gain access to the Court in contentious cases, except for the integration of their submissions in the arguments of a State party, seems to be through Article 50 of the ICJ Statute, which allows the Court to collect expert opinions. Lance, above n 301, 216.

parties may intervene if they have a legal interest in doing so.[309] Like the procedural rules of the ICJ, Article 31 only grants the right to intervene to States. Furthermore, the ITLOS Rules accommodate the intervention of States and intergovernmental organisations as *amicus curiae*.[310] The organisations from which the Tribunal may request and receive information were expressly limited to 'intergovernmental organizations' of States at the time of the drafting.[311] While there may be borderline cases of organisations that have both State and non-State members, it is obvious that NGOs do not fall into this category.[312]

At least one State party has already included the report of a relevant intergovernmental organisation in its submission in the *'Volga' Case (Russian Federation v Australia)*.[313] The *'Volga'* case concerned a claim from Russia for the prompt release of a Russian ship that was detained by Australia for illegal fishing in the southern Antarctic Ocean. Russia found the bond set by Australia for the release of the vessel unreasonably high. In response, Australia attempted to prove that the high bond was justified in light of the gravity of the offences and, therefore, attached a report from the Commission for the Conservation of Antarctic Marine Living Resources to its written submission.[314] To date, the Tribunal itself has not yet used the opportunity to collaborate directly with an intergovernmental organisation in it contentious cases.[315] The reason for this can probably be found in the urgency of the proceedings that have been instituted.[316]

Although the ITLOS has not yet officially accepted *amicus curiae* briefs of NGOs, the Seabed Disputes Chamber did give some recognition to such submissions in its recent *Advisory Opinion on Responsibilities and obligations of States sponsoring persons and entities with respect to activities in the Area*.[317] In this case two NGOs, Greenpeace International and the World Wide Fund for Nature, filed an *amicus curiae* brief. While the Seabed Dispute Chamber did not

---

309 Article 31 Annex VI United Nations Convention on the Law of the Sea of 10 December 1982, UN Treaty Series, vol. 1833, 3; Article 62 Statute of the International Court of Justice of 26 June 1945, Treaty Series, 993.

310 Articles 84 and 133 ITLOS Rules of the Tribunal of 17 March 2009, available at <www.itlos.org>; Articles 34 and 66 Statute of the International Court of Justice of 26 June 1945, Treaty Series, 993.

311 To avoid confusion that existed with regard to Article 34 Statute of the International Court of Justice of 26 June 1945, Treaty Series, 993. See Lance, above n 301, 229–30.

312 Gautier, above n 194, pp 239–40. Some argue that NGOs also have standing (Benzing, above n 84, 403).

313 ITLOS, *The 'Volga' Case (Russian Federation v Australia), Prompt Release*, Judgment of 2002.

314 Gautier, above n 194, p 240.

315 UNEP did submit a written statement (after the expiry of the time limit) in ITLOS Seabed Disputes Chamber, *Case of Responsibilities and obligations of States sponsoring persons and entities with respect to activities in the Area, Advisory Opinion*.

316 Rao and Gautier, above n 122, p 236.

317 ITLOS Seabed Disputes Chamber, *Case of Responsibilities and obligations of States sponsoring persons and entities with respect to activities in the Area, Advisory Opinion*.

make this submission part of the case file, it did link to it on the ITLOS website[318] despite the fact that no Treaty rule or internal ruling of the Tribunal provides for such a procedure.[319] However, in the later contentious *Arctic Sunrise Case (Kingdom of the Netherlands v Russian Federation)* on provisional measures, the Tribunal preferred not to publish the *amicus* brief of Greenpeace International on its website.[320] This may be explained by the adversarial nature of the latter case and the NGO's direct involvement in the dispute, which concerned the detention of the crew of one of their ships in Russia.[321]

2.5.3. INTERNATIONAL CENTRE FOR SETTLEMENT OF INVESTMENT DISPUTES

The admission of *amicus curiae* is the primary example of a procedural decision that may have a large impact on the consideration of public interest at the substantial level in the context of investment disputes. In general, the participation of NGOs in investment arbitration as *amicus curiae* provides a broader perspective to investment tribunals in cases of high public interest. Case law confirms that NGOs primarily participate in cases that involve issues of public interest, such as environmental protection and public services (in particular water provision). *Amici curiae* submissions may voice the interests of specific groups of individuals or investors; but they may also highlight 'the general interests of the international community that transcend the policy concerns of the host State'.[322]

---

318 See <http://www.itlos.org/index.php?id=109> (last accessed June 2015).

319 To the surprise of many, because no rules exists concerning such a link. D. Anton, R. Makgill and C. Payne, *Advisory Opinion on Responsibility and Liability for International Seabed Mining (ITLOS Case No. 17): International Environmental Law in the Seabed Disputes Chamber*, Research Paper, no. 11–08, Australian National University, ANU College of Law, available at <ssrn.com>, 2.

320 ITLOS, *The Arctic Sunrise Case (Kingdom of the Netherlands v Russian Federation), Provisional Measures*, Judgment of 2013.

321 A. Dolidze, 'The Arctic Sunrise and NGOs in International Judicial Proceedings' (2014) 18 *Asil Insights* 1.

322 F. Francioni, 'Access to Justice, Denial of Justice, and International Investment Law' in P.M. Dupuy, F. Francioni and E.U. Petersmann (eds), *Human Rights in International Investment Law and Arbitration*, Oxford University Press, Oxford 2009, p 743. Nevertheless, NGOs are non-democratic entities and concerns may be expressed with regard to the *amici*'s legitimacy as representing 'civil society as a whole' and their independence from the parties. E. De Brabandere, 'NGOs and the "Public Interest": The Legality and Rationale of Amicus Curiae Interventions in International Economic and Investment Disputes' (2011) 12 *Chicago Journal of International Law* 85; P. Wieland, 'Why the Amicus Curia Institution is Ill-Suited to Address Indigenous Peoples' Rights before Investor-State Arbitration Tribunals: Glamis Gold and the Right of Intervention' (2011) 3 *Trade Law & Development* 334, 340–41.

One of the main differences between a typical judicial process and investment arbitration is the limitation of public participation. Because the investor–State arbitration is based on international commercial arbitration, there is a great emphasis on confidentiality and secrecy. In an attempt to increase its transparency, the ICSID rules now allow third parties to attend the hearings unless the parties disagree.[323] A related measure was the revision of the ICSID Arbitration Rules in 2006 to allow tribunals to accept written *amicus curiae* briefs, a direct source of public input in the arbitration process.[324] The original ICSID Convention and arbitration rules did not explicitly allow for the intervention of *amicus curiae*. Because of this lack of explicit provisions, the Tribunal in the 2005 case of *Aguas del Tunari v Bolivia* did not find that it had the power to allow a non-party submission.[325] Nevertheless, the ICSID tribunals in later cases interpreted Article 44 of the Convention to allow the tribunal the discretionary power to accept *amicus curiae* submissions.[326] It thereby explicitly referred to the interpretation of the UNCITRAL Rules by the *Methanex* Tribunal, the first international investment tribunal that decided that it had the discretionary power to accept *amicus curiae* submissions.[327] In this context, it is important to note that the *Methanex* Tribunal explicitly based its authority to receive the submission on the fact that public interest issues were involved.[328]

Following these developments in practice, the ICSID rules were revised in 2006 and now explicitly provide that the tribunal has the power to allow certain non-disputing parties to file a written submission.[329] The new ICSID Arbitration Rule 37(2) was first used in the case of *Biwater Gauff v Tanzania*, a dispute on a private water concession that involved the right to water. In *Biwater Gauff*, the Tribunal stressed the public interests involved in the dispute when granting the *amicus*

---

323 Several arbitrations, including *Methanex*, were even broadcasted live from Washington. Rule 32 ICSID Rules of Procedure for Arbitration Proceedings of 10 April 2006, available at <icsid.worldbank.org>.

324 This rule was established in response to a request for transparency by civil society in cases such as *Aguas del Tunari* and *Aguas Argentinas*. Ibid, Rule 37(2).

325 The case concerned a water company that could not develop its project because the citizens of the city of Cochabamba protested massively against the privatisation of the water and sewage services and the concession was rescinded. ICSID, *Aguas del Tunari, S.A. v Republic of Bolivia, Decision on Jurisdiction*, ICSID case no. ARB/02/3, 21.10.2005, appendix III.

326 See, for example, ICSID, *Aguas Argentinas, S.A., Suez, Sociedad General de Aguas de Barcelona, S.A. and Vivendi Universal, S.A. v the Argentine Republic, Order in Response to a Petition for Transparency and Participation as Amicus Curiae*, ICSID case no. ARB/03/19, 19.05.2005.

327 UNCITRAL, *Methanex Corporation v United States of America, Decision on Petitions from Third Persons to Intervene as 'Amici Curiae'*, 15.01.2001.

328 Ibid, para. 49.

329 Such an *amicus curiae* submission must fulfil several requirements. First, it must bring a perspective to the dispute not represented by the parties; secondly, it must address a matter within the scope of the dispute; and, thirdly, the third party must have a significant interest in the proceeding. By posing these demands the ICSID balances the need for input on public interest issues with the disadvantages of added costs and more broadly defined, thus lengthier, disputes. Choudhury, above n 83, 816.

the right to submit a brief.[330] *Amicus curiae* submissions were subsequently allowed in the mining cases of *Piero Foresti et al. v South Africa*[331] and *Pac Rim Cayman v El Salvador*[332] without much explicit motivation. In *Foresti*, foreign investors filed a complaint against South Africa concerning its racial quota in the context of natural resource exploitation. In this case, the ICSID Tribunal granted several human rights NGOs authorisation to file an *amicus curiae* brief, which argued that the South African legislation was necessary to remedy the existing inequality with regard to access to natural resources.[333] The dispute of *Pac Rim Cayman LLC v El Salvador* concerned El Salvador's withdrawal of a concession for mining activities after the initial investments were already made. In this case, NGOs pointed out the human rights dimensions of the planned exploitation, including the environmental and health impact on the affected communities.[334]

The cases mentioned above seem to indicate that investment tribunals (relatively) easily grant *amici* the possibility to submit a written brief that centres on public interest issues, including human rights and environmental protection. However, in the summer of 2012 Rule 37(2) was interpreted much more restrictively in the joined cases of *Pezold/Border Timbers v Zimbabwe*.[335] These disputes relate to the expropriation by Zimbabwe of several timber plantations of the claimants, a group of European investors. In this case, four indigenous communities of Zimbabwe, joined by a German NGO (ECCHR), petitioned for *amicus curiae* participation stating that they had a claim on the land in dispute. Although the Tribunal acknowledged that the proceedings could affect the rights of the indigenous communities it rejected their request to intervene as *amicus*. In its decision the Tribunal reintroduced a set of procedural criteria for *amicus curiae* submission that were used before the revision of the ICSID rules in 2006.[336] In this specific case, the Tribunal found that the petitioners

330 The Tribunal thereby referred to the decision in ICSID, *Methanex. Biwater Gauff (Tanzania) Limited v United Republic of Tanzania, Procedural Order No. 5*, ICSID case no. ARB/05/22, 02.02.2007, para. 51.

331 ICSID, *Piero Foresti, Laura De Carli and Others v the Republic of South Africa, Procedural Order*, ICSID case no. ARB(AF)/07/1, 25.09.2009. This was decided on the basis of Rule 41(3) ICSID Additional Facility Rules of April 2006, available at <icsid.worldbank.org>, which wording is identical to that of Rule 37(2) ICSID Rules of Procedure for Arbitration Proceedings of 10 April 2006, available at <icsid.worldbank.org>.

332 ICSID, *Pac Rim Cayman LLC v Republic of El Salvador, Procedural Order No. 8*, ICSID case no. ARB/09/12, 23.03.2011. This was decided under Rule 37(2) and Article 10.20.3 of the Central American–Dominican Republic–United States Free Trade Agreement of 05.08.2004. They explicitly allow *amicus curiae* participation.

333 The *Foresti* case was discontinued. ICSID, *Piero Foresti, Laura De Carli and Others v the Republic of South Africa, Award*, ICSID case no. ARB(AF)/07/1, 04.08.2010.

334 ICSID, *Pac Rim Cayman LLC v Republic of El Salvador, Decision on Jurisdiction*, ICSID case no. ARB/09/12, 01.06.2012, para. 2.36.

335 ICSID, *Von Pezold/Border Timbers v Republic of Zimbabwe, Procedural Order No. 2*, ICSID case no. ARB/10/15 and ARB/10/25, 26.06.2012.

336 Ibid, paras. 49–62. First, they have to present insight that is independent of the arguments made by the parties. Secondly, *amici* submissions have to assist in determining a factual or

lacked independence because their claim on the disputed land was incompatible with the claimants' position as property owners and because the petitioners had received support from an NGO whose director politically supports the Zimbabwean policy.[337] Moreover, the petitioner's submission was not, in the eyes of the Tribunal, related to the matters brought before the Tribunal. The Tribunal noted that the disputes concerned the measures taken by Zimbabwe against the claimants, while the petitioners asked to make a submission on the putative rights of the indigenous communities, an issue that does not fall within the scope of the disputes.[338] The Tribunal expressly stated that 'the reference to "such rules of general international law as may be applicable" in the relevant BITs does not incorporate the universe of international law into the BITs or into disputes arising under the BITs'.[339]

Whether or not this restrictive interpretation of granting *amicus curiae* rights is followed, the impact of this specific procedural opening to common interests is currently diminished by the time and attention investment tribunals are willing to give to the contents of the briefs. It is not very promising that, at the moment, only written submissions are accepted and they are often restricted to a limited number of pages. While it is hard to establish the impact of *amicus curiae* submissions, it is acknowledged that in several disputes on water concessions the tribunals considered issues that were not presented as such by the disputing parties.[340] In the case of *Biwater Gauff*, however, the arbitrators did not grant deference to the State to justify its measures on the basis of the human rights considerations and, in the end, decided the case purely on the basis of investment law.[341] It should therefore be concluded that due to the limitations placed on *amicus curiae* briefs, the system remains a discretionary and informal mechanism that does not ensure that common interest arguments can be brought forward in the arbitration process.[342] Furthermore, even if the submissions are accepted, this does not guarantee the consideration of the rights of specific third parties or the general public.

---

legal issue related to the proceedings. Thirdly, they have to address a matter within the scope of the dispute. And fourthly, the petitioners have to demonstrate a significant interest in the proceedings.

337 Ibid, paras. 50–56. This narrow interpretation was never followed in previous ICSID cases (S. Schadendorf, 'Human Rights Arguments in Amicus Curiae Submissions: Analysis of ICSID and NAFTA Investor-State Arbitrations' (2013) 10 *Transnational Dispute Management* 10, available at <ssrn.com>.

338 ICSID, *Von Pezold/Border Timbers v Republic of Zimbabwe, Procedural Order No. 2*, ICSID case no. ARB/10/15 and ARB/10/25, 26.06.2012, para. 60.

339 Ibid, para. 57.

340 Choudhury, above n 83, 818.

341 Schadendorf, above n 337, 20.

342 E. Levine, 'Amicus Curiae in International Investment Arbitration: The Implications of an Increase in Third-Party Participation' (2011) 29 *Berkeley Journal of International Law* 200, 212; Wieland, above n 322, 345.

2.5.4. WTO DISPUTE SETTLEMENT MECHANISM

The intervention of third parties is arguably one of the most controversial procedural issues in the context of the WTO. This is especially true for third party interventions that could introduce (common) interests other than those of the parties into the WTO's adversarial dispute settlement system. In this context, a difference must be made between the intervention of Member States and that of private parties. The DSU explicitly allows Member States to intervene in a dispute if they have a 'substantial interest in a matter before a panel'.[343] Because this substantial interest is not further qualified as a trade or legal interest, this provision could, hypothetically, be used to intervene in the common interest.[344]

In contrast, private parties have neither been given the right to standing nor the right to intervene by the DSU. Therefore, if a private party seeks to bring its insights to the attention of the panel/AB, it has to do this in the form of an *amicus curiae* brief. Although these *amicus curiae* briefs sometimes function as purely legal advice or evidence of certain facts, they are often used to draw attention to certain issues of common interest.[345] At the outset, neither the panel nor the AB considered such submissions. For example, in a dispute on the WTO consistency of the US Clean Air Act, *United States – Standards for Reformulated and Conventional Gasoline*, *amicus curiae* briefs of NGOs were completely ignored.[346]

However, the AB adopted a different approach in *United States – Import Prohibition of Certain Shrimp and Shrimp Products* (*Shrimp/Turtle* case).[347] In this case it was disputed whether the US import ban of shrimp coming from countries that did not use a specific turtle-friendly fishing technique could be justified under the GATT because it was aimed at the conservation of natural resources (Article XX(g) GATT). Before issuing its ruling, the panel received two *amicus* briefs from environmental NGOs. In the end, it agreed to consider only those parts of the briefs that were explicitly endorsed by the US in its

343 Article 10§2 Understanding on Rules and Procedures Governing the Settlement of Disputes, Marrakesh Agreement Establishing the World Trade Organization, Annex 2 of 15 April 1994, UN Treaty Series, vol. 1869, 401.

344 Benzing, above n 84, 400.

345 L. Johnson and E. Tuerk, 'CIEL's Experience in WTO Dispute Settlement: Challenges and Complexities from a Practical Point of View' in T. Treves (ed), *Civil Society, International Courts and Compliance Bodies*, Cambridge University Press, Cambridge 2005, p 249.

346 WTO Appellate Body Report, *United States – Standards for Reformulated and Conventional Gasoline*, WT/DS2/AB/R, adopted 29.04.1996; A. I. Padideh, 'Judicial Lobbying at the WTO: The Debate over the Use of Amicus Curiae Briefs and the U.S. Experience' (2000) 24 *Fordham International Law Journal* 62, 68–69.

347 WTO Appellate Body Report, *United States – Import Prohibition of Certain Shrimp and Shrimp Products*, WT/DS58/AB/R, adopted 12.10.1998.

submission.[348] The Appellate Body confirmed this approach, holding that on the basis of Article 13 DSU,[349] '[a] panel has the discretionary authority either to accept and consider or to reject information and advice submitted to it, whether requested by a panel or not'.[350]

The AB even took its acceptance of *amicus curiae* briefs one step further in the case of *European Communities – Measures Affecting Asbestos and Products Containing Asbestos.*[351] This dispute concerned the French import ban on asbestos and asbestos products for the protection of public health. Because the WTO expected to receive a large number of *amicus* briefs on this issue, it disseminated procedural rules beforehand for *amicus curiae* seeking to participate in the dispute.[352] This formalisation of the recognition of *amicus curiae* by the AB was much criticised by WTO members, who found that the AB had overstepped its authority, and at the time of writing it was being discussed in the context of the DSU reform.[353]

In *Softwood Lumber*, the WTO accepted an indigenous *amicus curiae* brief, which held that Canada's failure to recognise Aboriginal land titles and consult with indigenous peoples was inconsistent with WTO law because it provided an unfair advantage to Canadian softwood lumber producers.[354] Although the panel accepted the NGO submission and distributed the brief to all parties, it was not dealt with substantively. While the formal acceptance of *amicus curiae* briefs may lead to the conclusion that the WTO's judicial bodies provide an opening for (common) interests other than those of the parties, the practice of both the panels and the AB paint a different picture altogether. In all of the selected cases, only those *amicus curiae* interventions that were added to or cited by one of the party submissions were considered. Because of this practice, only

---

348 WTO Panel Report, *United States – Import Prohibition of Certain Shrimp and Shrimp Products*, WT/DS58/R, adopted 15.05.1998, para. 155.

349 The DSU provides that 'panels may seek information from any relevant source and may consult experts to obtain their opinion on certain aspects of the matter' (Article 13.2 Understanding on Rules and Procedures Governing the Settlement of Disputes, Marrakesh Agreement Establishing the World Trade Organization, Annex 2 of 15 April 1994, UN Treaty Series, vol. 1869, 401).

350 WTO Appellate Body Report, *United States – Import Prohibition of Certain Shrimp and Shrimp Products*, WT/DS58/AB/R, adopted 12.10.1998, para. 108.

351 WTO Appellate Body Report, *European Communities – Measures Affecting Asbestos and Asbestos-containing Products*, WT/DS135/AB/R, adopted 12.03.2001.

352 Ibid.

353 The WTO General Council discussed the additional procedures in a special session on 22.11.2000 (WTO Doc. WT/GC/M/60). The meeting concluded with a note of caution to the AB, which subsequently decided to reject all requests for leave to submit an *amicus curiae* brief. D. Wirth, 'European Communities – Measures Affecting Asbestos and Asbestos-Containing Products' (2002) 96 *American Journal of International Law* 435, 439; Johnson and Tuerk, above n 345, pp 246–47.

354 WTO Panel Report, *United States – Final Countervailing Duty Determination with Respect to Certain Softwood Lumber from Canada*, WT/DS257/R, adopted 29.08.2003.

interests that are endorsed by the parties to the dispute are considered and there seems to be little added value to the acceptance of *amicus curiae* briefs.[355] In conclusion it can be said that, by only allowing briefs that are endorsed by one of the parties, the WTO DSU strikes a balance between third party (civil society, businesses, industry) concerns and the reluctance of Member States to allow non-trade concerns to be deliberated in WTO proceedings.[356]

2.5.5. REGIONAL HUMAN RIGHTS MECHANISMS

2.5.5.1. European Court of Human Rights

Since the entry into force of Protocol 11, Article 36(2) of the ECHR confirms the power of the Court to invite 'any person concerned who is not the applicant to submit written comments or take part in hearings'. Thus, the European Court welcomes third party interventions, and in particular those that concern common interests, in the form of *amicus curiae* interventions. Nevertheless, the case law on Article 36(2) is very limited and none of the examined cases include *amicus* interventions. The main reason for this is the low number of briefs that are submitted to the Court. To give an example, in the 1998–2011 period, the Court accepted third party interventions in 39 out of 40 cases pursuant to Article 36(2).[357] Taking account of the more than 12,000 cases the Court decided in that period, only a fraction of all ECtHR cases include non-State third party interventions. This (relative) lack of submissions can be attributed to the Court's huge body of case law and the fact that NGOs tend to focus their efforts on those cases that have the highest impact or prefer to act as the victims' representatives.[358] The conclusion may thus be drawn that the interventions of third parties in the cases of the ECtHR are limited but focused on high-impact cases.

2.5.5.2. Inter-American Court of Human Rights

Although neither the American Convention nor the original rules of procedure of the Court specifically mentioned the procedure for *amicus curiae*

[355] Johnson and Tuerk, above n 353, p 253.

[356] N. Bernasconi-Osterwalder, D.B. Magraw, M.J. Oliva, M. Orellana and E. Tuerk, *Environment and Trade: A Guide to WTO Jurisprudence*, Earthscan, London, Sterling, VA 2006, p 325.

[357] Numbers of a HUDOC database search on Article 36(2) for the period (01.11.1998–01.11.2011). The Court refused third party intervention to the Polish Association of Tenants in the case ECtHR, *Hutten-Czapska v Poland*, no. 35014/97, 22.02.2005; Lance, above n 301, 235.

[358] Lance, above n 301, 236.

submissions,[359] the Court accepted third party briefs, individual as well as non-governmental, from its inception.[360] These interventions are generally accepted to acquire complete knowledge on all elements of a case. While the Commission and the State will both raise different aspects of a case, they do not necessarily possess sufficient expertise to explain all issues in full and it is unlikely that they would always raise all interests at stake. The Court's frequent acceptance of *amicus curiae* briefs may therefore confirm that it is willing to look beyond the individual complaint. This conclusion is drawn from the fact that most of the submitted briefs concern common rather than individual interests. In more than half of the examined cases, at least one *amicus* brief was submitted to the Court that stressed the importance and consequences of the case to the general public. For example, in the case of the *Mayagna (Sumo) Awas Tingni Community v Nicaragua* and the case of *Kawas-Fernández v Honduras*, the Center for International Environmental Law (CIEL)[361] and the Environmental Defense Law Center, respectively, informed the Court of the important environmental consequences of the case.[362]

The effect of these submissions on the decision-making process of the Inter-American Court is, however, hard to determine. The Court indicates whether it has received *amicus curiae* briefs in its summary of the proceedings, but it rarely expressly refers to these briefs in its decision on the merits. Comparing the reasoning of the Court with that represented by the *amici* is further complicated by the fact that *amicus curiae* briefs are not included in the case record.[363] Nevertheless, it is possible to conclude that in most of the selected cases at least one of the interests brought forward in an *amici* submission was held to be decisive by the Court. Like the European Court, the IACtHR thus allows and takes account of *amicus curiae* submission. In contrast to the ECtHR, however, the IACtHR receives *amicus curiae* briefs on a regular basis.

---

359 Since 2009, *amicus curiae* submissions are explicitly allowed under Article 44 Rules of Procedure of the Inter-American Court of Human Rights of November 2009, available at <www.corteidh.or.cr>. Concerning the interpretation of previous procedural rules to allow *amicus curiae*, see T. Buergenthal, 'The Advisory Practice of the Inter-American Human Rights Court' (1985) 79 *American Journal of International Law* 1, 15; M. Pinto, 'NGOs and the Inter-American Court of Human Rights' in T. Treves (ed), *Civil Society, International Courts and Compliance Bodies*, Cambridge University Press, Cambridge 2005, p 54.

360 The Court already accepted *amicus curiae* briefs in its first contentious case. Inter-American Court of Human Rights, *Case of Velásquez-Rodríguez v Honduras*, Judgment of 29.07.1988, para. 38.

361 See <www.ciel.org>.

362 Inter-American Court of Human Rights, *Case of Mayagna (Sumo) Awas Tingni Community v Nicaragua*, Judgment of 31.08.2001, para. 42; Inter-American Court of Human Rights, *Case of Kawas-Fernández v Honduras*, Judgment of 03.04,2009, para. 13.

363 Pasqualucci, above n 125, p 214.

2.5.5.3. *African Commission on Human and Peoples' Rights*

Because NGOs enjoy direct access to the African Commission, it is not common for them to join as *amici*. This possibility may, however, gain in importance at the level of the African Court. Because NGOs will not have direct access to the African Court[364] the possibility of an *amicus curiae* intervention may become the most effective way of introducing common interests to the Court.

2.5.6. SUMMARY: THIRD PARTY INTERVENTIONS AND COMMON INTEREST

The study above has shown that third party interventions that focus on common interests are generally accepted in the rules of procedure at the level of the regional human rights regimes, although with varying effect on the number of submissions. The other studied mechanisms initially did not provide for the submission of *amicus curiae* briefs by parties other than public intergovernmental organisations in their rules of procedure. While the ICJ has interpreted this lack of provisions as an impediment to accepting such briefs, the ITLOS has shown itself to be more willing to refer to 'outsider' opinions. Although non-State actors have been allowed to intervene in a WTO dispute by way of *amicus curiae* briefs, practice shows that only those parts of the briefs that are explicitly endorsed by one of the parties will be formally considered by the judicial bodies. This is not surprising given the initial negative reaction of the State parties after the judicial bodies first developed a formal acceptance mechanism for *amicus curiae* briefs.

2.6. PROVISIONAL MEASURES

Of the institutions considered only two bodies have used provisional measures to protect the rights of the parties during the proceedings in the selected natural resource cases (the ICJ and the ITLOS). The WTO AB does not indicate provisional measures but works with a tight time schedule to prevent conflicts from deteriorating.[365] Although the regional human rights bodies have made extensive use of provisional measures, these measures are not studied here because they generally deal with different issues from those discussed in this book, for example expulsion and extradition. Provisional measures are found

[364] Article 30 Protocol on the Statute of the African Court of Justice and Human Rights of 1 July 2008, available at <www.au.int>.

[365] Reports are circulated 90 days after the appeal, although it must be noted that recently the AB has not managed to consistently meet this deadline.

to be less controversial because they are not determinative of the claim on the merits.[366] Nevertheless, it is of interest to look at this element here because recently the ICJ and the ITLOS have used the indication of provisional measures to go beyond the protection of the rights of the parties and into the realm of protecting common interests.

2.6.1. INTERNATIONAL COURT OF JUSTICE

In contrast with the prudent interpretation of most of its procedural rules, the Court has itself created an opening for the consideration of a common interest goal in its procedure on provisional measures. According to Article 41(1) of the ICJ Statute, the Court has the power to grant binding provisional measures under certain conditions.[367] First, the ICJ may only grant provisional measures if it has prima facie jurisdiction over a dispute.[368] Secondly, the ICJ Statute provides that measures should only be indicated if the Court 'considers that circumstances so require to protect the rights which might form the subject matter of a judgment'.[369] Traditionally the Court interpreted this to mean that measures are only justified if there is urgency, pending the final decision of the case, to protect the rights of the parties.[370] However, it has been noted that the ICJ widened its power to indicate provisional measures in situations in which they are needed to prevent the escalation or aggravation of a dispute.[371] The power to indicate provisional measures that are not requested by the parties is supported by the ICJ's power to grant provisional measures *proprio motu* but has been criticised

---

366 Brown, above n 53, p 234.

367 The ICJ for the first time confirmed that its provisional measures are binding in ICJ, *Case of LaGrand (Germany v United States of America), Judgment*, Judgment of 2001, para. 102. The concept that provisional measures are always binding, irrespective of the parties' consent, is criticised as unlawful in K. Oellers-Frahm, 'Expanding the Competence to Issue Provisional Measures – Strengthening the International Judicial Function' (2011) 12 *German Law Journal* 1279, 1290–92.

368 ICJ, *Case of Armed Activities on the Territory of the Congo (New Application: 2002) (Democratic Republic of the Congo v Rwanda), Provisional Measures, Order*, Judgment of 2002; ICJ, *Case of Pulp Mills on the River Uruguay (Argentina v Uruguay), Provisional Measures Order*, Judgment of 2006, para. 57.

369 Article 41(1) Statute of the International Court of Justice of 26.06.1945, Treaty Series, 993.

370 On the requirement of urgency: ICJ, *Case of Pulp Mills on the River Uruguay (Argentina v Uruguay), Provisional Measures Order*, Judgment of 2006, para. 62. On the protection of rights: ICJ, *Case of Armed Activities on the Territory of the Congo (New Application: 2002) (Democratic Republic of the Congo v Rwanda), Provisional Measures, Order*, Judgment of 2002, para. 1190.

371 K. Oellers-Frahm, 'Article 41' in A. Zimmermann, C. Tomuschat and K. Oellers-Frahm (eds), *The Statute of the International Court of Justice: A Commentary*, Oxford University Press, Oxford 2006, pp 931–32.

for going beyond the Court's mandate.[372] That the Court, nevertheless, extended its provisional measures to include the prevention of (possibly violent) conflict can be seen as an incorporation of the common interest of peace and security in its procedure.[373]

The ICJ's focus on the prevention of violent conflict is confirmed in the provisional measures order of *Armed Activities on the Territory of the Congo (DRC v Rwanda)*. In this case, the Court did not find that it had prima facie jurisdiction and therefore refrained from indicating provisional measures. However, instead of ending its decision there, the ICJ went on to urge the parties to prevent grave violations of human rights and international humanitarian law.[374] Again, this evolution in the Court's case law can be explained in light of the importance that the ICJ attaches to the maintenance of international peace and security, a fundamental interest of the international community.[375] This was further confirmed by the 2011 *Request for Interpretation of the Judgment of 15 June 1962 in the Case concerning the Temple of Preah Vihear (Cambodia v Thailand)*. In this case, Cambodia asked the ICJ to order an immediate withdrawal of all Thai forces from the area of the Temple of Preah Vihear, a religious site situated near the border between the two countries. The Court, however, did not grant the requested measures. Instead, it indicated provisional measures addressed to both the parties and ordered the parties to respect a demilitarised zone around the Temple.[376] Although the Court did not explain why it chose this approach, it can be deduced from its overall function and previous case law that the protection of international peace and security was its main goal in this case.

2.6.2. INTERNATIONAL TRIBUNAL FOR THE LAW OF THE SEA

Article 290 of UNCLOS provides that the ITLOS may prescribe binding provisional measures if certain conditions are fulfilled. First, the Tribunal must have prima facie jurisdiction. This implies that the dispute has been submitted

---

372 Article 75 ICJ Rules of the Court of 14 April 1978, available at <www.icj-cij.org>. This has nevertheless been criticised for going beyond the ICJ's mandate in Oellers-Frahm, above n 371, p 932.

373 Benzing, above n 84, 379.

374 ICJ, *Case of Armed Activities on the Territory of the Congo (New Application: 2002) (Democratic Republic of the Congo v Rwanda), Provisional Measures, Order*, Judgment of 2002, paras. 54–56, 93.

375 Benzing, above n 84, 380. For the time being, this conclusion may be over-enthusiastic because the rights of the parties in this case were intertwined with the protection of individual lives. Thus, the decision can be explained without referring to a common interest.

376 ICJ, *Case of Request for Interpretation of the Judgment of 15 June 1962 in the Case concerning the Temple of Preah Vihear (Cambodia v Thailand), Provisional Measures*, Judgment of 2011.

to the ITLOS in accordance with the rules of Part XV of the UNCLOS. Secondly, the suggested measures must be necessary to preserve the rights of the parties or to prevent serious harm to the marine environment.[377] Thirdly, pending the constitution of a tribunal that will decide on the merits, the urgency of the situation must require the institution of provisional measures.[378] All three of these requirements could be influenced by considerations of common interest.

The Tribunal in the *Southern Bluefin Tuna* case interpreted the requirement of prima facie jurisdiction. This dispute arose when Japan unilaterally decided to carry out a scientific exploratory fishing programme that went beyond the quota agreed upon between Australia, Japan and New Zealand in the 1993 Conservation of Southern Bluefin Tuna Convention. Australia and New Zealand chose to bring the issue to the ITLOS as a violation of the UNCLOS rather than settling it under the 1993 Convention. Japan argued that this choice was contrary to the dispute settlement procedure provided in the 1993 Convention. Nevertheless, the ITLOS established prima facie jurisdiction. The Annex VII arbitral Tribunal deciding on the merits did not follow this decision. It rejected jurisdiction and revoked the provisional measures.[379]

In contrast to the ICJ, the necessity of the provisional measure under UNCLOS may depend on the prevention of serious harm to the marine environment. This provision gives the ITLOS the option to base provisional measures exclusively on a common interest ground. The Tribunal has considered the preservation of the marine environment *proprio motu* in the *Southern Bluefin Tuna* case, which could indicate that the ITLOS found it to be the main reason for prescribing provisional measures.[380] The protection of the marine environment was also of crucial importance in the *MOX Plant* case. In this case, Ireland claimed that provisional measures were necessary both to preserve its rights and to prevent the pollution of the marine environment.[381] In its order, the Tribunal only granted provisional measures to preserve the marine environment.

---

377 Article 290(1) United Nations Convention on the Law of the Sea of 10 December 1982, UN Treaty Series, vol. 1833, 3 (pending ITLOS' final decision on the merits); ibid, Article 290(5) (pending the constitution of an arbitral tribunal).

378 Under ibid, Article 290(5). In his separate opinion on *Southern Bluefin Tuna*, Judge Treves suggests that urgency is also a requirement under ibid, Article 290(1), when ITLOS will also decide on the merits. ITLOS, *Southern Bluefin Tuna Case (New Zealand v Japan; Australia v Japan), Separate Opinion of Judge Treves*, Judgment of 1999, 1644.

379 See C. Romano, 'The Southern Bluefin Tuna Dispute: Hints of a World to Come ... Like It or Not' (2001) 32 *Ocean Development & International Law* 313, 313–48. In the end, the provisional measures restarted negotiations between the parties that led to a revitalisation of the Southern Bluefin Tuna Commission. Tuerk, above n 122, 301.

380 ITLOS, *Southern Bluefin Tuna Case (New Zealand v Japan; Australia v Japan), Provisional Measures*, Judgment of 1999, para. 70; B. Kwiatkowska, 'Southern Bluefin Tuna (New Zealand v. Japan; Australia v. Japan), Order on Provisional Measures (ITLOS Cases Nos. 3 and 4)' (2000) 94 *American Journal of International Law* 150, 155.

381 ITLOS, *The MOX Plant Case (Ireland v United Kingdom), Provisional Measures*, Judgment of 2001, 81–83.

The third requirement, urgency, was also clarified in the *MOX Plant* case. In light of the short time it would take to establish an arbitral tribunal, the Tribunal did not consider the circumstances to be urgent enough to answer Ireland's demand for the suspension of the planned commissioning of the MOX Plant.[382] This decision was influenced by the assurance given by the UK that it would not export additional MOX fuel before the constitution of an arbitral tribunal.[383] However, the Tribunal decided to use its power to prescribe different provisional measures under Article 89(5) of its rules of procedure. The Tribunal considered that 'prudence and caution require that Ireland and the United Kingdom cooperate in exchanging information concerning the risks or effects of the operation of the MOX plant and in devising ways to deal with them'.[384]

After establishing that it lacked the power to order provisional measures because the situation was not urgent, the Tribunal's decision to order different provisional measures is remarkable.[385] The reason for this apparent contradiction cannot be deduced from the order. It is possible that the ITLOS found the situation to be sufficiently urgent to merit less far-reaching measures than those proposed by Ireland.[386] It can be observed that the Tribunal in both the *MOX* and the *Southern Bluefin Tuna* Orders offered the applicants 'the benefit of a great many doubts'.[387] The loose interpretation of the requirements of prima facie jurisdiction[388] as well as urgency could be explained by considering the prevention of harm to the marine environment as the 'Tribunal's overriding objective' in these cases.[389]

One issue on which the ITLOS has adopted a relatively progressive approach to the consideration of common interests, namely a precautionary approach, is the issue of uncertain risks to serious environmental harm. The precautionary principle prescribes that scientific uncertainty on a serious risk of environmental

---

382 Taking account of the short time it would take to establish an arbitral tribunal. Ibid, 81.

383 Ibid, 78.

384 Ibid, 84. Thirteen of the Tribunal's 21 judges appended a declaration to the MOX Plant Order. The Annex VII Tribunal confirmed this Order (Arbitral Tribunal Constituted Pursuant to Article 287 and Article 1 of Annex VII of the UNCLOS, *The MOX Plant Case (Ireland v United Kingdom), Request for further provisional measures*, Judgment of 2003).

385 This was described by Judge Treves and Judge ad hoc Székely in their respective Separate Opinions. ITLOS, *The MOX Plant Case (Ireland v United Kingdom), Provisional Measures, Separate Opinion Judge* ad hoc *Székely*, Judgment of 2001; ITLOS, *The MOX Plant Case (Ireland v United Kingdom), Provisional Measures, Separate Opinion Judge Treves*, Judgment of 2001.

386 Brown, above n 247, 282.

387 Kwiatkowska, above n 380, 154.

388 Jurisdiction was later rejected by the arbitral tribunal. (Arbitral Tribunal constituted under Part XV ('Settlement of Disputes') Annex VII ('Arbitration') of the UNCLOS, *Southern Bluefin Tuna Case (Australia and New Zealand v Japan), Award on Jurisdiction and Admissibility*, Judgment of 2000).

389 Kwiatkowska, above n 380, 155.

harm should not preclude protective measures.[390] As described above, a first hint to this principle could already be found in the Tribunal's order on provisional measures in the *Southern Bluefin Tuna* case:

> [T]he parties should in the circumstances act with prudence and caution to ensure that effective conservation measures are taken to prevent serious harm to the stock of southern bluefin tuna;[391] ...
> although the Tribunal cannot conclusively assess the scientific evidence presented by the parties, it finds that measures should be taken as a matter of urgency to preserve the rights of the parties and to avert further deterioration of the southern bluefin tuna stock.[392]

Although the order 'studiously avoids' using the term and does not prescribe compliance with the precautionary principle as a provisional measure, clear references to both the element of scientific uncertainty and serious risk to the environment can be found throughout the decision.[393] Thus, it could be assumed that the ITLOS adopted a precautionary reasoning.[394] This assumption was confirmed in the *Advisory Opinion on activities in the Area* where the Seabed Disputes Chamber stated that the precautionary approach was implicit in the *Southern Bluefin Tuna* cases and that there is 'a trend towards making this approach part of customary international law'.[395] The Tribunal's use of the precautionary principle is interesting because it is not included in the UNCLOS and its meaning and status in general international law is at the very least arguable.[396]

In the later *MOX Plant* case on provisional measures, Ireland explicitly based its claim on the precautionary principle. In its order, the Tribunal found the precautionary principle inapplicable because of the lack of proof delivered by

---

390 Article 15 Rio Declaration on Environment and Development of 1992 UN Doc. A/CONF. 151/26.

391 ITLOS, *Southern Bluefin Tuna Case (New Zealand v Japan; Australia v Japan), Provisional Measures*, Judgment of 1999, para. 77.

392 Ibid, para. 80. The provisional measures were revoked by the ICSID Tribunal, which rejected jurisdiction (Arbitral Tribunal constituted under Part XV ('Settlement of Disputes') Annex VII ('Arbitration') of the UNCLOS, *Southern Bluefin Tuna Case (Australia and New Zealand v Japan), Award on Jurisdiction and Admissibility*, Judgment of 2000).

393 Boyle, above n 122, 373.

394 Benzing, above n 84, 392.

395 ITLOS Seabed Disputes Chamber, *Case of Responsibilities and obligations of States sponsoring persons and entities with respect to activities in the Area, Advisory Opinion*, para. 132. The Chamber referred, inter alia, to the precautionary approach adopted in ICJ, *Case of Pulp Mills on the River Uruguay (Argentina v Uruguay), Judgment*, Judgment of 2010.

396 P. Sands and J. Peel, *Principles of International Environmental Law*, Cambridge University Press, Cambridge 2012, p. 950.

Ireland on the risk of serious environmental harm.[397] Nevertheless, the ITLOS stated that Ireland and the United Kingdom should cooperate at two levels. First, in exchanging information concerning the risks or effects of the operation of the MOX plant and, secondly, in devising ways to deal with these risks.[398]

It further established the duty of cooperation as a fundamental principle in the prevention of pollution of the maritime environment under UNCLOS and general international law.[399] This is in accordance with the view that the *erga omnes* nature of certain obligations entails a duty to cooperate.[400] The Tribunal interpreted the duty to cooperate to include an exchange of information, risk monitoring and preventive measures.[401]

In his separate opinion on the case, Judge Wolfrum found that the duty to cooperate reflects a more general shift in international law from the bilateral to the consideration of common interests. He stated that the duty to cooperate 'balances the principle of sovereignty of States and thus ensures that community interests are taken into account vis-à-vis individualistic State interests'.[402] Judge Wolfrum further clarified the difference between the *Southern Bluefin Tuna* case and the *MOX Plant* case. While in the former case, the parties agreed that the stock of bluefin tuna was at an historical low and measures should be taken, the parties in the MOX case disagreed on the risk of serious environmental harm and therefore there was no room for the application of the precautionary principle.[403] This difference might also explain the perceived difference in the standard of proof in both cases, which was discussed in the section on evidence.[404]

In 2003, the Tribunal was again asked to decide on the issue in the provisional measures order in the *Case concerning Land Reclamation by Singapore in and around the Straits of Johor (Malaysia v Singapore)*. Malaysia asked the Tribunal to

397 ITLOS, *The MOX Plant Case (Ireland v United Kingdom), Provisional Measures*, Judgment of 2001, para. 75.

398 Ibid, para. 84.

399 Ibid, para. 82.

400 SHELTON, above n 102, 39.

401 ITLOS, *The MOX Plant Case (Ireland v United Kingdom), Provisional Measures*, Judgment of 2001, para. 89. This reflects the articles on prevention of transboundary harm from hazardous activities adopted by the ILC (ORELLANA, above n 243, 472).

402 ITLOS, *The MOX Plant Case (Ireland v United Kingdom), Provisional Measures, Separate Opinion Judge Wolfrum*, Judgment of 2001. Rashbrooke comments that while the procedural requirements prescribed by the Tribunal may benefit the environment, it is not guaranteed that they will. Moreover, he argues that because the ITLOS apparently did not find sufficient scientific evidence as to the environmental risk, the measures were aimed at preserving the parties' rights and not at protecting the marine environment (G. RASHBROOKE, 'The International Tribunal for the Law of the Sea: A Forum for the Development of Principles of International Environmental Law?' (2004) 19 *International Journal of Marine and Coastal Law* 515, 529–30).

403 ITLOS, *The MOX Plant Case (Ireland v United Kingdom), Provisional Measures, Separate Opinion Judge Wolfrum*, Judgment of 2001.

404 See pp 50ff.

suspend certain land reclamation projects started by Singapore near Malaysia's territorial waters and to order Singapore to provide information and negotiate with Malaysia on the projects. During the proceedings, the parties themselves proposed and agreed on provisional measures. This attitude was encouraged by the Tribunal, which found that, because of the environmental risks, 'prudence and caution' required it to order the parties to exchange information, apply risk assessments and address those risks.[405]

As in the *MOX Plant* case, the Tribunal connects the precautionary approach, or a prudent and cautious approach, in cases of environmental risk to the duty to cooperate. Ad hoc Judges Hossain and Oxman observed that in the *Land Reclamation* case, this decision was based on a 'fundamental principle' of the UNCLOS, namely the principle that the right of a State to use marine areas and natural resource is limited by 'the duty to have due regard to the rights of other States and to the protection and preservation of the marine environment'.[406] This reasoning also seems applicable to the more recent order on provisional measures in the *M/V 'Louisa' Case (Saint Vincent and the Grenadines v Kingdom of Spain)*.

In the *M/V 'Louisa'* case, Saint Vincent and the Grenadines asked the Tribunal to order the release of the *M/V Louisa*, a ship seized by Spain. Saint Vincent argued that there was a significant risk that the vessel would leak oil while in the Spanish harbour, and therefore a release was necessary to prevent harm to the marine environment. While the Tribunal confirmed that 'the parties should in the circumstances act with prudence and caution to prevent serious harm to the marine environment', it found that, in light of the assurances given by Spain concerning the monitoring of the ship and the protocols in place, it was not necessary to order provisional measures.[407] Because Spain had proven to take due regard of the protection and preservation of the marine environment, there was no need to limit its rights.

In light of developing international environmental law, the ITLOS case law has been criticised as 'Delphic to the point of being totally obscure'.[408] The vagueness of the ITLOS case law may be attributed to the short time it often

---

405 ITLOS, *Case concerning Land Reclamation by Singapore in and around the Straits of Johor (Malaysia v Singapore), Provisional Measures*, Judgment of 2003, para. 99. In 2005 the parties signed an agreement settling their dispute.

406 ITLOS, *Case concerning Land Reclamation by Singapore in and around the Straits of Johor (Malaysia v Singapore), Provisional Measures, Joint declaration of Judges ad hoc Hossain and Oxman*, Judgment of 2003, para. 1.

407 ITLOS, *M/V 'Louisa' Case (Saint Vincent and the Grenadines v Kingdom of Spain), Provisional Measures*, Judgment of 2010, paras. 76–77.

408 Rashbrooke, above n 402, 534, Rashbrooke referring to M.D. Evans, 'The Southern Bluefin Tuna Dispute: Provisional Thinking on Provisional Measures?' (1999) 10 *Yearbook of International Environmental Law* 7.

has to reach a conclusion and the focus on the dispute at hand.[409] Nevertheless, some conclusions can be drawn from the Tribunal's approach to environmental concerns in cases on provisional measures. First, ITLOS only orders preventive measures to be taken if the parties agree on the risk and it has not been proven that the measures already in place are sufficient.[410] Secondly, ITLOS generally orders procedural measures if the parties do not agree on the risk. Under the duty to cooperate, it orders the parties to exchange information, apply risk assessments and prevent any risks that are established. Therefore, it can be concluded from the case law that ITLOS plays a progressive role in the protection of the marine environment.

2.6.3. SUMMARY: PROVISIONAL MEASURES AND COMMON INTEREST

The only clear conclusion that can be drawn from the case law analysis on provisional measures is that they are more easily granted when the core values of the relevant regime are at stake. In the application of the procedural rules regarding provisional measures, the ICJ showed more flexibility in its consideration of one specific issue of common interest. While in principle provisional measures serve merely to protect the rights of the parties, the Court extended its provisional measures to include the prevention of (possibly violent) conflict, even if this not requested by either of the parties. It thereby incorporates the protection of international peace and security in its case law. A similar observation can be made with regard to the ITLOS. While the ITLOS uses a flexible interpretation of the requirements of prima facie jurisdiction, necessity and urgency, flexibility is inherent in the procedure for granting provisional measures and does not necessarily depend on the subject of the case. Nonetheless, provisional measures, albeit not necessarily those sought by the claimant, were easily granted in cases involving the preservation of the marine environment.

---

409 Most of the cases examined by the Tribunal have been cases on provisional measures or prompt release. Ibid, 534–535.

410 See ITLOS, *Southern Bluefin Tuna Case (New Zealand v Japan; Australia v Japan), Provisional Measures*, Judgment of 1999; ITLOS, *Case concerning Land Reclamation by Singapore in and around the Straits of Johor (Malaysia v Singapore), Provisional Measures*, Judgment of 2003.

CHAPTER 3
SUBSTANTIVE CONSIDERATIONS AND COMMON INTERESTS

3.1. INTRODUCTION

When studying the case law of international courts and tribunals, two types of cases can be identified in which the common interest is invoked. First, the common interest is often invoked by the defending State as an exception ground. Most international Treaties include provisions that allow a State to take measures that are inconsistent with some or all of the Treaty rules 'in the public interest'. These provisions are called 'public interest exceptions'. Although public interest exceptions are generally included in a Treaty to allow a State to defend its national, domestic, interests, they are often used to protect domestic interests that coincide with common interests. Some of these provisions explicitly refer to 'the' public interest or the specific interests that could qualify as an exception ground, others do not. Under the latter category, this study will also consider certain interpretations of provisions, which differentiate between public interest norms and other norms on the basis of the public interest purpose, as exceptions. The reason for this is that the purpose or effect of those interpretations is to allow the State to regulate in the public interest, to provide some leeway for State measures, when no technical legal exception is available. This is different from the second type of legal argument in which the violated Treaty norm obliges the State to regulate in the common interest. In the latter situation, the common interest is used to highlight or add weight to the norm that is allegedly violated. Thus, in most of these cases the common interest will be invoked by the claimant rather than the defendant. Furthermore, the role of the court will be different here. Instead of reviewing an exception to the relevant Treaty it will review whether a strict enforcement of the Treaty is in order.

3.2. PUBLIC INTEREST EXCEPTIONS

3.2.1. INTERNATIONAL COURT OF JUSTICE

3.2.1.1. Emergency Clauses

A first occasion on which the ICJ has to consider public interest issues invoked by the State is when it interprets emergency and necessity clauses. A variety of international Treaties include a public interest clause, namely a provision that allows for an exception to the Treaty rules 'in the public interest'. When a State invokes such a provision to justify its actions, the ICJ has to consider whether the purpose of the action was to protect an issue of public interest and whether the action was necessary for that purpose. Public interest clauses are not only relevant in the context of Treaty obligations; they also appear in the International Law Commission's (ILC) Draft Articles on State Responsibility.[411]

The public interest clause included in Article 33 of the Draft Articles was discussed in the case of the *Gabčíkovo-Nagymaros Project (Hungary/Slovakia).*[412] In this case, the ICJ had to determine whether the termination by Hungary of the Treaty on the construction of a system of dams on the river Danube was wrongful. A first point of interest in this case was the finding of the Court that the public interest clause included in the Articles on State Responsibility was applicable. The ICJ established that while the validity of the termination had to be determined by the Vienna Convention, the law of State responsibility could determine the circumstances under which an illegal termination's wrongfulness is precluded. This ended an earlier discussion on whether or not States, by adopting the Vienna Convention, forfeited their right to use arguments of public interest to suspend or terminate a Convention.[413]

A second reason to consider the *Gabčíkovo-Nagymaros* decision in this section is the Court's adjudication of the necessity of Hungary's action. To shed light on the ICJ's general approach to common interests it is not only the Court's recognition of the protection of the environment as an 'essential interest', but also its rejection of the necessity of Hungary's termination that is relevant.[414] From the ILC's clarification of the Draft Articles, the Court deduced that 'the state of necessity can only be invoked under certain strictly defined conditions

---

411 Chapter V Draft Articles on Responsibility of States for Internationally Wrongful Acts, International Law Commission of 2001 UN Doc. A/56/10.

412 ICJ, *Case of Gabčíkovo-Nagymaros Project (Hungary/Slovakia), Judgment*, Judgment of 1997.

413 M. Evans, 'Case Concerning the Gabcikovo-Nagymaros Project (Hungary v. Slovakia)' (1998) 47 *International & Comparative Law Quarterly* 688, 691–92.

414 ICJ, *Case of Gabčíkovo-Nagymaros Project (Hungary/Slovakia), Judgment*, Judgment of 1997, para. 53.

which must be cumulatively satisfied; and the State concerned is not the sole judge of whether those conditions have been met'.[415]

The Court subsequently identified five conditions necessary to invoke the state of necessity. First, the action must be taken to protect an essential interest of the State. Secondly, that essential interest must have been threatened by a grave and imminent peril. Thirdly, the State's action must have been the only means of protecting that interest. Fourthly, the act must not have seriously damaged an essential interest of the other State. And lastly, the state of necessity may not have been caused by the State invoking that necessity in any way.[416]

Although the quoted statement of the Court seems to imply that the State still has some measure of discretion in determining whether these conditions are fulfilled, the Court left little margin to Hungary.[417] It rejected the necessity defence for two reasons: first, because Hungary could not provide evidence that there was a grave and imminent peril to the environment at the time that it suspended the work on the dam; and secondly, because Hungary had other means available to respond to the situation.[418] Especially the first reason for this decision was criticised because demanding evidence of certainty and inevitability of a risk makes it near to impossible to claim environmental necessity in a preventive way.[419]

In the 2003 *Oil Platforms (Islamic Republic of Iran v United States of America)* case, the ICJ was asked to review the legality of an attack on Iranian oil platforms by the US military in reaction to attacks, which were attributed to both Iran and Iraq, on international oil tankers in the Persian Gulf.[420] The Court's jurisdiction in this case was based on a bilateral Treaty of Amity between the US and Iran. Iran based its claim for reparations on the fact that the attack interfered with the freedom of commerce and navigation, which was provided for in the Amity Treaty between the two countries.[421] In its defence, the US relied on a clause of the Amity Treaty that provided that the Treaty would not preclude measures 'necessary to protect its essential security interests'.[422] This is a typical public interest exception that is inherent in many Treaties. The Court interpreted the

415 Ibid, para. 51.
416 Ibid, para. 52.
417 Y. Shany, 'Toward a General Margin of Appreciation Doctrine in International Law?' (2005) 16 *European Journal of International Law* 907, 934.
418 ICJ, *Case of Gabčíkovo-Nagymaros Project (Hungary/Slovakia), Judgment*, Judgment of 1997, paras. 55–57.
419 E. Preiss, 'The International Obligation to Conduct an Environmental Impact Assesment: the ICJ Case Concerning the Gabcikovo-Nagymaros Project' (1999) 7 *New York University Environmental Law Journal* 307, 366.
420 ICJ, *Case of Oil Platforms (Islamic Republic of Iran v United States of America), Judgment*, Judgment of 2003.
421 Ibid, para. 31.
422 Ibid, para. 32.

exception in line with the general international law rules on the use of force. Thus, to justify the attacks on the Iranian oil platforms as self-defence the US had to prove that the attacks by Iran were 'armed attacks' in the sense of Article 51 of the UN Charter, which provides for the individual right of self-defence. Because the majority of the Court did not consider the attacks against the oil tankers to be armed attacks within the meaning of the UN Charter the US defence was rejected.[423] Nevertheless, the ICJ went on for the purpose of discussion to consider when self-defence is considered necessary to protect essential security interests under international law. In this context, it can be observed that the Court does not leave any margin of deference to the State in determining whether a measure was necessary. In considering whether the disputed actions would have answered the requirements of Article 51 of the UN Charter, the Court stated that 'the requirement of international law that measures taken avowedly in self-defense must have been necessary for that purpose is strict and objective, leaving no room for any "measure of discretion"'.[424]

What is remarkable in this case is that the ICJ chose to examine the US defence to Iran's claim for reparations before establishing whether the Treaty of Amity between Iran and the US was violated in the first place. Iran had claimed that by attacking and destroying the oil platforms the US had prevented Iran from exploiting and exporting its natural resources to the US, thereby violating the freedom of commerce agreed upon in the Amity Treaty.[425] The Court, however, found that at the time of the attacks there was no relevant commerce between the countries and therefore the freedom of commerce was not interfered with by the US attacks on the oil platforms.[426]

Why the ICJ chose to clarify its case law on the right to self-defence, while in the end it did not establish that the Treaty between the US and Iran was violated, may be explained by the position that the Court assumes. The Court's decision in this case proves that it does not consider its task to be limited to the settlement of specific disputes between certain States but to ensure respect for international law and the maintenance of peace and security, a more 'community-oriented perspective'.[427] That the individual judges struggle with this decision is shown in the separate and dissenting opinions, which represent very different understandings of what the Court should and should not engage in. In his separate opinion, Judge Simma states that the Court applied inappropriate restraint and draws a conclusion based

423 Ibid, paras. 64, 72.
424 Ibid, para. 73.
425 Ibid, para. 86.
426 Note that Iran's original claim was based on multiple Articles but was narrowed at the preliminary objections stage.
427 Cf. ICJ, *Corfu Channel Case (United Kingdom v Republic of Albania), Judgment*, Judgment of 1949. The Court is possibly led by the need for legal guidance in sensitive cases, such as those including *jus cogens* norms. Shany, above n 417, 938.

on a much broader range of legal sources, going far beyond those provided for in Article 38 of the ICJ Statute.[428] He states that the Court should not accept a reading of a bilateral Treaty that permits conduct prohibited by the law of the use of force.[429] Judge Simma indicates that the Court has to reinforce the rules on the use of force in order to uphold the law beyond the concrete case.[430] Judge Koojimans, on the other hand, found that the Court should have applied more restraint in the determination of 'essential security interests'. In his view, determining whether essential security interests are at stake is a political question that the Court should only examine when it is clearly unreasonable; instead the Court should focus on reviewing the State's choice of means.[431]

3.2.2. WTO DISPUTE SETTLEMENT MECHANISM

3.2.2.1. Like Products in the NT Provisions

One of the fundamental principles of the WTO system is non-discrimination. This principle forms the basis of the principle of national treatment (NT) and the most favoured nation (MFN) principle. The NT principle is included in Article III GATT and provides that once foreign products have entered the domestic market they should be treated equally to domestically produced 'like' goods. The aim of this Article is to avoid protectionism through domestic measures and ensure the same competitive conditions for imported and domestic goods that are alike. A similar rule applies to like services, like trademarks, copyrights and patents.[432] The MFN principle guarantees non-discrimination between imported goods and services originating from different WTO members, although some exceptions are allowed, such as free trade agreements that are concluded between a specific group of WTO members. The MFN principle is included in the agreements that cover the main areas of trade governed by the WTO.[433] Both non-discrimination principles are also included in Article 2.1 of

---

428 R. Teitel and R. Howse, 'Cross-Judging: Tribunalization in a Fragmented But Interconnected Global Order' (2009) 41 *New York University Journal of International Law and Politics* 959, 961.

429 ICJ, *Case of Oil Platforms (Islamic Republic of Iran v United States of America), Judgment, Separate Opinion Judge Simma*, Judgment of 2003.

430 Paulus, above n 82, pp 128–29. (In the same vein, Simma interprets the Treaty's freedom of commerce clause to protect free commerce as a value belonging to the State parties and does not confine it to the protection of specific transactions between the parties.)

431 ICJ, *Case of Oil Platforms (Islamic Republic of Iran v United States of America), Judgment, Separate Opinion Judge Kooijmans*, Judgment of 2003.

432 Article XVII GATS and Article III Agreement on Trade Related Aspects of Intellectual Property Rights (TRIPS).

433 Article I GATT, Article II General Agreement on Trade in Services (GATS) and Article IV TRIPS.

the Agreement on Technical Barriers to Trade (TBT). This Article holds that imported products 'shall be accorded treatment no less favourable than that accorded to like products of national origin and to like products originating in any other country'. The interpretation of Article 2.1 TBT Agreement will be discussed below.[434] The remainder of this section will focus on the interpretation of 'likeness' in the NT provisions, and not the MFN provisions, because it was mainly the interpretation of the NT provisions that was discussed in the selected case law.

When products are not considered 'like' because of public or common interest considerations, for example because they pose different risks to public health, they do not fall within the ambit of the principle of NT. Therefore, the first substantive question in which common interest considerations may play a role is the determination of the likeness of different foreign and local products. The review below will primarily focus on the interpretation of 'like' in the context of Article III:4 GATT. Although 'like' may be interpreted differently depending on the provision applied (for example, Article III:2 or III:4 GATT), there is a strong process of cross-fertilisation.[435]

In the WTO case law, different factors have been identified to determine whether products are 'like' and a differentiation has been made between the definitions of 'like' in different Articles. In the context of Article III:4 of the GATT, the WTO case law generally refers to four elements to establish whether product are like; the product's end use, consumer tastes and habits, the properties, nature and quality of the product, and its tariff classification.[436] In the case of *EC – Asbestos*, regarding the French import ban on asbestos and asbestos products, Canada claimed that the French ban did not respect the principle of NT (under Article III:4 GATT) because it treated asbestos-free building materials with the same function as asbestos products differently. In the end, the panel confirmed that the ban was inconsistent with the principle of NT, but found it to be justified under one of the general exceptions of Article XX, which is discussed below.[437] However, the AB reversed this finding because it did not consider the disputed products to be like products and, therefore, held that the principle of NT did not apply.

The AB primarily based this conclusion on the difference in physical properties between the products and, alternatively, on the presumed difference in consumers' tastes and habits.[438] '[C]onsumers' tastes and habits regarding

---

434 See discussion on p 100.

435 H. Hestermeyer, 'Article III GATT' in R. Wolfrum, P.-T. Stoll and H. Hestermeyer (eds), *WTO – Trade in Goods*, Martinus Nijhoff Publishers, Leiden/Boston 2011, p 130.

436 These elements were developed in the pre-WTO, WTO GATT Working Party Report, *Border Tax Adjustments*, L/3464, adopted 02.12.1970.

437 The panel found the ban to be justified by Article XX(b) because asbestos is a manifest risk to human health.

438 WTO Appellate Body Report, *European Communities – Measures affecting Asbestos and Asbestos-containing Products*, WT/DS135/AB/R, adopted 12.03.2001, paras. 114, 122.

fibers, even in the case of commercial parties, such as manufacturers, are very likely to be shaped by the health risks associated with a product, which is known to be highly carcinogenic.'[439]

By defining toxicity as a physical property and assuming the effect of health risks on consumers' tastes and habits, the AB in *EC – Asbestos* applied a broad interpretation of the traditional elements determining likeness. This broad interpretation shows that the WTO judicial bodies are willing to interpret their own established case law in an evolutionary manner to allow Member States to enforce common interest issues, such as public health, within their territory. Nevertheless, the AB did reiterate in its decision that the question of likeness refers to the competitive relationship between products.[440] Thus, it remains uncertain how much room is left for the consideration of non-economic concerns, especially in cases where a less broad consensus exists on the risks related to a certain product.[441]

Whereas Article III applies to internal measures on like products, in other words measures that apply to the product, Article XI applies to border measures. Article XI prohibits certain measures imposed on the importation or exportation of products, more specifically non-tariff restrictions such as quotas and import licences. For the purposes of this review, the main difference between these provisions is that Article III allows internal measures if they are non-discriminatory, whereas Article XI:1 prohibits non-tariff restrictions.[442] In the past a prohibition on the import *and* sale of a product was considered under Article XI. However, in *EC – Asbestos*, the French prohibition on the import and the sale of a product were considered, as a whole, under Article III.[443] This interpretation offers an opportunity for trade restrictions based on public or common interest grounds.

A related topic, which is still highly debated, is whether products that could be considered different on the basis of their PPMs (processes and production methods) should be considered like products under Article III. The goal of this type of measure is to minimise the negative effects caused by the production or harvest of a certain product. Therefore, the element of consumer tastes and habits could provide an argument for defining such products as not-like. However, consumers may not know the PPMs of certain products unless they are labelled, thus treated differently. Furthermore, a differentiation on the basis of PPMs would allow States to circumvent the application of Article XX, which

439 Ibid, para. 122.
440 Ibid, para. 99.
441 Bernasconi-Osterwalder et al., above n 356, p 14.
442 See also R. Wolfrum, 'Article XI GATT' in R. Wolfrum, P.-T. Stoll and H. Hestermeyer (eds), *WTO – Trade in Goods*, Martinus Nijhoff Publishers, Leiden/Boston 2011, p 293.
443 Hestermeyer, above n 435, p 126.

is discussed below. Therefore, such products are generally considered to be like products under WTO law.[444]

Although the AB found that the dispute in *EC – Asbestos* did not fall under Article III:4 of the GATT because it did not concern 'like' products, the AB still elaborated on the Article's requirement of not according 'less favourable' treatment on imported products. In its decision, the AB held that the prohibition of 'less favourable' treatment does not automatically prohibit a differentiation between 'like' products.[445] In other words, a formal regulatory distinction is not conclusive evidence of less favourable treatment, the panel has to look at the conditions of competition. In *Dominican Republic – Cigarettes*, the AB confirmed that in some cases the detrimental impact could be explained by other factors than the origin of the products.[446] In the case of *EC – Biotech* concerning the EC's moratorium on the approval of biotech products, the panel furthermore stated that a different treatment of imported products is not necessarily less favourable if the difference can be explained through origin-neutral factors, such as 'a perceived difference in terms of the required care in their safety assessment, risk for the consumer, etc.'.[447] This interpretation seemed to offer additional leeway for considering non-trade interests that are supported by consumer behaviour. However, in the more recent case of *EC – Seals*, the AB clarified its earlier decisions and explicitly stated that the question of whether the detrimental impact of a measure stems exclusively from a legitimate regulatory distinction should not be considered under Article III:4 GATT.[448] When examining less favourable treatment, the only consideration is whether the measure, rather than unrelated market conditions, explains the disparate impact on the conditions of competition. Thus, the AB made a clear division of labour between both Articles and leaves no room for common interest considerations at this stage of its assessment.[449] This interpretation has the consequence that many national public interest measures are now prima facie illegal under WTO law, although some leeway still exists in determining whether a disparate impact on the competitive conditions exists. The disparate impact test requires that a group, a critical mass,

444 Ibid, 146–47.

445 WTO Appellate Body Report, *European Communities – Measures affecting Asbestos and Asbestos-containing Products*, WT/DS135/AB/R, adopted 12.03.2001, para. 100.

446 WTO Appellate Body Report, *Dominican Republic – Measures affecting the Importation and Internal Sale of Cigarettes*, WT/DS302/AB/R, adopted 25.04.2005, para. 96.

447 WTO Panel Report, *European Communities – Measures affecting the Approval and Marketing of Biotech Products*, WT/DS291/R; WT/DS292/R; WT/DS293/R, adopted 29.09.2006, para. 7.2411.

448 WTO Appellate Body Report, *European Communities – Measures Prohibiting the Importation and Marketing of Seal Products*, WT/DS400/AB/R, adopted 22.05.2014, para. 5.117.

449 M. Du, 'Treatment No Less Favorable'and the Future of National Treatment Obligation in GATT Article III: 4 after EC–Seal Products', 2015, available at <ssrn.com> (later published in *World Trade Review* (2016) 1, 139–163), 16.

of foreign market actors is disproportionately disadvantaged in comparison to a domestic group. In the case of a non-protectionist public interest measures, it is more likely that only some actors are disadvantaged and not a critical mass.

3.2.2.2. General Exceptions Clause

The first thing that springs to mind when discussing WTO law and common interests are the explicit mechanisms provided in the WTO agreements to balance trade liberalisation and other policy objectives. The GATT includes explicit references to common interests in Article XX and Article XXI. These Articles provide that State measures that have been found inconsistent with one of the GATT rules may still be justified if they are, inter alia, necessary to protect public morals,[450] to protect human, animal or plant life or health,[451] relate to the conservation of exhaustible natural resources[452] or are necessary to protect international peace and security.[453] Article XIV of the GATS contains similar provisions as the GATT.[454] However, this overview will focus only on the GATT because, so far, no case law on trade in services has been closely linked to natural resource exploitation.[455]

Article XX GATT, also known as the General Exceptions Article, consists of two parts: (1) the chapeau, which provides certain limits to the application of the domestic measure, and (2) 10 subparagraphs describing the interests that may justify an exception to the GATT rules. In this context, it is important to note that the exceptions enumerated in Article XX are 'limited and conditional'. In other words, members may only justify their WTO-inconsistent measures with the policy objectives provided for in the subparagraphs of Article XX, no other grounds are accepted, and the measures must satisfy both the conditions of the subparagraph and the chapeau of Article XX.[456] In the landmark decision of *US – Gasoline*,[457] in which the AB had to determine whether the US Clean Air

450 Article XX(a) GATT.
451 Article XX(b) GATT.
452 Article XX(g) GATT.
453 Article XI(c) GATT.
454 Despite some textual differences, the purpose and language of the exception clauses are largely similar and, therefore, most of the observations made below also apply to the GATS.
455 For an interesting take on the relationship between public policy regulation and GATS see D. Prévost, 'Services and Public Policy Regulation in WTO Law: The Example of the US-Gambling case' in J. Van De Gronden (ed), *The EU and WTO Law on Services: Limits to the Realisation of General Interest Policies within the Services Markets?*, Kluwer Law International, Alphen aan den Rijn 2009, p 293.
456 WTO Appellate Body Report, *United States – Import Prohibition of Certain Shrimp and Shrimp Products*, WT/DS58/AB/R, adopted 12.10.1998, para. 157.
457 WTO Appellate Body Report, *United States – Standards for Reformulated and Conventional Gasoline*, WT/DS2/AB/R, adopted 29.04.1996.

Act's discrimination against imported gasoline could be justified under Article XX, the dual structure of Article XX was used to elaborate a two-tiered test for the judicial examination of compliance. The AB stated that it must first be assessed whether the design of the disputed measure falls within the scope of one of the public interest objectives provided for in Article XX(a)–(j). Next, it must be examined whether the application of the measure is consistent with the first paragraph – the chapeau – of Article XX GATT, which prohibits 'arbitrary or unjustifiable discrimination' and 'disguised restriction on international trade'.[458] The WTO DSM's elaboration of both tests is of interest when examining its approach to common interest issues.

Concerning the first question, the design of the measure, the AB emphasises that the task of the WTO dispute settlement body is neither to examine the necessity of the protection of a public interest nor to establish the level of protection that should be pursued. This was expressly stated in the 2001 case of *EC – Asbestos*. In this case, the AB was asked to reverse the panel's finding that the French ban on (products containing) asbestos fell under Article XX(b), which justifies measures necessary for the protection of human life or health. However, the AB upheld the panel's finding and, in addition, established that 'it is undisputed that WTO Members have the right to determine the level of protection of health that they consider appropriate in a given situation'.[459]

The assessment of the design of a measure is thus limited to an examination of (1) whether the objective of the measure falls within the scope of one of the objectives described under Article XX(a)–(j) GATT and (2) depending on the objective, whether the domestic policy is necessary to protect that objective[460] or relates to the protection of the objective.[461] While Article XX provides only a limitative list of public and common interests, the WTO dispute settlement bodies have interpreted the scope of these provisions broadly. The earliest examples of this broad interpretation can be found in the WTO's case law on Article XX(g), which justifies measures relating to the protection of exhaustible natural resources. For example, in *US – Gasoline*, a case concerning the US Clean Air Act's discrimination against imported gasoline, the panel held that clean air is an exhaustible natural resource.[462] It did not consider it an objection that the resource, air, was renewable and defined by its quality.[463]

---

458 Ibid.

459 WTO Appellate Body Report, *European Communities – Measures affecting Asbestos and Asbestos-containing Products*, WT/DS135/AB/R, adopted 12.03.2001, para. 168.

460 For example Article XX(b) GATT 'necessary to protect human, animal or plant life or health'.

461 For example Article XX(g) GATT 'relating to the conservation of exhaustible natural resources'.

462 WTO Panel Report, *United States – Standards for Reformulated and Conventional Gasoline*, WT/DS2/R, adopted 29.01.1996, para. 6.37.

463 Ibid.

An even more remarkable interpretation of the same subparagraph was put forward in *United States – Import Prohibition of Certain Shrimp and Shrimp Products* (*Shrimp/Turtle* case).[464] In this case the AB had to determine whether the US import ban on shrimp coming from countries that did not use a specific turtle-friendly fishing technique could be justified under Article XX(g). Despite a clear focus on mineral and non-living resources in the drafting history of Article XX(g), the AB contented that the protection of sea turtles falls within the goal of conserving exhaustible natural resources.[465] The DSM thus uses an evolutionary interpretation and reads the WTO agreements 'in the light of contemporary concerns of the community of nations about the protection and conservation of the environment'.[466] In justifying this approach, the AB explicitly referred to the 'acknowledgement by the international community of the importance of concerted bilateral or multilateral action to protect living natural resources' and the Convention on International Trade in Endangered Species of Wild Fauna and Flora (CITES), which lists sea turtles as a species threatened with extinction.[467]

More recent case law has explored the scope of the public morals exceptions under Article XX(a). According to the panel in *US – Gambling*, a case on the restriction of internet gambling services in the US, public morals are 'standards of right and wrong conduct maintained by or on behalf of a community or nation'.[468] This interpretation was confirmed and clarified further in the 2014 case of *EC – Seals*.[469] The latter case concerned the 2009 EU import ban on seal products on the basis of protection of the public morals related to animal welfare. This ban included an exception for products made by indigenous hunters and was challenged by Canada and Norway at the WTO because they felt it constituted a discrimination against their, mostly non-indigenous, industries, in favour of Greenland, which has a large percentage of indigenous hunters. In determining the scope of public morals, the AB granted the State a wide margin 'to define and apply for themselves the concept of public morals according to their own systems and scales of values'.[470] This broad interpretation could allow

---

464 WTO Appellate Body Report, *United States – Import Prohibition of Certain Shrimp and Shrimp Products*, WT/DS58/AB/R, adopted 12.10.1998.

465 Ibid, para. 128.

466 Ibid, para. 129. This interpretation of Article XX is criticised as being an implausible and ahistorical interpretation of Article XX(g) that exceeds the authority of the AB and undermines the WTO governance structure. J.P. Kelly, 'The Seduction of the Appellate Body: Shrimp/Turtle I and II and the Proper Role of States in WTO Governance' (2005) 38 *Cornell International Law Journal* 459, 466, 491.

467 WTO Appellate Body Report, *United States – Import Prohibition of Certain Shrimp and Shrimp Products*, WT/DS58/AB/R, adopted 12.10.1998, paras. 131–32.

468 WTO Appellate Body Report, *United States – Measures affecting the Cross-Border Supply of Gambling and Betting Services*, WT/DS285/AB/R, adopted 07.04.2005, para. 296.

469 WTO Appellate Body Report, *European Communities – Measures Prohibiting the Importation and Marketing of Seal Products*, WT/DS400/AB/R, adopted 22.05.2014, para. 5.199.

470 Ibid.

States to use the protection of the common interests that are discussed in this study as justification grounds under the GATT.[471]

That the scope of Article XX's subparagraphs cannot be stretched endlessly was illustrated in the 2011 panel decision in the case of *China – Measures Related to the Exportation of Various Raw Materials*. This dispute concerned the inconsistency of the Chinese export restraint on raw materials, which caused scarcity and high prices outside China, with China's Accession Protocol to the WTO. In its defence, China stated that some of the challenged restraints are justified because they reduce pollution and consequently lead to an improvement of public health, which is protected under Article XX(b).[472] However, the panel established that no mention was made of environmental objectives in the disputed measures and that the (future) environmental benefits of the measures were insufficiently proven. The panel in *China – Raw Materials* further noted that if it were to accept China's argument under Article XX(b) 'this provision could then be interpreted to allow the use of export restrictions on any polluting products on the ground that export restrictions reduce the production of these products and thus pollution'.[473] The decision indicates that a connection between the effect of the disputed measure and one of the objectives protected under Article XX does not suffice to establish that the measure falls within the scope of Article XX.[474] If the measure does fall within the *scope* of one of the objectives listed in the subparagraphs of Article XX, it must also be necessary for or relate to the protection of that objective to be justified under Article XX.[475]

In its case law, the AB has defined the requirement of 'necessary to' as more than 'making a contribution to' and close to 'indispensable'.[476] In the previously discussed case of *EC – Asbestos*, the AB enumerated the factors that are decisive in determining whether a domestic measure can be considered necessary to obtain a certain public interest goal. To summarise, account has to be taken of the extent of the contribution to the objective, the trade restrictiveness of the measure and the importance of the interests at stake.[477] Furthermore, the complainant must

---

471 At least when the disputed measure protects the morals of its own population, it remains unclear if extraterritorial protection is possible under Article XX(b) GATT. R. Howse, J. Langille and K. Sykes, 'Sealing the Deal: The WTO's Appellate Body Report in EC – Seal Products' (2014) 18 *Asil Insights* 4.

472 WTO Panel Report, *China – Measures related to the Exportation of Various Raw Materials*, WT/DS394/R; WT/DS395/R; WT/DS398/R, adopted 05.07.2011, para. 7.498.

473 Ibid, para. 7.515.

474 G. Ayres and A. Mitchell, *General and Security Exceptions under the GATT and GATS*, Pre-publication Draft, 2012, available at <ssrn.com> (published in *International Trade Law and WTO*, Federation Press, 2012), 11.

475 For example Article XX(g) GATT 'relating to the conservation of exhaustible natural resources'.

476 WTO Appellate Body Report, *Korea – Measures Affecting Imports of Fresh, Chilled and Frozen Beef*, WT/DS161/169/AB/R, adopted 11.12.2000, para. 161.

477 Ibid, para. 164; Mitchell, above n 123, p 198.

prove that no 'reasonably available' less trade-restrictive measure exists that attains the same level of protection.[478] The first element that attracts attention is the AB's consideration of the importance of the values or interests at stake. In the *EC – Asbestos* and *China – Raw Materials* cases, the AB emphasised that the preservation of human life and health is 'both vital and important in the highest degree'.[479] It seems logical that '[t]he more vital or important those common interests or values are, the easier it would be to accept as "necessary" a measure designed as an enforcement instrument'.[480] However, this reasoning implies that a judicial body has to assess the importance of a State's policy goal that is already explicitly recognised under Article XX GATT. It is therefore not surprising that, in practice, the dispute settlement bodies have time and again recognised that the stated objectives, ranging from the preservation of human life to the fight against tax evasion, are 'most important'.[481]

Subsequently, the contribution of the contested measure to the objective and its degree of trade restrictiveness are examined. In its assessment of the material contribution of the measure the AB takes account of the fact that common interest issues, such as public health and environmental problems, 'may be tackled only with a comprehensive policy'. Therefore, it accepts that in certain cases the respondent does not prove the contribution that the measure makes but demonstrates that the measure is 'apt' to obtain the objective in the future.[482] The fact that the AB accepts a qualitative link and does not require quantitative proof of the relationship between the measure and the policy goal makes it much easier to invoke the exceptions under Article XX.[483] In the *EC – Seals* case, for example, the panel found that the contested measure 'makes a contribution to reducing the demand for seal products within the European Union' on the basis of the 'design, structure, and expected operation' of the import ban and not on the basis of the limited data available on the operation

---

478 WTO Appellate Body Report, *Brazil – Measures affecting Imports of Retreaded Tyres*, WT/DS332/AB/R, adopted 03.12.2007, para 156.

479 WTO Appellate Body Report, *European Communities – Measures affecting Asbestos and Asbestos-containing Products*, WT/DS135/AB/R, adopted 12.03.2001, para. 172; WTO Panel Report, *China – Measures related to the Exportation of Various Raw Materials*, WT/DS394/R; WT/DS395/R; WT/DS398/R, adopted 05.07.2011, para. 7.482.

480 WTO Appellate Body Report, *Korea – Measures Affecting Imports of Fresh, Chilled and Frozen Beef*, WT/DS161/169/AB/R, adopted 11.12.2000, para. 162.

481 For example, in *Dominican Cigarettes* measures to combat tax evasion are considered a most important interest (WTO Appellate Body Report, *Dominican Republic – Measures affecting the Importation and Internal Sale of Cigarettes*, WT/DS302/AB/R, adopted 25.04.2005, para. 7.215). Ayres and Mitchell, above n 474, 18.

482 WTO Appellate Body Report, *Brazil – Measures affecting Imports of Retreaded Tyres*, WT/DS332/AB/R, adopted 03.12.2007, para. 151.

483 M. Matsushita, 'The Dispute Settlement Mechanism at the WTO: The Appellate Body – Assessment and Problems' in A. Narlikar, M. Daunton and R. Stern (eds), *The Oxford Handbook on the World Trade Organization*, Oxford University Press, Oxford 2012, p 517.

of the measure.[484] Nevertheless, the panel and the AB also found that the Inuit exception reduced the contribution of the measure to seal welfare because it did not subject the Inuit hunts to animal welfare regulations and did not exclude the products from commercial hunts by the Inuit people.[485] Thus, the decision of the State to balance different non-trade interests is reviewed at this level, which could compromise its freedom to set the desired level of protection.

The last step in the assessment of necessity is to determine whether no reasonably available less trade-restrictive measures exist that reach the member's desired level of protection.[486] Whether a measure is reasonably available depends on whether the costs and technical difficulties of implementing the alternative measure impose an undue burden on the member.[487] In this last step, the AB uses cost-benefit analyses to find the correct balance between the (administrative and technical) costs of enforcing an alternative measure and its trade benefits.[488] It must be noted that the latter test does not involve an appreciation of the interest pursued by the measure vis-à-vis the interest of free trade.

Although it is sometimes stated that the AB weighs the importance of a measure pursuing a non-trade policy against the trade cost of that measure when addressing necessity, some observations should be made in this regard. First, we have noted that the DSM does not intervene in the member's appreciation of the importance of the policy goal and the level of protection that it deems necessary. Secondly, it can be argued that there is no true 'weighing and balancing' between the contribution of the measure to the policy goal and its trade restrictiveness because these elements are inherently interlinked. The more a measure achieves, the less likely it is that another measure exists which is less trade restrictive and achieves the same level of protection.[489]

484 WTO Panel Report, *European Communities – Measures Prohibiting the Importation and Marketing of Seal Products*, WT/DS400/R, adopted 25.11.2013, para. 7.459.

485 Ibid; WTO Appellate Body Report, *European Communities – Measures Prohibiting the Importation and Marketing of Seal Products*, WT/DS400/AB/R, adopted 22.05.2014, para. 5.225.

486 The burden of proof lies on the claimant.

487 WTO Appellate Body Report, *United States – Measures affecting the Cross-Border Supply of Gambling and Betting Services*, WT/DS285/AB/R, adopted 07.04.2005, para. 308; WTO Appellate Body Report, *China – Measures affecting Trading Rights and Distribution Services for Certain Publications and Audiovisual Entertainment Products*, WT/DS363/AB/R, adopted 21.12.2009, para. 327.

488 D. Regan, 'The Meaning of "Necessary" in GATT Article XX and GATS Article XIV: The Myth of Cost–Benefit Balancing' (2007) 6 *World Trade Review* 347, 358.

489 Ibid, 357. The link between the contribution to the policy goal and the trade restrictiveness of a measure is, however, more complicated when multiple non-trade interests are involved. It is quite plausible that a less restrictive alternative improves the contribution to one of the interests to such an extent that it makes up for a slightly diminished contribution to the other non-trade interest protected by the measure. (On this issue, see D. Regan, *Measures with Multiple Purposes: Puzzles from EC-Seal Products*, AJIL Unbound, 2015, available at <asil.org>.)

In contrast with subparagraphs (a) and (b), subparagraph (g) requires that the domestic measure *relates to* the conservation of exhaustible natural resources. The requirement of *relating to* was clarified by the AB in the case of *US – Gasoline*. In its decision, the AB provided that, although 'relating to' requires a lesser degree of connection as 'necessary for', a substantial relationship must still exists between the design of the measure and the policy goal.[490] This was reaffirmed in the *US – Shrimp/Turtle* case, where the AB added that a measure should not be disproportionally wide in its scope in relation to the public or common interest objective. In other words, there must be 'a close and genuine relationship of ends and means'.[491]

The panel in *China – Raw Materials* used the interpretations presented above to determine that China's export restrictions on natural resources did not relate to their conservation. In its decision, the panel held that

> a policy of restricting extraction would be more in line with a policy to achieve conservation than one confined to restricting exports. For the purpose of conservation of a resource, it is not relevant whether the resource is consumed domestically or abroad; what matters is its pace of extraction.[492]

The second part of the general exceptions test, concerning the measure's consistency with the chapeau of Article XX, focuses on the application of the disputed measure. In *EC – Seals*, the AB clarified that the application can often be determined by examining the design, architecture and structure of the measure.[493] Nevertheless, it remains unclear whether 'application' refers to the purpose or effect of the measure, or both.[494] The chapeau was established as a measure to prevent abuse of the exceptions provided for in Article XX (a)–(j)[495] and, consequently, prevent a devaluation of the Agreement's obligations and rights to merely facultative guidelines.[496] The chapeau establishes that a measure, even if it falls within the scope of one of the subparagraphs of Article XX, may

---

490 WTO Appellate Body Report, *United States – Standards for Reformulated and Conventional Gasoline*, WT/DS2/AB/R, adopted 29.04.1996, p 19.

491 WTO Appellate Body Report, *United States – Import Prohibition of Certain Shrimp and Shrimp Products*, WT/DS58/AB/R, adopted 12.10.1998, paras. 136–41.

492 WTO Panel Report, *China – Measures related to the Exportation of Various Raw Materials*, WT/DS394/R; WT/DS395/R; WT/DS398/R, adopted 05.07.2011, para. 7.428.

493 WTO Appellate Body Report, *European Communities – Measures Prohibiting the Importation and Marketing of Seal Products*, WT/DS400/AB/R, adopted 22.05.2014, para. 5.302.

494 L. Bartels, *The Chapeau of Article XX GATT: A New Interpretation*, University of Cambridge Faculty of Law Research Paper, 2014, available at <ssrn.com>, 6.

495 WTO Appellate Body Report, *United States – Standards for Reformulated and Conventional Gasoline*, WT/DS2/AB/R, adopted 29.04.1996, p 22.

496 WTO Appellate Body Report, *United States – Import Prohibition of Certain Shrimp and Shrimp Products*, WT/DS58/AB/R, adopted 12.10.1998, para. 156.

still violate the GATT if it constitutes an arbitrary or unjustifiable discrimination or a disguised restriction on international trade.

Initially, the AB held that discrimination between countries where the same conditions prevail is not permitted 'when the reasons given for this discrimination bear no rational connection to the objective falling within the purview of a paragraph of Article XX, or would go against that objective'.[497] An example of arbitrary and unjustifiable discrimination can be found in the *US – Shrimp/Turtle* case. In this case, the AB accepted that the US could ban the import of shrimp (products) caught without the use of TEDs (Turtle Excluder Devices). However, it considered the application of this ban to be arbitrary because the certification process was not transparent and denied due process to the members. In determining whether the measure was unjustifiable the AB examined whether the US had cooperated with the WTO members to address the conservation of endangered sea turtles. It found that the US refused to certify countries without taking account of their specific conditions and strictly prohibited import from non-certified countries, even if the shrimp were in fact caught using TEDs. Moreover, the US did not allow the same time for adaptation to all members, it did not provide a comparable number of TEDs to all members and failed to seriously negotiate with the complainants. To comply with the AB's decision, the US changed its requirement to all measures 'comparable in effectiveness' to that of the US and actively participated in cross-border negotiations. Although these negotiations did not lead to an environmental Treaty, the WTO AB found this new application of the import ban to be consistent with WTO law. By drawing attention to the failure of the US to take account of alternative fishing methods and to cooperate with the complainants, the AB indirectly enforced the duty to cooperate in environmental protection.[498]

In contrast to the *Shrimp/Turtle* case, the AB in *EC – Seals* no longer required that the provisional justification under one of the subparagraphs of Article XX bears a rational connection to the reason for discrimination. Although the connection between the objective falling under one of the subparagraphs and the

---

497 WTO Appellate Body Report, *Brazil – Measures affecting Imports of Retreaded Tyres*, WT/DS332/AB/R, adopted 03.12.2007, para. 151.

498 Shaffer and Trachtman describe this as a process-based review, a review in which the national decision-making process is examined to determine whether it takes account of the interest of the affected States. G. Shaffer and J. Trachtman, 'WTO Judicial Interpretation' in A. Narlikar, M. Daunton and R.M. Stern (eds), *The Oxford Handbook on the World Trade Organization*, Oxford University Press, Oxford 2012, pp 541–42, 555. Andenas and Zleptnig defined this part of the AB's review as 'the procedural side of the balancing test or proportionality inquiry, recognising that rights and interests can only be realised through fair and equitable domestic procedures': M. Andenas and S. Zleptnig, 'Proportionality and Balancing in WTO Law: A Comparative Perspective' (2007) 20 *Cambridge Review of International Affairs* 71, 82.

discrimination remains 'one of the most important factors', it is 'not the sole test that is relevant to the assessment of arbitrary or unjustifiable discrimination'.[499] Thus, in theory, the protection of the Inuit culture (a common interest) could have justified the discriminatory effect of the seals measure under the chapeau, while the protection of public morals (a different interest) justified the inconsistency of the measure with the GATT under Article XX(a). In practice, however, the AB found that the Inuit exception, which de facto discriminated between seal producers of different States, violated the chapeau because of the way it was designed and implemented, first, because it facilitates the import of products from Inuit in Greenland better than those from other States, and secondly, because it does not prevent the import of products from commercialised Inuit hunts, which goes against the objective of seal welfare.[500] The latter argument shows that in this case the AB balanced non-trade interests pursued by the measure, animal welfare and the welfare of indigenous peoples to come to the conclusion that the measure constituted an arbitrary and unjustifiable discrimination. The question is whether this balancing act should not be left to the States.[501]

3.2.2.3. Health Concerns and SPS Agreement

Aside from their recognition in Article XX of the GATT, common interest concerns are also explicitly recognised in the SPS Agreement. The SPS Agreement elaborates the rules for the application of Article XX(b) GATT to sanitary and phytosanitary measures, i.e. measures that are designed to protect human, animal or plant life or health from certain risks.[502] The SPS Agreement mainly targets the SPS measures' design, not the level of protection that the State is pursuing.[503] It includes requirements similar to those of Article XX(b) GATT. SPS measures may not be more trade restrictive than 'required to achieve their appropriate level of sanitary or phytosanitary protection', and they may not unjustifiably discriminate against another member 'where identical or similar

499 WTO Appellate Body Report, *European Communities – Measures Prohibiting the Importation and Marketing of Seal Products*, WT/DS400/AB/R, adopted 22.05.2014, para. 5.321.

500 Ibid, para. 5.338.

501 This was suggested by, among others, Qin (J. Qin, *Accommodating Divergent Policy Objectives under WTO Law: Reflections on EC—Seal Products*, AJIL Unbound, 2015, available at <asil.org>).

502 Preamble SPS Agreement.

503 In the words of the AB '[t]he right of a Member to determine its own appropriate level of sanitary protection is an important right'. WTO Appellate Body Report, *EC Measures Concerning Meat and Meat Products (Hormones)*, WT/DS26/AB/R; WT/DS48/AB/R, adopted 16.01.1998, para. 172.

conditions prevail' or be used as disguised barriers to trade.[504] In addition, the SPS Agreement determines that SPS measures must be 'based on scientific principles' and 'not maintained without scientific evidence'.

Although none of the examined case law on natural resource exploitation focuses on the SPS Agreement, the SPS case law will briefly be considered here because of its influence on the consideration of common interest concerns throughout the WTO's case law. In the *EC – Asbestos* case, the AB explicitly stated that some of the principles developed in the SPS case law are also applicable to Article XX(b) of the GATT. These principles include the Member States' right to determine their own level of protection, to evaluate scientific risks in qualitative, rather than quantitative, terms and to rely on respected sources of divergent scientific opinion, rather than majority opinions. The recognition of the AB of these principles in *EC – Asbestos*, seems to leave some room for a precautionary approach when common interests are at stake. However, this is not confirmed in the SPS case law. The European Community first invoked the precautionary principle before the WTO AB in the SPS case of *EC – Hormones*, a dispute on the EU import ban on hormone-treated meat. In its defence, the EC claimed that the SPS Agreement did not prohibit members from implementing preventive measures in the situation of scientific uncertainty. While the AB agreed that the precautionary principle is incorporated in the preamble and certain provisions of the SPS Agreement, it held that the principle does not affect the obligation of the Member States to support existing risks with sufficient scientific evidence (Article 2.2 SPS Agreement) and to undertake a risk assessment (Article 5.1 SPS Agreement) before establishing trade-restrictive measures with a view to achieving their chosen level of protection.[505]

In the same decision, in *EC – Hormones*, the AB for the first time interpreted the requirement of undertaking a risk assessment. The AB adopted a broad interpretation of this demand, stating that Member States could also base SPS measures on scientific views that are not those of the majority, especially if the risk concerned is 'life-threatening in character and is perceived to constitute a clear and imminent threat to public health and safety'.[506] Despite this broad interpretation, the AB upheld the panel's decision that the risk assessment used by the EC was not up to standard because the scientific evidence invoked by the EC was too general in nature. In its decision, the AB established that it is within the power of the panel to assess whether a reasonable linkage exists between the scientific evidence and the measure, using the advice of experts. That the

[504] Articles 2.3 and 5.6 SPS Agreement.

[505] WTO Appellate Body Report, *EC Measures Concerning Meat and Meat Products (Hormones)*, WT/DS26/AB/R; WT/DS48/AB/R, adopted 16.01.1998, para. 177. For the dispute settlement organs to accept that the measure is based on that risk assessment is has to be sufficiently specific (ibid, para. 200).

[506] Ibid, para. 194.

standard of linkage required by the panels is not easily reached was proven in the subsequent case law, in which risk assessments were rejected because of their lack of scientific evidence.[507] Nevertheless, the AB stresses that it is not the task of the panel to act as a risk assessor, the panel must only assess whether the risk assessment 'is supported by coherent reasoning and respectable evidence'.[508]

The EC again invoked the precautionary principle in the more recent dispute of *EC – Biotech*, concerning the EC's moratorium on the approval of biotech products.[509] The EC referred to several documents of international law to justify the fact that the precautionary principle is now a general rule of international law that has to be considered in the interpretation of the WTO Agreements. However, the panel established that it does not have to take account of rules of international law that have not been ratified by all WTO members in its interpretation of WTO law.[510] It did consider it within the discretion of the panel to interpret WTO law in light of an international Treaty ratified by all the parties to the dispute, in the specific circumstances of that dispute. The panel thus limited its power to look at international law outside the WTO regime and thereby shifted the task of balancing different Treaty regimes back to the political process.[511] This refusal to take into account international agreements that are not ratified by all WTO members is implicitly rejected by the AB in *EC – Aircraft*.[512] In this case, the AB clarifies that it is important to strike a balance between the individual obligations of each individual member and the need for a consistent and harmonious interpretation of WTO law among all the members.[513]

3.2.2.4. PPMs and TBT Agreement

Like the SPS Agreement, the TBT Agreement establishes rules that specific kinds of allowed public interest regulations have to comply with. The TBT Agreement is applicable to technical regulations and standards, i.e. 'document[s] which lay down product characteristics or their related processes and production

507 For example, in WTO Panel Report, *European Communities – Measures affecting the Approval and Marketing of Biotech Products*, WT/DS291/R; WT/DS292/R; WT/DS293/R, adopted 29.09.2006; WTO Appellate Body Report, *Japan – Measures affecting the Importation of Apples*, WT/DS245/AB/R, adopted 26.11.2003.

508 WTO Appellate Body Report, *United States – Continued Suspension of Obligations in the EC – Hormones Dispute*, WT/DS320/AB/R, adopted 16.10.2008, para. 590.

509 WTO Panel Report, *European Communities – Measures affecting the Approval and Marketing of Biotech Products*, WT/DS291/R; WT/DS292/R; WT/DS293/R, adopted 29.09.2006.

510 This case is not discussed at length because it concerns agriculture (see section on definitions).

511 Shaffer and Trachtman, above n 498, pp 544–45.

512 WTO Appellate Body Report, *European Communities and Certain Member States – Measures Affecting Trade in Large Civil Aircraft*, WT/DS316/AB/R, adopted 19.05.2011.

513 Ibid, para. 845.

methods'.[514] This Agreement may prove to be of specific importance when considering the *exploitation* of natural resources because it could provide an opening for non-product-related PPMs, measures that attempt to minimise the negative effects caused by the production or harvest of a certain product.

The AB applied the TBT Agreement in the case of *US – Tuna/Dolphin III*, a dispute regarding the US dolphin-safe label for tuna.[515] In this case, Mexico challenged the United States' labelling scheme because it affected the sale of Mexican tuna products that did not receive the label. The AB started its examination by assessing whether the labelling scheme was a technical regulation. As stated above, this assessment is important because it may allow States to regulate how natural resources are exploited if they have a legitimate objective to do so. In *US – Tuna/Dolphin III*, the AB determined that the measure was a technical regulation because it 'sets out a single and legally mandated definition of a "dolphin-safe" tuna product and disallows the use of other labels on tuna products that do not satisfy this definition'.[516] With this conclusion, the AB left open the applicability of the TBT Agreement to regulations that attempt to minimise the negative effects caused by the production or harvest of a certain product.[517]

Nevertheless, the measure was found to be inconsistent with Article 2.1 of the TBT Agreement. This Article incorporates the NT and the MFN principle and holds that imported products 'shall be accorded treatment no less favourable than that accorded to like products of national origin and to like products originating in any other country'. Although the measure was origin neutral, the AB found that the labelling scheme provided less favourable treatment to Mexican tuna products. The AB came to this conclusion in two steps. First, the AB established that the measure modifies the conditions of competition in a way that has a detrimental impact on the Mexican tuna products.[518] In the second step, which is especially relevant here, the AB examined whether the detrimental

514 For example packaging, marking and labelling requirements, and procedures for assessment of conformity with technical regulations and standards. Preamble TBT Agreement Annex 1, para. 1.

515 WTO Panel Report, *United States – Measures concerning the Importation, Marketing and Sale of Tuna and Tuna Products*, WT/DS381/R, adopted 15.09.2011.

516 WTO Appellate Body Report, *United States – Measures concerning the Importation, Marketing and Sale of Tuna and Tuna Products*, WT/DS381/AB/R, adopted 16.05.2012, para. 199.

517 E. Trujillo, 'The WTO Appellate Body Knocks Down U.S. "Dolphin-Safe" Tuna Labels But Leaves a Crack for PPMs' (2012) 16 *Asil Insights* 1 in conclusion. In the more recent case of *EC – Seals*, the contested EU regulations concerned both product composition and hunting methods. In the end, the AB examined the measure under the GATT because it found that it mainly concerned the process and not the product. Thus, the AB never determined whether the measure was a PPM under Annex 1.1 TBT Agreement and the scope of the TBT Agreement remains uncertain. (The *EC – Seals* case is discussed on p 96.) See also Howse et al., above n 471, 18; J. Trachtman, *The WTO Seal Products Case: Doctrinal and Normative Confusion*, AJIL Unbound, 2015, available at <www.asil.org>.

518 WTO Appellate Body Report, *United States – Measures concerning the Importation, Marketing and Sale of Tuna and Tuna Products*, WT/DS381/AB/R, adopted 16.05.2012, para. 240.

impact of the measure was exclusively the consequence of a legitimate regulatory distinction.[519] Thus, according to the AB, finding a detrimental effect on trade is not enough to conclude that the non-discrimination principles in Article 2.1 TBT Agreement are violated.[520] In *US – Tuna/Dolphin III* the detrimental impact was the consequence of a focus on a specific fishing technique (setting on dolphins) in a specific area (the Eastern Tropical Pacific) and a failure to equally address the risks to dolphins arising from different fishing techniques in different areas of the ocean. Therefore, it was concluded that the impact was not exclusively due to a legitimate regulatory distinction and the measure was inconsistent with Article 2.1 TBT Agreement.[521]

A second Article of the TBT Agreement that is highly relevant in the context of common interests is Article 2.2 TBT Agreement. This Article provides that 'technical regulations shall not be more trade-restrictive than necessary to fulfil a legitimate objective'. In contrast to the GATT and the SPS Agreement, which include a limited list of public interest objectives, Article 2.2 TBT Agreement only gives examples of the objectives that could justify a technical barrier to trade, including the protection of human health or safety, animal or plant life or health, and the environment. In the case law discussed above, consumer information and dolphin protection were also recognised as legitimate objectives under the TBT Agreement. At first sight, this open-ended list allows a wider variety of public interest policies than the closed list included in Article XX of the GATT. However, in the *EC – Seals* case, the AB stated that any imbalance between the different agreements should be addressed by the members and hinted that it will interpret Article XX to include all possible legitimate objectives, which was confirmed by the broad interpretation of public morals in this case.[522]

519 In *US – Clove* the AB determined that the existence of a detrimental effect is not sufficient to demonstrate less favourable treatment under Article 2.1. A 'panel must further analyze whether the detrimental impact on imports stems exclusively from a legitimate regulatory distinction rather than reflecting discrimination against the group of imported products'. WTO Appellate Body Report, *United States – Measures Affecting the Production and Sale of Clove Cigarettes*, WT/DS406/AB/R, adopted 04.04.2012, para. 182.

520 Note that this approach is different from the one taken under Article III:4 GATT, discussed above.

521 WTO Appellate Body Report, *United States – Measures concerning the Importation, Marketing and Sale of Tuna and Tuna Products*, WT/DS381/AB/R, adopted 16.05.2012, paras. 297–99.

522 WTO Appellate Body Report, *European Communities – Measures Prohibiting the Importation and Marketing of Seal Products*, WT/DS400/AB/R, adopted 22.05.2014, para. 5.129. 'Hint' identified in Du, above n 449, 20. Trachtman suggest that this more liberal interpretation of Article XX GATT could counterbalance the rejection of the regulatory purpose test under Article III:4 in Trachtman, above n 517.

3.2.3. INTERNATIONAL CENTRE FOR SETTLEMENT OF INVESTMENT DISPUTES

3.2.3.1. Like Circumstances in the NT and MFN Provisions

Most investment Treaties include NT and MFN provisions. These are non-discrimination standards that prevent States from treating foreign investors less favourably than domestic or other foreign investors in like circumstances. The impact of the interpretation of the NT and MFN standards on the State's ability to regulate with the aim of realising specific public interests should not be underestimated. When measures that have a differential effect on foreign and domestic investors potentially lead to investment arbitration and high compensation awards, the host State will automatically be discouraged from adopting differential measures. Domestic regulation to promote, for example, sustainable development is significantly more difficult when categorisation on the basis of sector, product, production method, etc. may easily lead to the attribution of significant damages.[523] In this section, the focus will be on the interpretation of the NT standard. However, the conclusions drawn can also be applied to the MFN standard because a similar rationale is used for both standards when it comes to assessing domestic measures that aim to contribute to public interests.[524]

Describing the 'general' method of review for the standard of NT in investment arbitration is not without difficulties. Besides the lack of an official doctrine of precedence, the number of tribunals that have so far dealt with the NT standard is relatively limited. The reason for this lack of 'precedents' is that NT only truly became relevant in the late 1990s, when the treatment of domestic investors in developing countries finally went beyond the minimum standards for the protection of foreign investors included in most international investment agreements. It is only since that evolution in domestic law that making an appeal to this standard has become beneficial for foreign investors.[525] The NT standard is generally interpreted to include not only the prohibition of formal discrimination, but also the prohibition of material discrimination. In other words, it extends to the prohibition of measures that have the effect of discrimination between domestic and foreign investors without formally differentiating on the basis of nationality. This prohibition is not considered to be absolute. While an absolute prohibition on formal discrimination might

---

523 Orellana, above n 243, 3.

524 Ibid. In contrast to international trade law, where a clear distinction is drawn between the principles used in assessing the NT and MFN standards.

525 N. DiMascio and J. Pauwelyn, 'Nondiscrimination in Trade and Investment Treaties: Worlds Apart or Two Sides of the Same Coin?' [2008] *American Journal of International Law* 48, 67.

be acceptable, it seems hard to legitimise a prohibition of measures that have a discriminatory effect without taking account of the public policy grounds that underlie such measures.[526]

Because of the relative nature of the NT standard, most investment tribunals use a two-pronged test to determine whether it is complied with. First, it is determined whether the contested measure constitutes a discrimination based on nationality and, secondly, the question is answered whether the discriminatory measure is justified on the basis of a public interest. The first test, discrimination on the basis of nationality, can be further disentangled into two components: likeness and less favourable treatment.[527] To determine whether a measure is discriminatory, tribunals first examine the circumstances under which domestic and foreign investors operate. Although not all investment Treaties use the criterion of 'like circumstances' in qualifying the NT standard, many of the arbitrations to date have dealt with Treaties that explicitly mentioned likeness.[528] Furthermore, one ICSID Tribunal has stated that 'the absence of the term "like" in … the BIT is not decisive since this element is inherent in an evaluation of discrimination'.[529] Likeness has been interpreted in different ways by investment tribunals.[530] While some have required the compared investors to be in identical situations,[531] others have focused on the competitive relationship between different businesses,[532] or rejected both these 'narrow' interpretations and looked beyond the relevant business sector.[533] If domestic and foreign investors are found to operate in like circumstances, the investment tribunal verifies whether the treatment given to the foreign investor is less favourable. Again, there is room for interpretation in examining this issue. The arbitrators may focus on the effect of the challenged measure or they may look only at the intent of the State to accord some investors less favourable treatment.[534]

526 F. Ortino, 'Non-Discriminatory Treatment in Investment Disputes' in P.-M. Dupuy, F. Francioni and E.U. Petersmann (eds), *Human Rights in International Investment Law and Arbitration*, Oxford University Press, Oxford 2009, pp 352–53.

527 Ibid, 354–60.

528 Ibid, 354. For example, the Energy Charter Treaty does not include the criterion of likeness in Article 10(7).

529 ICSID, *Total S.A. v Argentine Republic, Award*, ICSID case no. ARB/04/1, 27.12.2010, para. 213. See also ICSID, *Parkerings-Compagniet AS v Lithuania, Award*, ICSID case no. ARB/05/8, 11.09.2007, para. 369.

530 DiMascio and Pauwelyn, above n 525, 71.

531 For example, UNCITRAL, *Methanex Corporation v United States of America, Award*, 09.08.2005, para. 17.

532 For example, UNCITRAL, *S.D. Myers, Inc. v Government of Canada, Partial Award*, 13.11.2000, para. 251.

533 UNCITRAL, *Occidental Exploration and Production Company v the Republic of Ecuador, Award*, 01.07.2004, para. 173. Ortino, above n 526, pp 354–56.

534 Ortino, above n 526, pp 356–60.

In both scenarios, positive evidence on the nationality-basis of the discrimination is required, differential treatment *an sich* is not enough.[535]

The arbitrators' interpretation of what constitutes discrimination on the basis of nationality may affect the host State's ability to regulate in general. However, it is especially the second step in the NT test, justification on the basis of public interest, which is of interest for the current discussion. This is what Ortino describes as the 'second function' of the test of like circumstances.[536] In the landmark case of *Pope & Talbot Inc. v Government of Canada*, Canada's allocation of fee-free export quota for softwood lumber was challenged. In this context, the Tribunal found that measures are justified under the standard of NT if they

> have a reasonable nexus to rational government policies that (1) do not distinguish, on their face or de facto, between foreign-owned and domestic companies, and (2) do not otherwise unduly undermine the investment liberalizing objectives of NAFTA. … A formulation focusing on the like circumstances … will require addressing any difference in treatment, demanding that it be justified by showing that it bears a reasonable relationship to rational policies not motivated by preference of domestic over foreign-owned investment.[537]

What is remarkable in this interpretation of 'like circumstances' is that it establishes a de facto general exceptions clause (comparable to Article XX GATT) in the interpretation of international investment agreements that do not include such a provision (for example, the NAFTA). By providing that a foreign investor that is affected by a measure that relates to public policy is not in like circumstances as a domestic investor not affected by this measure, it leaves a significant opening for the State to pursue common interests. For example, it allows the State to introduce a measure of environmental protection that only targets investments in hazardous activities and has no impact on investments in non-hazardous activities.[538]

To establish that the foreign investor is not in like circumstances due to a public policy measure, the State must show that the challenged measure has a public policy ground that is effectively linked to the measure. The grounds that have so far been examined in investment cases were mainly of an economic nature.[539] One

---

535 DiMascio and Pauwelyn, above n 525, 72.

536 Ortino, above n 526, p 360.

537 UNCITRAL, *Pope & Talbot v Canada, Award*, 10.04.2001, paras. 78–79.

538 Example in R. Pavoni, 'Environmental Rights, Sustainable Development, and Investor-State Case Law: A Critical Appraisal' in P.-M. Dupuy, F. Francioni and E.U. Petersmann (eds), *Human Rights in International Investment Law and Arbitration*, Oxford University Press, Oxford 2009, p 540.

539 For example, ensuring the economic strength of domestic producers to ensure that the country will be able to domestically produce certain products in the future. UNCITRAL, *S.D. Myers, Inc. v Government of Canada, Partial Award*, 13.11.2000, 255.

important exception is the *Parkerings* case. In *Parkerings* the Tribunal considered that a legitimate ground for distinguishing between two underground parking projects in the old centre of Vilnius, Lithuania, was the impact of both projects on historical and archaeological preservation and environmental protection. In this decision the scope of accepted interests clearly extends beyond the economic sphere. Besides providing a legitimate public purpose, the State must also establish that there is a relation between the purpose and the challenged measure. The standard applied in the interpretation of this requirement determines how easy or difficult it will be for a State to take measures based on public interest grounds. Especially in the context of sustainable development, it is often difficult to establish a one-on-one relationship between the initial policy objectives and concrete measures, because the latter are often taken in reaction to the public perception of threats or evolving scientific insights. As stated above, the Tribunal in *Pope & Talbot* only required a 'reasonable nexus'. However, the Tribunal in the *GAMI* case (on Mexico's regulation of the sugar industry) found a plausible connection to be sufficient and thus upheld a different standard of review.[540] While most tribunals require at least a reasonable nexus, investment arbitrations generally do not demand a strict necessity of the measure for the fulfilment of the public purpose in reviewing the host State's public purpose defence.[541] It could, therefore, be concluded that the interpretation of the NT standard in *Pope & Talbot* offers a method of review that allows tribunals to balance common interests and investment protection in the examination of differential treatment of foreign and domestic investors. In practice, however, it is hard to determine the effect of the NT standard in international investment law on the protection of common interests at the domestic level. As shown above, upholding the NT standard has led tribunals to apply different standards of review and, as a consequence, remains unpredictable in its outcome.[542]

3.2.3.2. *Regulatory Takings*

A second protection standard that is raised in the majority of investment arbitrations is the protection against expropriation. Expropriation has always

540 UNCITRAL, *GAMI Investments, Inc. v United Mexican States, Award*, 15.11.2004, para. 144.

541 A. Mitchell and C. Henckels, *Variations on a Theme: Comparing the Concept of 'Necessity' in International Investment Law and WTO Law*, Pre-publication Paper, 2012, available at <ssrn.com> (published in (2014) 14 *Chicago Journal of International Law* 93), 27.

542 Ortino argues that the positive side of the variety of interpretations that currently exists in the context of investment arbitration is that it allows States to take account of possibilities in the jurisprudence when drafting their IIAs. Because these agreements are bilateral and no strong unified interpretation exists, it is relatively easy to change the standards included in favour of protection of common interests. Ortino, above n 526, pp 363–66.

been a hot topic in international investment law. After decolonisation, concern in Western nations soared over the potential use by newly independent countries of their sovereign powers to expropriate assets of Western companies. As a consequence, most, if not all, international investment agreements include an expropriation prohibition that aims to balance the host State's right to take regulatory measures with the investor's protection against arbitrary or uncompensated expropriations. These provisions were developed after the Second World War to facilitate investments abroad and start from the assumption that investors cannot trust the domestic judicial bodies of the host State to provide security for their investments.[543] While regulatory takings are necessary at times and are generally accepted as an inevitable risk of business, foreign investors are more willing to make long-term and substantial investment if they are subject to a stable transnational legal framework.

Most expropriation provisions include not only direct but also indirect expropriation. The first form, direct expropriation, involves a formal expropriation through which the title of the property is transferred or the property is physically seized. The second form, indirect expropriation, does not involve a change in the title of the property but interferes in the use or enjoyment of property in such a way that it deprives the owner of its benefits. In other words, expropriation provisions apply to all State measures that deprive the owner of the use or reasonably-to-be-expected economic benefit of property.[544] However, this prohibition is subject to public interest exception clauses. Under the so-called police-powers exception a State measure is not considered an expropriation if it is a lawful exercise of governmental powers. Most international investment agreements include this exception and allow regulatory expropriations if the State measure is non-discriminatory and aimed at a public purpose and if the investor receives 'full, prompt and adequate compensation'.[545] While the number of publicly available arbitrations that have examined expropriation measures

---

[543] A. Kawharu, 'International Law's Protection of Foreign-Owned Property against Uncompensated Expropriation: Preserving Host State Regulatory Freedom' in D. Grinlinton and P. Taylor (eds), *Property Rights and Sustainability: The Evolution of Property Rights to Meet Ecological Challenges*, Martinus Nijhoff Publishers, Leiden 2011, p 343.

[544] ICSID, *Metalclad Corporation v the United Mexican States, Award*, ICSID case no. ARB(AF)/97/1, 30.08.2000, para. 104.

[545] This is the so-called Hull standard of compensation, coined by US Secretary of State Cordell Hull in the context of Mexico's nationalisation of US oil companies in 1938 (Van Harten, above n 114, p 91); the NAFTA, for instance, provides that an expropriation is permissible for a public interest purpose. Article 1110 NAFTA provides that 'no Party may directly or indirectly nationalize or expropriate an investment of an investor of another Party in its territory or take a measure tantamount to nationalization or expropriation of such an investment ('expropriation'), except: (a) for a public purpose; (b) on a non-discriminatory basis; (c) in accordance with due process of law and Article 1105(1); and (d) on payment of compensation in accordance with paragraphs 2 through 6'.

justified by the State under the public powers doctrine is still limited, some general tendencies can be drawn from this jurisprudence because of the de facto doctrine of precedent.

In the interest of reaching an agreement, many IIAs include vague property protection provisions that do not provide any criteria for distinguishing non-compensable regulatory measures from compensable expropriations.[546] As a consequence, investment arbitrators enjoy a lot of discretion in this matter. The current tendencies in investment arbitration to strictly scrutinise indirect takings claims can be traced back to the 2005 case of *Methanex*.[547] Before Methanex, indirect takings were more easily considered to be expropriations. The 1999 landmark *Metalclad* case is often referred to as an example of how broadly ICSID tribunals interpreted the prohibition on expropriation and favoured 'investor's economic interests over a State's regulatory ones'.[548] In *Metalclad*, the Tribunal was asked to determine whether an environmental measure issued by Mexico could be considered an indirect expropriation measure if, as a consequence of this measure, one specific foreign investment became worthless. In its decision, the Tribunal determined that the prohibition on expropriation includes regulations that have 'the effect of depriving the owner, in whole or in significant part, of the use or reasonably-to-be-expected economic benefit of property' even if, as in this specific case, the measure does not provide any economic benefits to the State.[549]

With the *Methanex* case, however, investment arbitration has turned to a more restrictive definition of illegal expropriations. In this case, the ICSID Tribunal expressly recognised that non-discriminatory regulations enacted for a public purpose are in principle not expropriations and therefore do not give the investor a right to compensation.[550] One explanation that has been put forward

546 N. Jansen Calamita, *International Human Rights and the Interpretation of International Investment Treaties – Constitutional Considerations*, Pre-publication Draft, 2013, available at <ssrn.com> (published in *The Interaction of International Investment Law with other Fields of Public International Law*, Cambridge University Press, Cambridge 2013), 10–11.

547 It goes without saying that investors have favoured an extensive interpretation of property protection, including adopting a wide definition of the protected investment and including indirect expropriation as a basis for compensation. A minority of tribunals have shared this view. For example, UNCITRAL, *Methanex Corporation v United States of America, Award*, 09.08.2005.

548 ICSID, *Metalclad Corporation v the United Mexican States, Award*, ICSID case no. ARB(AF)/97/1, 30.08.2000; D. Allen, *'This Business Will Never Hold Water' International Investment Arbitration on Public-Private Water Service Provision – A Comment on Biwater Gauff (Tanzania) Limited v. United Republic of Tanzania*, Working Paper, 2010, available at <ssrn.com>. Nevertheless, one paper argued that the challenged measure was not a regulatory taking but a failure by the State to live up to its promise of delivering the necessary permits for the landfill because of environmental regulations. Brower and Schill, above n 119, 487.

549 ICSID, *Metalclad Corporation v the United Mexican States, Award*, ICSID case no. ARB(AF)/97/1, 30.08.2000, para. 103.

550 UNCITRAL, *Methanex Corporation v United States of America, Award*, 09.08.2005, part 4, chapter d, para. 7.

for the more restrictive definition of expropriation used since *Methanex* is that developed nations now increasingly function as host countries and are concerned for their policy space.[551] Three methods have been used by arbitral tribunals to determine whether a measure should be seen as an indirect expropriation: looking at the effect of the measure (sole effect doctrine), looking at the objective of the State measure (police power doctrine) and balancing the objective with the effect (proportionality test).[552] Most recent cases have implicitly followed the latter method.[553] The *Tecmed* case, concerning Mexico's denial to renew the licence of a hazardous waste landfill, is one of the few cases where the Tribunal put explicit emphasis on the principle of proportionality when deciding if a State measure is justified in the public interest: '[W]hether such actions or measures are proportional to the public interest presumably protected thereby and to the protection legally granted to investments, taking into account that the significance of such impact has a key role upon deciding the proportionality.'[554]

When proportionality analysis is applied strictly the arbitrators play a controversial role in determining the value of a public interest compared to an investor right. An important element in this analysis is therefore the applied standard of review, in other words the extent to which investment tribunals substitute the State's assessment with their own opinion of how to exercise public power. One of the main reasons to be sceptical of proportionality analysis is that it does not present guidelines to set the standard of review but can be extremely intrusive when combined with a high standard of review. In the *Tecmed* case, for example, the Tribunal offered no deference to the State and substituted the State's assessments of the appropriate balance between public and private interests with its own.[555] The standard proportionality analysis consists of four elements: legitimacy, suitability, necessity and proportionality *stricto sensu*. The

551 J. Waincymer, 'Balancing Property Rights and Human Rights in Expropriation' in P.-M. Dupuy, F. Francioni and E.U. Petersmann (eds), *Human Rights in International Investment Law and Arbitration*, Oxford University Press, Oxford 2009, p 303. Pelc argues that an increasing number of disputes concern democratic states and seem to be instituted with the sole aim of deterring government regulation. K. Pelc, *Does the International Investment Regime Induce Frivolous Litigation?*, Paper, 2016, available at <ssrn.com>.

552 Y. Radi, 'Realizing Human Rights in Investment Treaty Arbitration: A Perspective from within the International Investment Law Toolbox' (2012) 37 *North Carolina Journal of International Law and Commercial Regulation* 1107, 1173–74.

553 C. Henckels, 'Indirect Expropriation and the Right to Regulate: Revisiting Proportionality Analysis and the Standard of Review in Investor-State Arbitration' (2012) 15 *Journal of International Economic Law* 223, 225.

554 ICSID, *Tecnicas Medioambientales Tecmed S.A. v the United Mexican States, Award*, ICSID case no. ARB (AF)/00/2, 29.05.2003, para. 122. The use of the proportionality test was later explicitly confirmed in the case of *Azurix v Argentina* and a similar test was adopted in *LG&E v Argentine Republic.*

555 ICSID, *Tecnicas Medioambientales Tecmed S.A. v the United Mexican States, Award*, ICSID case no. ARB (AF)/00/2, 29.05.2003, para. 122.

first element, legitimacy, examines whether the challenged measure is based on a public interest objective. In terms of determining what kind of objective is of 'public interest', investment tribunals generally leave a large measure of discretion to the host State.[556] For example, in the case of *Antoine Goetz v Republic of Burundi* an ore-extracting company claimed that Burundi had withdrawn its free zone certificate, which exempted the company from paying taxes and customs, in violation of the expropriation provision in the relevant BIT. In its review of the legitimacy of the measure, the Tribunal stated that

> [e]n l'absence d'erreur de droit ou de fait, d'erreur manifeste d'appréciation ou de détournement de pouvoir, il n'appartient pas au Tribunal de substituer son propre jugement à l'appréciation faite discrétionnairement par le Gouvernement du Burundi des impératifs d'utilité publique … ou d'intérêt national.[557]

In other words, unless the host State has made a blatant error, the Tribunal will not substitute the State's determination of public interest purposes by its own vision of what is in the general or national interest. The second element, suitability, examines whether the challenged measure has the potential to contribute to the alleged public purpose. While the element of suitability is mainly based on an objective reasoning of whether the challenged measure could contribute to the fulfilment of the raised objective, 'necessity' leaves more room for interpretation. When applying a strict test of necessity only the alternative that reaches the specific goal of the measure and is least restrictive to investors' rights may be considered necessary. Thus, a strict necessity approach does not allow for the consideration of broader policy goals, such as environmental protection, that are potentially affected by the least restrictive measure.[558]

The final element, the test of strict proportionality is highly subjective. The value that is attributed to all the relevant interests will always depend on the normative values held by the arbitrators. Deference to the national authorities seems necessary in light of their expertise and democratic legitimacy. Only clearly disproportionate public interest measures should be considered expropriations. This approach was followed in the later *Argentina* cases, where it was found that regulatory measures should not be considered indirect expropriations unless they are 'obviously disproportionate' to the public interest they aim

556 One notable exception was the *Tecmed* case. In *Tecmed*, the Tribunal established that the grounds brought forward by the State were not the real purposes of the challenged measure and found that the real objective of the disputed measure was to respond to public pressure. The Tribunal rejected this objective as a legitimate public interest because it did not prevent an urgent crisis. Ibid. This reasoning can be criticised because it does not consider the (public interest) reasons for the public opposition.

557 ICSID, *Antoine Goetz et consorts v République du Burundi, Award*, ICSID case no. ARB/95/3, 10.02.1999, para. 126.

558 Henckels, above n 553, 249.

to fulfil or 'unreasonable, i.e. arbitrary, discriminatory, disproportionate or otherwise unfair'.[559] This deferential approach seems more in line with the text of the investment agreements that do not require a proportionality analysis. Despite the deference that is necessary in the context of strict proportionality, proportionality *stricto sensu* remains an indispensable step in the assessment of expropriation claims. While abuse of power will already be filtered out by the tests of suitability and necessity, the strict proportionality test prevents indirect expropriation from not being recognised in cases where the only possible measure to reach a (relatively unimportant) legitimate aim has a severe impact on the property right of the investor.[560] In general, investment arbitration tribunals have allowed an increasingly broad margin of deference to the host State in the context of regulatory takings, taking account of the purpose of the measure and its proportionality. However, it remains unclear what weight is given to these considerations in disputes on (indirect) expropriation.[561]

3.2.3.3. *FET and Proportionality*

Proportionality analysis is not only used in examining the justification of regulatory takings, it is also increasingly used in applying the standard of fair and equitable treatment (FET).[562] The standard of FET is an all-encompassing standard that is now considered a standard provision in investment Treaties.[563] Although there are some differences in the exact wording of this standard in different IIAs and in the interpretation of the standard by different investment tribunals, a uniform list of elements that are protected under this standard can still be identified.[564] In contrast with the NT standard, FET does not require a comparison between domestic and foreign investors and is not limited to

559 In *LG&E* the Tribunal took a more deferential approach that takes account of 'the context within which a measure was adopted' (ICSID, *LG&E Energy Corp. LG&E Capital corp. LG&E International, Inc. v Argentine Republic, Decision on Liability*, ICSID case no. ARB/02/1, 03.10.2006, paras. 189–95). Moreover, it applied a more flexible test of proportionality, holding that a host State's public interest measure must be accepted unless it is 'obviously disproportionate to the need being addressed' (ibid, para. 159).

560 Henckels, above n 553, 253–54.

561 Kawharu, above n 543, p 277.

562 Henckels, above n 553, 254.

563 B. Kingsbury and S. Schill, *Investor-state Arbitration as Governance: Fair and Equitable Treatment, Proportionality and the Emerging Global Administrative Law*, Public Law and Legal Theory Working Papers, Paper 146, New York University, 2009, available at <ssrn.com>, 8.

564 The FET principle is included in very similar wording in most BITs and therefore investment tribunals have developed a relatively uniform set of elements that are required to fulfil the FET standard (Mitchell and Henckels, above n 541, 20.) For example, NAFTA includes the FET standard in Article 1105.

discrimination on the basis of nationality. Because of this broad protection standard, FET features in most investment arbitrations. In the context of protecting public interest, the FET standard can be problematic because it is such an open-ended standard. One of the main objectives of the principle of FET is to 'maintain a stable framework for investments and maximum effective use of economic resources'.[565] In the investment tribunals' case law, five general elements can be identified that constitute the principle of FET.[566] In essence, the State has to provide a stable and predictable legal framework; make consistent decisions;[567] protect legitimate expectations; provide procedural due process and prohibit denial of justice; protect against discrimination and arbitrariness; and act transparently.[568] All of these elements are linked to a process-oriented understanding of legality and good governance.[569] In other words, FET means that the government has to act in accordance with the rule of law. In contrast to national commercial law, the FET requirements emphasise the specific role of the State and the additional requirements set in a public–private relationship. One exception is the requirement of protecting legitimate expectations, which may also be found in domestic contract law. In the context of protecting public interests, it is precisely this requirement that has proven to be problematic because it potentially restricts the host States' freedom to change old economic policies. For example, in the *Tecmed* case, the Tribunal stated that

> the foreign investor expects the host State to act in a consistent manner, free from ambiguity and totally transparently … so that it may know beforehand any and all rules and regulations that will govern its investments, as well as the goals of the relevant policies and administrative practices or directives.[570]

This interpretation of FET clearly limits the State's ability to react to changing public and common interest after the initial investment has been made. This strict interpretation has been altered in more recent case law where tribunals use

---

565 ICSID, *CMS Gas Transmission Company v Argentina, Award*, ICSID case no. ARB/01/8, 12.05.2005, paras. 273–74. This objective was inferred from the relevant BITs preamble, but similar provision can be found in most IIAs.

566 Kingsbury and Schill, above n 563, 10–16; Brower and Schill, above n 119, 487.

567 ICSID, *CMS Gas Transmission Company v Argentina, Award*, ICSID case no. ARB/01/8, 12.05.2005, para. 274; ICSID, *Metalclad Corporation v the United Mexican States, Award*, ICSID case no. ARB(AF)/97/1, 30.08.2000, para. 99; ICSID, *Tecnicas Medioambientales Tecmed S.A. v the United Mexican States, Award*, ICSID case no. ARB (AF)/00/2, 29.05.2003, para. 154.

568 ICSID, *Tecnicas Medioambientales Tecmed S.A. v the United Mexican States, Award*, ICSID case no. ARB (AF)/00/2, 29.05.2003, para. 154.

569 Kingsbury and Schill, above n 563, 18.

570 ICSID, *Tecnicas Medioambientales Tecmed S.A. v the United Mexican States, Award*, ICSID case no. ARB (AF)/00/2, 29.05.2003, para. 154.

the principle of proportionality to determine whether a State measure violates the legitimate expectations of the investor. Recent investment arbitrations have established that the requirement of protecting legitimate expectations does not imply that investors may expect that the regulatory framework is frozen at the time of the investment. On the contrary, the Tribunal in *EDF v Romania* stated that the legal framework can 'be adapted to changing circumstances'[571] and that 'except where specific promises or representations are made by the State to the investor, the latter may not rely on a bilateral investment treaty as a kind of insurance policy against the risk of any changes in the host State's legal and economic framework'.[572] Thus, the standard of FET does not require that the State refrains from regulatory measures, it only demands that the State give due consideration to the investors' interests when changing its regulations.

In determining which policy adaptations do not violate the principle of protecting legitimate expectations, the principle of proportionality is gradually entering the case law on the doctrine of legitimate expectations, similarly to the jurisprudence on expropriation.[573] The *Argentina* cases illustrate the evolution of the proportionality analysis used by the ICSID tribunals. In these cases the measures taken by Argentina to combat the economic crisis in 2002 were challenged. It is fair to say that these measures 'destroyed the regulatory environment on which foreign investors had relied'.[574] While the initial *Argentina* cases used only a strict proportionality analysis, more recent case law shows a shift to a proportionality analysis in addressing the FET standard. This more recent interpretation was also followed by the NAFTA Tribunal in the natural resource case of *Glamis Gold v US*.[575] In this case, the US domestic legislation addressing environmental and cultural concerns was challenged. In essence, the laws required that open mining pits were filled once they were no longer used and instituted certain regulatory controls for instances where Native American artefacts were found during the mining process.

Here, the Tribunal discussed the four elements of the proportionality analysis and allowed significant deference to the host State. First, it established that in looking at the legitimate objective of the measure, it did not have to determine what the importance of the objective was, but only 'whether or not there was a manifest lack of reasons for the legislation'.[576] In the context of the suitability

---

571 ICSID, *EDF (Services) Limited v Romania, Award*, ICSID case no. ARB/05/13, 08.10.2009, para. 277.

572 Ibid, para. 217.

573 Necessity analysis is not being used in the context of any other requirements of FET, most likely because in these cases no legitimate objective was found. Mitchell and Henckels, above n 541, 21.

574 Stone Sweet, above n 116, 69.

575 ICSID Additional Facility, *Glamis Gold, Ltd. v United States of America, Award*, 08.06.2009.

576 Ibid, para. 805.

of the measure, the Tribunal established that that the challenged measure was 'reasonably drafted to address its objectives' and 'rationally related to its stated purpose'.[577] In this context, the Tribunal referred to the State's' 'sufficient good faith belief that there was a reasonable connection between the harm and the proposed remedy' and offered deference on the ground that it should respect the State's expertise in assessing the underlying facts.[578] When addressing the necessity of the measure, the Tribunal again referred to the assessment of the State that had considered alternative measures, and came to the conclusion that the current law was 'necessary for the immediate preservation of the public general welfare'.[579] Thus, in *Glamis Gold* the Tribunal allowed a broad margin of deference to the State on the basis of its democratic legitimacy to compromise between the interests of its constituents.[580] The *Glamis Gold* assessment stands in stark contrast to the earlier ICSID cases of *InterAgua and Suez Vivendi v Argentina*, where the tribunals in their necessity analysis used the argument that less restrictive alternatives were available and therefore the challenged measures were not justified.[581] In both cases, it was found that the measures were an abuse of regulatory power. However, in both cases, Professor Nikken stated in his separate opinion that the necessity analysis should be applied less strictly and should (in light of the Tribunal's competence) be limited to investigating whether a measure falls 'within the range of decisions that any reasonable government could have adopted under the same circumstances'.[582]

In the context of the fourth element of proportionality, proportionality *stricto sensu*, it is interesting to look at the arbitration of *Occidental v Ecuador*.[583] Occidental or Oxy exploited hydrocarbons in a specific area of the Amazon in a participation contract with the national oil company Petroecuador. In 2000 Oxy transferred a 40 per cent economic interest in this area to the Alberta Energy Corporation (AEC). This unilateral action of Oxy violated the domestic law and the participation contract with Petroecuador. In reaction to this breach, but

577 Ibid, para. 803.

578 Ibid, para. 805.

579 Ibid, para. 181.

580 Ibid, paras. 803–05.

581 ICSID, *Suez, Sociedad General de Aguas de Barcelona S.A., and InterAgua Servicios Integrales del Agua S.A. v the Argentine Republic, Decision on Liability*, ICSID case no. ARB/03/17, 30.07.2010, para. 215; ICSID, *Suez, Sociedad General de Aguas de Barcelona, S.A., and Vivendi Universal S.A. v the Argentine Republic, Decision on Liability*, ICSID case no. ARB/03/19, 30.07.2010, para. 235.

582 ICSID, *Suez, Sociedad General de Aguas de Barcelona S.A., and InterAgua Servicios Integrales del Agua S.A. v the Argentine Republic, Separate Opinion of Arbitrator Pedro Nikken*, ICSID case no. ARB/03/17, 30.07.2010, paras. 37–42; ICSID, *Suez, Sociedad General de Aguas de Barcelona, S.A., and Vivendi Universal S.A. v the Argentine Republic, Separate Opinion of Arbitrator Pedro Nikken*, ICSID case no. ARB/03/19, 30.07.2010, paras. 37–42.

583 ICSID, *Occidental Petroleum Corporation, Occidental Exploration and Production Company v the Republic of Ecuador, Award*, ICSID case no. ARB/06/11, 05.10.2012.

mainly because of severe public pressure to protect the Amazon environment and redirect oil revenues to the domestic society, the State terminated the participation contract with Oxy and seized Oxy's offices and oil fields in Ecuador in 2006. Shortly thereafter Oxy initiated arbitrations. In its decision, the Tribunal states that 'the overriding principle of proportionality requires that any such administrative goal must be balanced against the Claimants' own interests and against the true nature and effect of the conduct being censured'.[584] In the end, it found that the termination of the contract was disproportionate to Oxy's transfer of rights to AEC, mainly because there were many alternative and less restrictive measures available. This decision led to ICSID's highest damages award to date, 2.3 billion US dollars.[585]

3.2.3.4. *Non-Precluded Measures*

Because of the (often unexpected) interpretations by investment tribunals of the protection standards discussed above, exceptions can increasingly be found in the so-called non-precluded measures (NPMs) provisions. In 2008, Choudhury argued that international investment law had been derailed from its initial purpose as a shield against the unlimited sovereign powers of the State and became a sword that is eagerly used to attack and limit public policy powers.[586] In what seems to be a counter-reaction to the restriction of sovereign powers by investment arbitration, States are increasingly including NPM clauses, which permit States to take actions that are inconsistent with the Treaty when necessary to protect common interests. While older IIAs rarely included exception clauses, some more recent Treaties allow for measures that protect the environment or public health.[587] NPM provisions are now relatively common in the IIAs of

---

584 Ibid, para. 450.

585 In this decision, it is clear that the host State is held to a higher standard than contractual, not public, parties that would be allowed to cancel a contract that is no longer upheld by the other party. Allen finds this troubling because the State is held at this high standard and at the same time, in certain cases, is treated as a commercial party that is not allowed to pursue its public interest in the context of the expropriation claim. D. ALLEN, *'This Business Will Never Hold Water' International Investment Arbitration on Public-Private Water Service Provision – A Comment on Biwater Gauff (Tanzania) Limited v. United Republic of Tanzania*, Working Paper, 2010, available at ssrn.com, 28.

586 CHOUDHURY, above n 83.

587 Some older BITs do include exception clauses for measures that protect international peace and security or public order. Examples can be found in W. BURKE-WHITE and A. VON STADEN, *Investment Protection in Extraordinary Times: The Interpretation and Application of Non-Precluded Measures Provisions in Bilateral Investment Treaties*, Scholarship at Penn Law, Paper 152, 2007, available at <lsr.nellco.org> (published in (2008) 48 *Virginia Journal of International Law* 307, 307). For an example of a public interest exception see the Energy Charter Treaty.

important economic actors such as Germany, India and the US.[588] For example, the 2012 US Model BIT states that investment should not be encouraged at the cost of reducing domestic standards relating to labour and environmental protection. Because these NPM provisions may drastically limit the protection of foreign investors in the context of international investment arbitration, it is argued here that the 'sword' of more recent investment law is somewhat blunt.

NPM clauses can be defined as provisions setting out 'the circumstances in which a state may promulgate a measure or otherwise act in a manner inconsistent with its substantive obligations towards investors'.[589] While some NPM provisions cover public interest exceptions in general, others point out more specific issues such as peace and security, public order, public health and public morality.[590] Besides targeting different public and common interests, NMP clauses also differ in the nexus they require between the measure and the goal. While some provisions require that the measure is necessary, others demand only a relation to the protected objective or explicitly bring the determination of the nexus under the scrutiny of the State.[591] Because of the effect NPM have on the protection standards offered, their interpretation is crucial for determining the scope of the relevant IIA. Until now, NPM provisions have only been discussed in few ICSID arbitrations, most notably on the measures taken by Argentina following the 2001 financial crisis in the country.[592] Argentina argued that the financial crisis excused it from compensating the complaining investors for violating the US–Argentina BIT. It referred to both the necessity exception used in customary international law and the exception included in the relevant BIT to underpin this argument. In the earlier cases, *CMS, Enron* and *Sempra v Argentine Republic*, the tribunals used the customary law standard of necessity, which is employed in the rules on State responsibility, to determine the justifiability of Argentina's actions.[593] Following this standard, Argentina was asked to show that there were no other measures that the State could have taken to counter the economic crisis.[594] Because of the use of this strict interpretation

---

588 Only a (growing) minority of investment Treaties include an NPM clause. The US and Canada, Germany, India and the BLUE (Belgian–Luxembourg Economic Union) include such provisions in their model BITs.

589 Mitchell and Henckels, above n 541, 10.

590 For examples of BITs including these specific concerns, see ibid, 11. The 2012 US Model BIT states that investment should not be encouraged at the cost of reducing domestic standards relating to labour and environmental protection.

591 Ibid, 12.

592 ICSID, *CMS Gas Transmission Company v Argentina, Award,* ICSID case no. ARB/01/8, 12.05.2005; ICSID, *Enron Corporation Ponderosa Assets, L.P. v the Argentine Republic, Award,* ICSID case no. ARB/01/3, 22.05.2007; ICSID, *Sempra Energy International v Argentine Republic, Award,* ICSID case no. ARB/02/16, 28.09.2007.

593 Burke-White and von Staden, above n 587, 297.

594 See for example, ICSID, *Sempra Energy International v Argentine Republic, Award,* ICSID case no. ARB/02/16, 28.09.2007, paras. 350–51.

of the customary standard of necessity, a defence based on the NPM clause included in the applicable BIT was, in practice, unavailable.[595] Therefore, the *CMS, Enron* and *Sempra* decisions are often quoted as typical examples of the ICSID tribunals' insensitivity to legitimate public interest regulation.[596]

However, in more recent cases concerning the measures taken by Argentina, the tribunals have taken a rather different approach, leaving more deference to the State and accepting Argentina's defence on the basis of the necessity provisions included in the relevant BITs. The first tribunal to move away from the strict necessity test in the first cases against Argentina was the Tribunal in the case of *LG&E*, which was decided in October 2006. In this case, the Tribunal used a balancing test, similar to that used by the WTO AB, to determine whether the State measures were necessary. Instead of looking at the mere existence of alternative measures it took account of the grave nature of the economic crisis and the infringement of the investor's rights.[597] The Tribunal indirectly allowed a margin of appreciation to the State by not examining whether less restrictive alternatives existed. Considering the urgency with which Argentina had to act, the Tribunal granted the State the freedom to choose the appropriate means.[598] In the later *Continental Casualty v Argentine Republic* case, the Tribunal explicitly drew upon the WTO's less restrictive alternative test. In this context, the Tribunal, which was led by the former WTO AB Judge Giorgio Sacerdoti, adopted the proportionality analysis elaborated by the WTO DSM in relation to Article XX GATT. Citing the reasoning of several WTO decisions, the Tribunal carefully examined whether there was (1) a contribution to legitimate aim and (2) no reasonable alternative for any of the measures taken by Argentina that would have been less in conflict with the applicable investment law. In the context of the first requirement, the Tribunal explicitly gave deference to the State, stating that 'a significant margin of appreciation' should be given to the State.[599] As far as the second requirement was concerned, the Tribunal established that

> the necessity of a measure should be determined through 'a process of weighing and balancing of factors' which usually includes the assessment of the following three factors: the relative importance of interests or values furthered by the challenged measures, the contribution of the measure to the realization of the ends pursued by it and the restrictive impact of the measure on international commerce.[600]

---

595 Burke-White and von Staden, above n 587, 298.

596 The annulment committee in the *CMS* case found that the Tribunal had failed to assess whether Argentina could invoke an NPM provision. ICSID, *CMS Gas Transmission Company v Argentina, Decision of the Ad Hoc Committee on the Application for Annulment of the Argentine Republic*, ICSID case no. ARB/01/8, 25.09.2007, paras. 158, 163.

597 Burke-White and von Staden, above n 587, 324.

598 Ibid, 325.

599 ICSID, *Continental Casualty Company v the Argentine Republic, Award*, ICSID case no. ARB/03/9, 05.09.2008, para. 181.

600 Ibid, para. 194.

In this context, the Tribunal did not apply a strict standard of review, recognising that it is not its mandate to censure Argentina's sovereign choices as an independent State. Thus although NPM clauses are not considered self-judging by the tribunals (it is exactly the purpose of most IIAs to put an end to host States' attempts to judge their own purpose when it comes to emergency legislation)[601] the strict necessity analysis has been replaced with a more nuanced approach based on proportionality analysis and allowing deference on the basis of democratic legitimacy.

3.2.4. REGIONAL HUMAN RIGHTS MECHANISMS

3.2.4.1. European Court of Human Rights

The European Convention explicitly refers to public interests when addressing non-absolute rights, in other words, rights that can be restricted under certain conditions. Two of those rights can be restricted by the State under the condition that the restriction is 'in the public interest'. Article 1 of Protocol 1 permits the State to expropriate or control the use of property and Article 2 of Protocol 4 provides that the liberty of movement and freedom to choose one's residence may be restricted 'in the public interest'.[602] However, these are not the only rights that may be limited for the purpose of public interests. The restriction of certain other rights may be justified by the protection of public safety,[603] public order,[604] health,[605] morals,[606] etc. In what follows, the restriction to the right to property and the right to private and family life will be examined more closely.

Before examining the Court's case law on public interest exceptions in natural resource exploitation cases, this section will take a look at the general approach of the Court when examining public interest exceptions. When generalising, it can be said that the ECtHR uses three questions to establish whether a State interference or restriction is consistent with the Convention. Was the State measure lawful? Was the purpose of the State measure of public interest? And

601 For the example of the US–Argentina BIT see J. ALVAREZ and K. KHAMSI, 'Argentine Crisis and Foreign Investors: A Glimpse into the Heart of the Investment Regime' [2008–09] *Yearbook on International Investment Law and Policy* 379, 420.

602 Article 1 Protocol 1 speaks of '*cause d'utilité générale*' in the official French text of the Convention, while Article 2(4) Protocol 4 mentions '*l'intérêt public*'. In the Spanish translation the same distinction is made between '*causa de utilidad pública*' and '*interés público*'. On the other hand, the German and Dutch translations use the same term in both Articles, respectively '*öffentliche Interesse*' and '*algemeen belang*'.

603 For example, Article 8 ECHR – right to respect for private and family life.

604 For example, Article 9 ECHR – freedom of thought, conscience and religion.

605 For example, Article 10 ECHR – freedom of expression.

606 For example, Article 11 ECHR – freedom of assembly and association.

was the State measure necessary?[607] It is especially the Court's answer to the latter question that has been the subject of much scholarly debate, because it is at this point that the Court 'balances' the different interests involved.

The Court uses a variety of instruments to determine the necessity of a measure.[608] However, the ECtHR's primary tool to establish necessity is the test of proportionality. While the proportionality test will be elaborated in more detail in the subsequent sections, it may be useful here to include the Court's description of the proportionality test as it was developed in the landmark case of *Belgian Linguistics*. In this case the ECtHR stated that Article 14 (non-discrimination) does not prohibit measures that are based on the public interest and 'strike a fair balance between the protection of the interests of the community and respect for the rights and freedoms safeguarded by the Convention'.[609]

It must, however, be noted that the balance required by the Court strongly depends on the rights at stake. When more fundamental rights are at stake, for example the freedom of expression or intimate aspects of private life, the Court uses a strict test of proportionality that demands the existence of a pressing social need, a proportionate response and relevant and sufficient reasons for that response.[610] The extent to which the interference restricts the very essence of the right also seems to affect the Court's finding of a fair balance.[611] Another instrument that is used by the Court to determine the proportionality of a measure is the availability of less restrictive means.[612]

All of these elements affect the margin of appreciation that is granted to the State. The margin of appreciation is a concept that has been developed by the ECtHR to allow the Member States a certain degree of flexibility in the fulfilment of their obligations under the ECHR. The Court first established the concept in the case of *Handyside v UK*. In this case, the Court was asked to determine whether the distribution of a book (freedom of expression) could be restricted on the ground of obscenity (moral grounds). In *Handyside*, the Court pointed out that its review is subsidiary to that of the State and that the State is better placed to determine the necessity of a restriction. Thus, it stated that the Convention 'leaves to the Contracting States a margin of appreciation'.[613]

---

607 However, not all limitation clauses are subjected to this test. See CHRISTOFFERSEN, above n 272, chapter 2.8.2.2.

608 J. VANDE LANOTTE and Y. HAECK, *Handboek EVRM: algemene beginselen*, Intersentia, Antwerp 2005, p 138.

609 ECtHR 23.07.1968, *Case 'relating to certain aspects of the laws on the use of languages in education in Belgium' (Belgian Linguistic case)*, no. 1474/62; 1677/62; 1691/62; 1769/63; 1994/63; 2126/64, para. 7.

610 ECtHR 07.12.1976, *Handyside v the United Kingdom*, no. 5493/72.

611 VANDE LANOTTE and HAECK, above n 608, p 145.

612 Ibid, 138.

613 ECtHR 07.12.1976, *Handyside v the United Kingdom*, no. 5493/72.

The scope of the margin allowed to the Member States depends on various factors such as the nature of the right and the individual interest at stake, the existence of a consensus among the Member States on the scope of the disputed right,[614] the nature of the disputed activity, the positive or negative nature of the human rights obligation, the emergency of the State action and the nature of the public interest pursued by the State.[615] Of special relevance here is the influence of the nature of the invoked interest. The case law of the Strasbourg organs on this factor is not an example of consistency. Nevertheless, it may be stated that States are allowed a wider margin of appreciation in the context of social and economic policies and planning or environmental policies.[616] However, even if the State is allowed a wide margin of appreciation, the ECtHR warns that the power of appreciation is never unlimited:

> The domestic margin of appreciation thus goes hand in hand with a European supervision. Such supervision concerns both the aim of the measure challenged and its 'necessity'; it covers not only the basic legislation but also the decision applying it, even one given by an independent court.[617]

Although the current section focuses on public interest clauses, it should be noted that the use of the margin of appreciation in the case law of the Court is not limited to determining the necessity of derogations. The margin of appreciation is used in a similar way in the context of positive obligations.[618] When determining whether the State has taken the necessary measures to implement certain rights, the Court recognises that the State is in principle better placed to apply the Convention to the concrete factual circumstances and should therefore be allowed a certain degree of flexibility in choosing the means to implement the Convention rights.[619]

A third, and often criticised, use of the concept exists that should be distinguished from the previous two because it does not concern the application of a right to specific circumstances, but rather the scope of certain rights.[620]

---

614 The so-called European consensus standard has played a crucial role in determining whether the margin of appreciation is to be wide or narrow. When the majority of Member States have developed a similar practice or regulation, the Member State involved in the dispute will enjoy only a narrow margin and must produce 'very weighty reasons' to justify its measure.

615 This list is problematic because it is only identified in literature and not used by the Court. Therefore, the width of the margin is unpredictable.

616 For example in ECtHR 08.07.2003, *Hatton and Others v the United Kingdom*, no. 36022/97.

617 ECtHR 07.12.1976, *Handyside v the United Kingdom*, no. 5493/72, para. 49.

618 Shany, above n 417, 935.

619 See ECtHR 08.07.2003, *Hatton and Others v the United Kingdom*, no. 36022/97; ECtHR 09.06.2005, *Fadeyeva v Russia*, no. 55723/00.

620 See J. Gerards and H. Senden, 'The Structure of Fundamental Rights and the European Court of Human Rights' (2009) 7 *International Journal of Constitutional Law* 619, 619–53.

The Court sometimes, and perhaps wrongfully, refers to the margin of appreciation to indicate that States may be better placed to interpret which obligations they have under the Convention.[621] For example, in the case of *Stec and Others* the Court had to determine whether the UK's enforcement of different retirement ages for men and women was discriminatory. In its decision, the ECtHR pointed out the wide margin of appreciation of the UK in cases involving economic and social policy and subsequently concluded that there was no violation of the Convention.

3.2.4.1.1. Restriction of the Right to Property

Against this general background, the following section will focus on cases involving the right to property. The majority of the ECtHR's litigation on natural resource exploitation involves disputes on property. The right to property is included in Article 1 of the Conventions' First Protocol. Like most Articles of the ECHR that include a public interest clause, Article 1 Protocol 1 has a twofold structure that first defines the right and then determines under what circumstances interferences or restrictions of this right are justified in the public interest.

Thus, Article 1 Protocol 1 provides that:

> … No one shall be deprived of his possessions except in the public interest and … [t]he preceding provisions shall not, however, in any way impair the right of a State to enforce such laws as it deems necessary to control the use of property in accordance with the general interest … .

Before addressing the Court's interpretation of the public interest clauses, it has to be noted that the Court applies a broad interpretation of the right to peaceful enjoyment of one's possessions. Well-known examples of situations that were considered to violate this right include the existence of an expropriation permit that is not being executed but lowers the value of the property to which it applies and the delayed payment of a pension in circumstances of high inflation. The Court also applies a broad interpretation of the two exception clauses. For example, it considers de facto expropriations to constitute deprivations of property and has found the legal control of rent prices to be a control of the use of property in the sense of paragraph 2.[622]

---

621 J. Kratochvíl, 'The Inflation of the Margin of Appreciation by the European Court of Human Rights' (2011) 29 *Netherlands Quarterly of Human Rights* 324, 324–57; G. Letsas, 'Two Concepts of the Margin of Appreciation' (2006) 26 *Oxford Journal of Legal Studies* 705, 705–32.

622 ECtHR 24.06.1993, *Papamichalopoulos and Others v Greece*, no. 14556/89; ECtHR 19.12.1989, *Mellacher and Others v Austria*, no. 10522/83; 11011/84; 11070/84.

Because of the case law selection, the control of the use of property, rather than deprivation will be the focus of the following section. In the 1991 landmark case of *Fredin v Sweden* the Court used the criteria included in the Convention to elaborate a set of questions to determine whether the control of the use of property is consistent with the Convention. The Court performed its assessment of the case on the basis of three questions. Was the interference lawful? Was the purpose of the interference of public or common interest? And was the control of the use of property proportional?[623] The same questions of lawfulness, public interest purpose and proportionality were also applied in other cases, including the exploitation cases of *Posti and Rahko v Finland* and *Alatulkkila and Others v Finland*.

The first requirement, *lawfulness*, i.e. the rule of law test, implies that the restriction of a right must be grounded in a domestic law. This was confirmed in the decision on *Fredin v Sweden*. In this case, the claimants asked the Court to establish that the revocation by the State of their permit to exploit a gravel site was inconsistent with Article 1 Protocol 1 of the ECHR. In examining the lawfulness of the legal provision facilitating the revocation, the Court examined (1) the measure's compliance with the domestic law, recognising that its 'competence to review the State's compliance with the domestic law is limited', (2) the measure's foreseeability and (3) the availability of legal protection in domestic law.[624] Thus, the requirement of lawfulness only governs the law's procedural qualities – its accessibility, preciseness and certainty; it does not affect the State's substantive choice.[625]

The second requirement, the *purpose of the disputed measure*, is dealt with only superficially in the examined case law.[626] For example, in the case of *Fredin v Sweden*, the Court limited itself to stating that 'the Court recognizes for its part that in today's society the protection of the environment is an increasingly important consideration'.[627] In the cases of *Posti and Rahko v Finland* and

623 ECtHR 18.02.1991, *Fredin v Sweden (No. 1)*, no. 12033/86, paras. 48–55.

624 Ibid, para. 50.

625 Ibid. 'The Court's competence to review the State's compliance with the domestic law is limited.' McHarg, above n 94, 685.

626 For example, in the case of *Fredin v Sweden*, the Court limited itself to stating that 'The Court recognizes for its part that in today's society the protection of the environment is an increasingly important consideration' (ECtHR 18.02.1991, *Fredin v Sweden (No. 1)*, no. 12033/86, para. 48). In the 2002 case of *Posti and Rahko v Finland* the Court stated, again without further explanation, that the limitation of the applicants' right to fish salmon and sea trout in State-owned waters was justified because it was pursuing 'the legitimate general interest in protecting the fish stock' (ECtHR 24.09.2002, *Posti and Rahko v Finland*, no. 27824/95, para. 77). In the subsequent case of *Alatulkkila and Others v Finland*, the Court referred to its concise statement in *Posti and Rahko v Finland* to justify the limitations of the applicants' fishing rights in their own waters (ECtHR 28.07.2005, *Alatulkkila and Others v Finland*, no. 33538/96, para. 67).

627 ECtHR 18.02.1991, *Fredin v Sweden (No. 1)*, no. 12033/86, para. 48.

Alatulkkila and Others v Finland, both cases on the limitation of the right to fish certain species for reasons of environmental protection, the Court stated, again without further explanation, that the limitation of the applicants' right to fish salmon and sea trout in State-owned waters was justified because it was pursuing 'the legitimate general interest in protecting the fish stock'.[628]

These examples confirm the idea that '[i]n practice, lawfulness and proportionality are the major tests. While the European Court often studies the criteria of public interest, the test is virtually always complied with.'[629] The fact that the public interest purpose put forward by the State's policy is hardly ever questioned may be explained by the subsidiary role of the European Court.[630] In cases concerning property, the Court has repeatedly stated that, taking account of the principle of subsidiarity, 'the national authorities are in principle better placed than the international judge to appreciate what is "in the public interest"'.[631]

Because of the subsidiarity of the Court's review, the State also enjoys a certain margin of appreciation with regard to the third question, the *proportionality* of the interference. In particular in the case of property rights, the government is granted a wide margin of appreciation because 'the decision to enact laws expropriating property will commonly involve consideration of political, economic and social issues, which require an expertise and democratic legitimacy that judicial organs generally do not enjoy'.[632] That the State enjoys a wide margin of appreciation does, however, not imply that its discretion is unlimited. While the increased weight given to the role of the national policy maker will inevitably attach more importance to the substantive issue defended by the State, the Court may still find that no fair balance has been struck between the different interests.[633]

While in the past the Court has held that it 'must restrict itself to supervising the lawfulness and the purpose of the restriction in question',[634] it is now

---

628 ECtHR 24.09.2002, *Posti and Rahko v Finland*, no. 27824/95, para. 77.

629 M. Sepulveda, T. van Banning, G.D. Gudmundsdottir and C. Chamoun, *Universal and Regional Human Rights Protection: Cases and Commentaries*, University for Peace, Ciudad Colon 2004, p 384.

630 The width of the margin depends on different elements: the character of the provision, the nature of the provision for the claimant, the nature of the activity, the nature of the justification given by the state and the presence of a clear consensus between the Member States. Vande Lanotte and Haeck, above n 608, p 216.

631 First established by the Court in ECtHR 21.02.1986, *James and Others v the United Kingdom*, no. 8793/79, para. 46.

632 Y. Arai-Takahashi, *The Margin of Appreciation Doctrine and the Principle of Proportionality in the Jurisprudence of the ECHR*, Intersentia, Antwerp 2002, p 154. Arai-Takahashi herein refers to ECtHR 21.02.1986, *James and Others v the United Kingdom*, no. 8793/79, para. 46.

633 For example, if the applicant has to bear an individual and excessive burden, ECtHR 23.09.1982, *Sporrong and Lönnroth v Sweden*, no. 7151/75; 7152/75, para. 73.

634 ECtHR 07.09.1976, *Handyside v the United Kingdom*, no. 5493/72, para. 62.

established case law that the courts' supervision of public interest exceptions includes a test of proportionality.[635] Since the case of *Sporrong and Lönnroth v Sweden*, the Court has stressed that it 'must determine whether a fair balance was struck between the demands of the general interest of the community and the requirements of the protection of the individual's fundamental rights'.[636] With regard to the right to property, the Court quotes different elements, such as the effects of the interference[637] and the applicant's legitimate expectations,[638] as important in striking a fair balance.[639]

Taking account of these considerations, the Court found the interferences with the right to property to be proportional in all the studied cases. This is not surprising because, in general, the margin of appreciation is so wide in the context of the control of the use of property that a lack of proportionality is rarely found. In essence, the Court only checks whether the State took account of the interests involved when implementing its measure. This is especially clear in the case of *Posti and Rahko v Finland* on the limitation of fishing permits for environmental reasons.[640] In this case, the Court highlights the efforts made by the State, including the availability of compensation and alternative fishing grounds, to find a balance without really assessing whether these efforts balance out the restriction of the right.

3.2.4.1.2. Restrictions of the Right to Private and Family Life

Aside from general derogation clauses 'in the public interest', such as those included in the provision on the right to property, the ECHR also allows derogation from specific rights for the purpose of specific public interests. These specific public interest exception clauses are most frequently appealed to in

---

635 The proportionality test was first developed in the case of *Handyside v the United Kingdom*, a freedom of expression case, and was only later introduced into the case law on the right to property.

636 ECtHR 23.09.1982, *Sporrong and Lönnroth v Sweden*, no. 7151/75; 7152/75, para. 69.

637 ECtHR 18.02.1991, *Fredin v Sweden (No. 1)*, no. 12033/86, para. 53; ECtHR 24.09.2002, *Posti and Rahko v Finland*, no. 27824/95, para. 77; ECtHR 28.07.2005, *Alatulkkila and Others v Finland*, no. 33538/96, para. 67.

638 ECtHR 18.02.1991, *Fredin v Sweden (No. 1)*, no. 12033/86, para. 54.

639 While compensation is not required for the control of the use of property, it enforces the fair balance. A. Mowbray, 'A Study of the Principle of Fair Balance in the Jurisprudence of the European Court of Human Rights' (2010) 10 *Human Rights Law Review* 289. ECtHR 18.02.1991, *Fredin v Sweden (No. 1)*, no. 12033/86, paras. 51–56; ECtHR 24.09.2002, *Posti and Rahko v Finland*, no. 27824/95, para. 77; ECtHR 28.07.2005, *Alatulkkila and Others v Finland*, no. 33538/96, para. 67. Because of the case law selection, this review focuses on the control of the use of property rather than the deprivation of property. The main difference in the Court's assessment of these two exception clauses is that the ECtHR has established that the deprivation of property may only be proportional if reasonable compensation is paid.

640 ECtHR 24.09.2002, *Posti and Rahko v Finland*, no. 27824/95.

cases concerning Articles 8–11 ECHR.[641] In the case law on natural resource exploitation, special attention goes to Article 8§2 of the Convention, which allows for certain restrictions of the right to private and family life.

Again, it should be stressed that the European Court uses a broad interpretation of the Convention's rights. In its case law, the ECtHR has brought a large variety of issues under the right to private and family life, including the right of prisoners to associate with others and the right of transsexuals to change their official papers. Restrictions to these rights are allowed if they (1) are in accordance with the law, (2) have a legitimate aim and (3) are necessary in a democratic society. Since the latter requirement is evaluated using the principle of proportionality, a three-fold test can be distinguished similar to that established in the context of Article 1 Protocol 1.

On the issue of lawfulness, the Court has drawn a parallel between the concept 'in accordance with the law' in Article 8§2 and Article 10 of the Convention.[642] Therefore, the principles established in the *Sunday Times* judgment also apply to Article 8 cases. In *Sunday Times* the ECtHR stated that a restriction is lawful if it (1) has a basis in domestic law, (2) is adequately accessible and (3) is formulated with sufficient precision.[643] These principles are also reflected in *Noack and Others v Germany*, a case concerning the forced relocation of the applicants for the purpose of the expansion of lignite-mining operations in the area. Here, the Court focused on the existence of precise domestic laws governing the displacement of the applicants.[644] In line with the right to property cases, the ECtHR's focus is on the procedural qualities of the domestic law.

As far as the second requirement is concerned, the purpose pursued by the interference, it can be stated that the Court does not scrutinise the aims of the Member State's policies. For example, in the lignite-mining case of *Noack and Others v Germany*, the Court simply confirmed the State's claim that ensuring a long-term, low-cost energy supply and creating jobs is a legitimate aim that allows the State to derogate from Article 8 of the Convention.[645] In another exploitation case, *Dubetska and Others v Ukraine*, the ECtHR also recognised economic concerns as interests capable of outweighing the rights protected in the

641 S. Greer, '"Balancing" and the European Court of Human Rights: A Contribution to the Habermas-Alexy Debate' (2004) 63 *Cambridge Law Journal* 412, 424.

642 In *Silver and Others v UK* the ECtHR first stated that 'the principles enounced in the Sunday Times judgment concerning the expression "prescribed by law/prévues par la loi" in Article 10 (Article 10) were also applicable to the expression "in accordance with the law/prévue par la loi" in Article 8 (Article 8)'. ECtHR 25.03.1983, no. 5947/72; 6205/73; 7052/75; 7061/75; 7107/75; 7113/75; 7136/75, para. 85.

643 ECtHR 26.04.1979, *Sunday Times v the United Kingdom*, no. 6538/74, para. 49.

644 ECtHR 25.05.2000, *Noack and Others v Germany*, no. 46346/99, 8.

645 Ibid.

Convention. In this case, which concerned environmental pollution emanating from a State-owned mine, the Court confirmed that the State had to strike a balance between the applicants' rights and nationwide economic concerns.[646] This leads to the conclusion that the Court interprets the justifications described in Article 8§2 broadly and that, in most Article 8 cases, the legitimate aim is not an element of controversy.[647] Again, the subsidiarity of the Court's review may serve as an indication of why the Court is unwilling to perform a more thorough assessment.

Most of the debate on Article 8§2 ECHR concerns the necessity of the State measure. While the Court stresses that it is primarily the task of the State to determine whether the interference or restriction is necessary in a democratic society, it does exercise supervision on this issue. Because the national authorities are in principle better placed to evaluate local needs and conditions they enjoy a wide margin of appreciation. Nevertheless, the Court evaluates whether they struck a fair balance in the specific circumstances of the case.[648] According to the ECtHR's established case law, a restriction can only be 'necessary in a democratic society' if it answers to a pressing social need, is proportional to its aim, is based on relevant and sufficient reasons and strikes a fair balance between the interests involved.[649]

Although the Court has frequently reiterated these conditions, it does not expressly apply all of the criteria in its case law. In the case of *Noack and Others v Germany*, concerning the relocation of the applicants for the purpose of expanding mining operations, the Court does not explicitly deal with the questions of social need or relevant and sufficient reasons. Instead, it considers the specific circumstances of the case, in particular the wide public and parliamentary debate and the procedural safeguards, to conclude that the interference was not disproportionate to the aim pursued.[650] A similar conclusion can be drawn from the case of *Dubetska and Others v Ukraine*. In this dispute on pollution caused by a State-owned mine, the Court did not seem to use its traditional requirements. It only scrutinised the State's decision-making process and the implementation of its policy. On this basis, the Court concluded that the interference violated the Convention because it was contrary to domestic law and because no effective solution was found in 12 years.[651] Thus, the ECtHR de facto mainly focused on

646 ECtHR 10.02.2011, *Dubetska and Others v Ukraine*, no. 30499/03, para. 155.

647 Arai-Takahashi, above n 632, p 62.

648 ECtHR 10.02.2011, *Dubetska and Others v Ukraine*, no. 30499/03, para. 141.

649 The Court first enumerated these requirements with regard to Article 8 in ECtHR 25.03.1983, *Silver and Others v the United Kingdom*, no. 5947/72; 6205/73; 7052/75; 7061/75; 7107/75; 7113/75; 7136/75.

650 The Court considers the seriousness of the interference, the measures taken to ease the transfer of the population, etc. ECtHR 25.05.2000, *Noack and Others v Germany*, no. 46346/99, 9–10.

651 ECtHR 10.02.2011, *Dubetska and Others v Ukraine*, no. 30499/03, para. 144.

procedural factors to determine the proportionality of the measures taken in the examined cases.

3.2.4.2. *Inter-American Court of Human Rights*

Like the European Convention, the American Convention on Human Rights contains several non-absolute rights, i.e. rights that may be restricted by the State in the interest of society. In the selected case law on natural resource exploitation, two non-absolute rights are of special importance: the right to property, which may be subordinated to 'the interest of society',[652] and the freedom of thought and expression, which can be restricted to protect 'national security, public order, or public health or morals'.[653]

3.2.4.2.1. Restriction of the Right to Property

Although the Court confirms that it is the sovereign choice of the State to let public interests prevail over a non-absolute human right or vice versa, it emphasises that it is within the competence of the Court 'to analyse whether the State ensured the human rights' of those whose rights are restricted.[654] With regard to the restriction of the right to property, this implies that four requirements have to be fulfilled (1) lawfulness, (2) necessity, (3) proportionality and (4) legitimate purpose.[655]

These requirements were confirmed in the case of *Sawhoyamaxa v Paraguay*, where the Court found that it 'must assess in each case the legality, necessity, proportionality and fulfilment of a lawful purpose in a democratic society (public purposes and public benefit), to impose restrictions on the right to property, on the one hand, or the right to traditional lands, on the other'.[656] In this decision on the non-restitution of indigenous land, the IACtHR held it to be insufficient that the State prima facie rejects a claim because the disputed land is held privately and used productively.[657] The requirements set out by the Inter-American Court closely resemble those used by the European Court. It is clear that the Court does not accept State decisions that have not considered the effects of their decision in relation to community values.

---

652 Article 21 American Convention on Human Rights.

653 Article 13§2.b American Convention on Human Rights.

654 Inter-American Court of Human Rights, *Case of Sawhoyamaxa Indigenous Community v Paraguay*, Judgment of 29.03.2006, para. 136.

655 Inter-American Court of Human Rights, *Case of Yakye Axa Indigenous Community v Paraguay*, Judgment of 17.06.2005, paras. 144–45.

656 Ibid, para. 138.

657 Ibid, para. 141.

However, the Court does not analyse these requirements in all cases. In the case of *Saramaka v Suriname*, for example, the Court's focus is completely on the additional requirement that the disputed restriction may not deny the survival of the Saramaka people.[658] In this case, the Surinamese State awarded land concessions for forestry and mining on Community lands to third parties. The Court found this restriction on the right to property, in particular the Community's right to natural resources, to be justified[659] if it would not deny the survival of the Saramaka.[660] To ensure the latter, the State has to abide by three safeguards, which require (1) the possibility of effective participation for the affected people (and obtaining free prior informed consent in plans with profound impact), (2) reasonable benefit sharing with the affected people and (3) prior environmental and social impact assessments.[661] In this case, the Court found a violation of Article 21 because none of these safeguards were offered with regard to the disputed concessions.

The possibility of effective participation also proved to be of crucial importance in the case of *Xákmok Kásek v Paraguay*.[662] Ancestral land of the Xákmok Kásek Community had been transferred to private owners and (partly) declared a Protected Wildlife Area without taking account of the claims of the Community to this land. This lack of participation resulted in a loss of cultural identity for the Community and a lack of possibilities for subsistence practices, such as hunting and fishing.[663] In conclusion the Court therefore found that Paraguay had violated the Community's right to property by not taking account of its interests.[664] While, on the one hand, the body of safeguards set forward in *Saramaka v Suriname* noticeably strengthens the indigenous communities' right to property, on the other hand it limits the Court's review to procedural

---

658 Inter-American Court of Human Rights, *Case of the Saramaka People v Suriname*, Judgment of 28.11.2007, para. 128. While the Court defines this as an additional requirement, it could be seen as part of the proportionality analyses. It is hard to imagine that any goal would justify the denial of survival of a people.

659 'Although the Court recognizes the interconnectedness between the right of members of indigenous and tribal peoples to the use and enjoyment of their lands and their right to those resources necessary for their survival, said property rights, like many other rights recognized in the Convention, are subject to certain limitations and restrictions. ... the State will be able to restrict, under certain circumstances, the Saramakas' property rights, including their rights to natural resources found on and within the territory.' Ibid, para. 127.

660 Ibid, para. 128.

661 Ibid, para. 129. For a critical note on the Court's decision see J.M. Pasqualucci, 'International Indigenous Land Rights: A Critique of the Jurisprudence of the Inter-American Court of Human Rights in Light of the United Nations Declaration on the Rights of Indigenous Peoples' (2009) 27 *Wisconsin International Law Journal* 51, 51–98.

662 Inter-American Court of Human Rights, *Case of Xákmok Kásek Indigenous Community v Paraguay*, Judgment of 24.08.2010.

663 Ibid, paras. 171–81.

664 Ibid, para. 182.

matters.[665] A similar combination of a proportionality test and a de facto focus on procedural aspects was found in the case law of the European Court.

3.2.4.3. *African Commission on Human and Peoples' Rights*

Like its American and European counterparts, the African Charter includes many Articles that provide for derogation from the right or freedom therein protected 'in the public interest'.[666] The 'limits to these limitations' are defined differently per right or freedom included in the Charter. Some Articles explicitly define that restrictions are only permissible if provided for in law and applied for the purpose of very specific public and common interests;[667] others apply the vague criteria of 'law and order'[668] or do not require more than lawfulness as a justification.[669] The latter clause seems to suggest that the State has the freedom to derogate from the right for any reason as long as the derogation is not contrary to domestic law.[670] Nothing, however, could be further from the truth. The Commission has, time and again, stressed that these so-called 'claw back' clauses must not be interpreted against the principles of the Charter and that they should not be used as a means of giving credence to violations of the express provisions of the Charter.[671] To effectively protect human rights, the Commission has thus given itself the task of judging, on a case-by-case basis, whether the State has correctly balanced the human rights at stake with other interests. In the following paragraphs, it will be studied which elements the Commission deems essential for a restriction to be justified.

The case of the *Endorois Welfare Council v Kenya*[672] is the only one of the studied cases in which the defending State itself justified the disputed actions with reasons of public interest. The communication concerns the 1970s' eviction of the Endorois people by the Kenyan State to install a wildlife reserve and tourist facilities at Lake Bogoria. Before the Commission, the Endorois accused the Kenyan State of violating, inter alia, their right to property, freedom of

665 N. Bankes, 'International Human Rights Law and Natural Resources Projects Within the Traditional Territories of Indigenous Peoples' (2010) 47 *Alberta Law Review* 457, 490–91.

666 What is more, Article 27(2) of the Charter provides that '[t]he rights and freedoms of each individual shall be exercised with due regard to the rights of others, collective security, morality and common interest'.

667 For example, Article 11 – freedom of assembly and Article 14 – right to property.

668 For example, Article 8 – freedom of conscience.

669 For example, Article 9.2 – freedom of expression and Article 10 – freedom of association.

670 Heyns, above n 126, 108.

671 This was first stated in African Commission on Human and Peoples' Rights May 1999, *Amnesty International v Zambia*, no. 212/98.

672 African Commission on Human and Peoples' Rights November 2009, *Centre for Minority Rights Development (Kenya) and Minority Rights Group International on behalf of Endorois Welfare Council v Kenya*, no. 276/2003.

religion and right to development. It is in this context that the Commission further developed the requirements for a permitted derogation.[673] Article 14 of the African Charter provides that an encroachment upon the right to property is only permissible if it is 'in accordance with the provisions of appropriate laws' and 'in the interest of public need or in the general interest of the community'. With regard to the first requirement, the *lawfulness* of the interference with the right to property, the Commission states that 'appropriate laws' include domestic as well as international laws.[674]

As a consequence, for a restriction to the right to property of an indigenous community to be lawful, it should fulfil the three requirements of participation, benefit sharing, and prior environmental and social impact assessment.[675] The Commission assumes that a restriction of these rights is only justified in the public interest if all sources were consulted as part of the decision-making process. Concerning the second requirement, a public need or public interest goal, the Commission determines that is does not suffice for the State to act in pursuit of a public interest when restricting a human right. Any limitations on rights should also be proportionate to that aim.[676] Thus, the more important the restriction of the right is for the affected individual(s), the more important the interest has to be that is being pursued.

Several examples of proportionality may be found in the *Endorois Welfare Council v Kenya* case. As regards the Endorois' right to property, the Commission finds the public interest threshold to be set much higher when the property concerned is indigenous rather than individual private land, because the right to land is so closely linked to the right to life in the indigenous life style.[677] Accordingly, the Commission finds the displacement of the Endorois to be disproportionate to any public need served by the game reserve. In a similar vein, the Commission holds that a restriction to the Endorois' religious freedom should not only be in the interest of the public and lawful, it should also be necessary for and proportional to the public interest objective pursued: 'The raison d'être for a particularly harsh limitation on the right to practice religion, such as that experienced by the Endorois, must be based on exceptionally good reasons.'[678] Restricting the Community's access to religious sites is, according to

---

673 See also J. Cerone, 'Introductory Note to African Commission on Human and Peoples' Rights: Centre for Minority Rights Development (Kenya) & Minority Rights Group International on Behalf of Endorois Welfare Council v. Kenya' (2010) 49 *International Legal Materials* 858, 858–906.

674 African Commission on Human and Peoples' Rights November 2009, *Centre for Minority Rights Development (Kenya) and Minority Rights Group International on behalf of Endorois Welfare Council v Kenya*, no. 276/2003, para. 219.

675 Ibid, para. 228.

676 Ibid, para. 214.

677 Ibid, para. 212.

678 Ibid, para. 172.

the Commission, unnecessary to achieve environmental and economic public interest goals. Therefore, this restriction can never be proportionate to the interest pursued.[679]

3.2.5. SUMMARY: PUBLIC INTEREST EXCEPTIONS

In the context of public interest exceptions, two different situations could be identified. In the first situation, the judicial body interprets the relevant Treaty text in such a way that it includes an exception for a public interest concern. In the second instance, the Treaty explicitly provides a public interest exception. In the latter instance, the concept of proportionality balancing is most often used to determine whether the public interest warrants an exception to the relevant right or obligation. However, there are some notable exceptions for Treaty rights that themselves could be considered of common interest. The ICJ, for example, does not appear to leave much room for interpretation and requires strict necessity for the use of force in the context of the right to self-defence. Again, this decision shows the Court's devotion to ensuring respect for international law and in particular the maintenance of peace and security, a concern of common interest. Furthermore, it should be noted that not all versions of proportionality balancing are created equal. While in some contexts proportionality balancing is used to give discretion to the Court in reviewing the necessity and application of a State measure, for example in the WTO and some ICSID tribunals, other judicial bodies, such as the ECtHR, apply a more specific standard of review and, depending on the concrete circumstances, leave more or less discretion to the State. In trade law and investment Treaty arbitration such a standard has not crystallised yet.[680]

An example of how judicial bodies interpret Treaty texts in a way that introduces a public interest exception where there was none can be found in the interpretation of 'likeness' by both the WTO and the ICSID tribunals. It was found that the WTO AB has considered issues of common interest, in particular public health, to establish that products are not 'like products' and, therefore, the WTO obligation of NT does not apply to these products. The AB did not deviate from the GATT or its previous case law to come to this conclusion; it used the method of evolutionary interpretation to establish that the WTO criteria for differentiating between products include health risks. A similar reasoning can be found in the ICSID case law with regard to the interpretation of 'like circumstances' in the context of the NT standard.

679 Ibid, para. 173.

680 Henckels, above n 562, 241.

3.3. COMMON INTEREST NORMS

3.3.1. INTERNATIONAL COURT OF JUSTICE

3.3.1.1. Jus Cogens *and* Erga Omnes *Norms*

As discussed in the introductory section, the doctrines of *jus cogens* and *erga omnes* obligations reflect the acceptance of community interests on the international level by offering specific protection to those interests. Since there is no list that determines which rules have a *jus cogens* or *erga omnes* character, the ICJ's interpretation of these doctrines sheds light on which underlying interests it considers to be of common interest. Furthermore, the consequences that it attaches to the recognition of a rule as *jus cogens* or *erga omnes* indicate how much the Court's decisions are affected by such concerns. Coincidentally, the ICJ's first (and to date only) recognition of a *jus cogens* rule happened in a case that concerned, inter alia, the illegal exploitation of natural resources.[681] As stated in the section on jurisdiction, the Court expressly recognised the prohibition of genocide as a peremptory norm in *Armed Activities in the Territory of the Congo (DRC v Rwanda)* but did not consider the alleged breach of this norm to establish jurisdiction, because the parties did not consent to its jurisdiction. According to the Court, a peremptory norm may not trump the basis of its jurisdiction, a 'norm of general international law accepted and recognized by the international community of States'.[682] The Court thus established limits to the operation of *jus cogens* norms while, at the same time, recognising the underlying common values.

The recognition of the concept of obligations *erga omnes* by the ICJ has been discussed above.[683] Therefore, it suffices to reiterate that the ICJ's jurisdiction cannot be based on the concept but it does give a non-involved State standing to claim the breach of an obligation *erga omnes partes*. In contrast to the limited recognition of *jus cogens* rules, the Court recognised a variety of norms as *erga omnes* obligations in its case law. The ICJ identified the prohibition of acts of aggression and genocide, the protection of basic human rights (including protection from slavery and racial discrimination),[684] the right to

---

681 In ICJ, *Case of Gabčíkovo-Nagymaros Project (Hungary/Slovakia), Judgment*, Judgment of 1997, para. 112. The ICJ referred to *jus cogens*, but did not determine whether a norm had arisen with regard to the protection of the environment because none of the parties claimed that. While there is discussion that at least some rules of IEL have a *jus cogens* character, this does not seem to be the case in current international law. Vinuales, above n 243, 43.

682 ICJ, *Case of Armed Activities on the Territory of the Congo (New Application: 2002) (Democratic Republic of the Congo v Rwanda), Provisional Measures, Order, Separate Opinion of Judge Dugard*, Judgment of 2002, para. 13.

683 See pp 33ff on jurisdiction and pp 40ff on standing.

684 ICJ, *Case of Barcelona Traction, Light and Power Company, Limited, Judgment*, Judgment of 1970, para. 34.

self-determination[685] and the core obligations of international humanitarian law[686] as *erga omnes* obligations.[687]

In conclusion, it can be said that while the Court does recognise that certain obligations pertain to a special category, because they have been recognised as common interests by the international community as a whole, it has not yet attached specific consequences to this recognition. The Court has not granted hierarchical priority to *jus cogens* or *erga omnes* obligations, other than in the context of the indispensable third party doctrine and standing in violations of *erga omnes partes* obligations discussed above.[688] This conclusion was confirmed in the recent *Jurisdictional Immunities (Germany v Italy: Greece Intervening)* case, where the Court found that the rule of jurisdictional State immunity cannot become void by the gravity of the breach, even when peremptory norms are violated.[689]

3.3.1.2. Environmental Protection

A second issue of common interest, which has already been referred to in the section on procedural rules, is environmental protection and preservation. The first case in which the Court was asked expressly to take the legal developments in international environmental law into consideration was the dispute on the *Gabčíkovo-Nagymaros Project (Hungary/Slovakia)*.[690] Two questions that were answered in this case are of specific relevance for this research: whether it was wrongful of Hungary to refuse to further implement the project in Nagymaros for environmental reasons and whether Hungary could terminate the Treaty between Hungary and Slovakia on the project because international environmental law prohibited its performance.

On the former issue, Hungary argued that there was a situation of ecological necessity that precluded wrongfulness in its suspension of the 1977 Treaty. This claim has already been discussed under the heading of public interest exceptions. It was based on Article 33 of the Draft Articles on the International

685 ICJ, *Case of East Timor (Portugal v Australia), Judgment*, Judgment of 1995, para. 29; ICJ, *Case of Legal Consequences of the Construction of a Wall in the Occupied Palestinian Territory, Advisory Opinion*, Judgment of 2004, para. 88.

686 ICJ, *Case of Legal Consequences of the Construction of a Wall in the Occupied Palestinian Territory, Advisory Opinion*, Judgment of 2004, para. 157.

687 Benzing, above n 84, 372.

688 See pp 33ff on jurisdiction and pp 40ff on standing.

689 ICJ, *Case of Jurisdictional Immunities of the State (Germany v Italy; Greece Intervening), Judgment*, Judgment of 2012, para. 97.

690 Evans, above n 413, 688. The Court had itself already confirmed the importance of environmental protection in ICJ, *Case of Legality of the Threat or Use of Nuclear Weapons, Advisory Opinion*, Judgment of 1996.

Responsibility of States, which provides that a state of necessity may exist if an essential interest of the State is threatened by a grave and imminent peril.[691] Although the ICJ stressed the 'great significance that it attaches to respect for the environment, not only for States but also for the whole of mankind', it found that 'the perils invoked by Hungary ... were not sufficiently established in 1989, nor were they "imminent"'.[692]

Next, the Court had to examine whether international environmental law (IEL) prohibited the implementation of the 1977 Treaty between Hungary and Slovakia. Hungary brought detailed arguments of IEL before the Court, nevertheless the ICJ limited itself to an, albeit broad, interpretation of the 1977 bilateral Treaty. The Court interpreted the Articles of the Treaty that referred to the protection of the water quality, nature and fisheries as 'evolving provisions of environmental law' and thereby allowed itself to integrate modern concepts of common interest into the Treaty.[693] By using this approach, the Court avoided the conclusion that the Treaty could not be implemented. On the contrary, this interpretation allowed the Court to order the implementation of the 1977 Treaty in an altered manner, taking account of IEL. Although in this specific case the disputed Treaty explicitly included a provision on environmental protection, the Court stated in general terms that

> [s]uch new environmental norms have to be taken into consideration, and such new standards given proper weight, not only when the States contemplate new activities but also when continuing with activities begun in the past. This need to reconcile economic development with protection of the environment is aptly expressed in the concept of sustainable development.[694]

The Court thus refrained from specifying new environmental norms. It established that the 1977 Treaty included evolving provisions of environmental law and left it to the parties to reinterpret the Treaty accordingly.[695] In the words of Judge Simma, such a prudent approach 'reflects an old, tired view of international law ... according to which restrictions on the independence of

---

691 Draft Articles on Responsibility of States for Internationally Wrongful Acts, International Law Commission of 2001 UN Doc. A/56/10.

692 ICJ, *Case of Gabčíkovo-Nagymaros Project (Hungary/Slovakia), Judgment*, Judgment of 1997, paras. 53, 57.

693 E. Hey, 'International Water Law Placed in a Contemporary Environmental Context: The Gabcikovo-Nagymaros Case' (2000) 25 *Physics and Chemistry of the Earth* 303, 303.

694 ICJ, *Case of Gabčíkovo-Nagymaros Project (Hungary/Slovakia), Judgment*, Judgment of 1997, para. 140.

695 In this case, the Court could only make recommendations on the issue of international environmental law because the agreement by which the parties granted jurisdiction to the Court left it to the parties to determine how to implement the judgment. P. Bekker, 'Gabcikovo-Nagymaros Project (Hungary/Slovakia), Judgment International Court of Justice' (1998) 92 *American Journal of International Law* 273, 278.

States cannot be presumed because of the consensual nature of the legal order'.[696] Others feel that the Court was wise to leave the matter to the parties and not specify new norms of IEL. They argue that this decision is a good example of how the Court balances all interests involved to reach a conclusion that considers all legal aspects in an evolutionary manner and that will be accepted and complied with by both parties.[697]

Environmental concerns also played an important role in the 2010 *Pulp Mills on the River Uruguay (Argentina/Uruguay)* case. This dispute concerned Uruguay's omission to inform and consult with Argentina before issuing environmental authorisations for the construction of pulp mills on the river Uruguay. Argentina argued that Uruguay's actions breached the 1975 Statute on the use of the River Uruguay on two levels, first, by breaching the procedural obligations of information and consultation, and secondly, by violation of the substantive provisions of the Statute that provided for the prevention of pollution and the preservation of the aquatic environment. On the procedural level, the two countries agreed in the 1975 Statute that CARU (the Treaty body) would be informed of any construction that could affect the regime of the river. They further established the duty to consult and negotiate with each other on such issues. The Court found that Uruguay had not fulfilled these procedural obligations. With regard to the fact that Uruguay issued environmental authorisations before fulfilling its procedural obligations, the Court stated that it was 'contrary to the object and purpose of the 1975 Statute to embark on disputed activities before having applied the procedures'.[698] Next, the Court considered the alleged breach of substantive obligations by Uruguay.

Although the Court did not find it sufficiently proven that any of the substantive obligations of the 1975 Statute were breached, it did reach an important conclusion in the context of Article 41 of the Statute.[699] In the view of the ICJ, the obligation to prevent pollution and preserve the aquatic environment (Article 41) implies an obligation to carry out an environmental impact assessment (EIA) when transboundary harm could occur. The Court considered this practice to be a requisite in general international law.[700] However, it also found that general international law does not specify the scope and content of

---

696 ICJ, *Case of Accordance with International Law of the Unilateral Declaration of Independence in respect of Kosovo, Declaration of Judge Simma*, Judgment of 2010, para. 2.

697 Fitzmaurice, above n 31, 385; M. Fitzmaurice, 'The International Court of Justice and the Environment' (2004) 4 *Non-State Actors and International Law* 173, 187; Bekker, above n 695, 277; Guillermo et al., above n 233, 457.

698 ICJ, *Case of Pulp Mills on the River Uruguay (Argentina v Uruguay), Judgment*, Judgment of 2010, para. 143.

699 C.R. Payne, 'Pulp Mills on the River Uruguay (Argentina v. Uruguay), International Court of Justice' (2012) 105 *American Journal of International Law* 94, 99.

700 ICJ, *Case of Pulp Mills on the River Uruguay (Argentina v Uruguay), Judgment*, Judgment of 2010, para. 204.

an EIA. While the consideration of alternative locations and a consultation of the affected populations may be included, it remains up to the State to determine the content of this obligation.[701] The ICJ did not find evidence that Uruguay had violated its obligation to perform an EIA nor its substantive obligation to preserve the environment because it had prepared an EIA and no significant change had occurred in the aquatic environment since the pulp mills started functioning.[702] Therefore, the ICJ concluded that Uruguay had breached only its procedural obligations (Articles 7–12) and not its substantive obligations (Articles 35, 36, 41) under the Statute. The consequence of this decision was that the Court considers its recognition of the breach a sufficient satisfaction because only procedural provisions were violated.

Two explanations have been put forward for the Court's focus on procedure in this case. The first explanation is that the Court deems consultation and cooperation to be the best means to reach the parties' goal of 'achieving the optimum and rational utilization of the River Uruguay'. A second explanation is that in this kind of case it is extremely difficult for the applicant to prove its substantive claims.[703] It could be argued that, in such circumstances, the Court should appoint its own experts to tackle substantive issues or even perform a risk assessment to prevent environmental damage.[704] However, the litigants prefer to control the evidence presented to the Court themselves and the Court does not wish to deter future applicants.[705] From the *Gabčíkovo-Nagymaros* case it became clear that the international law of sovereign States is not absolute when the survival of humanity is at risk. Stec and Judge Weeramantry respectively appropriately pointed out, while referring to this case, that

> [l]imiting the self-interest of states by taking into account global concerns of humanity has become a fundamental aspect of international law.[706]

> [W]e have entered an era of international law in which international law subserves not only the interests of individual States, but looks beyond them and their parochial concerns to the greater interests of humanity and planetary welfare.[707]

---

701 Ibid, para. 205. In light of the emphasis on consultation of the affected population in most modern Treaties, it is remarkable that the Court does not consider consultation to be a compulsory element of an EIA. Payne, above n 699, 100.

702 ICJ, *Case of Pulp Mills on the River Uruguay (Argentina v Uruguay), Judgment*, Judgment of 2010, para. 219.

703 J. Cogan, 'The 2010 Judicial Activity of the International Court of Justice' (2011) 105 *American Journal of International Law* 477, 479.

704 ICJ, *Case of Pulp Mills on the River Uruguay (Argentina v Uruguay), Joint dissenting opinion of Judges Al-Khasawneh and Simma*, Judgment of 2010.

705 Cogan, above n 703, 481.

706 Stec, above n 32, 364.

707 ICJ, *Case of Gabčíkovo-Nagymaros Project (Hungary/Slovakia), Judgment, Separate Opinion Judge Weeramantry*, Judgment of 1997.

Nevertheless, it must be noted that, despite its express recognition of environmental protection as a concern of humankind as a whole, the ICJ remains very cautious in its approach.

The prudent approach was confirmed in the recent case of *Australia v Japan (Whaling)*.[708] This case revolved around the ICJ's interpretation of the International Convention for the Regulation of Whaling (ICRW). Under the Whaling Convention the majority of whaling activities are prohibited, with two exceptions. First, aboriginal whaling is allowed under the ICRW and, secondly, whaling for the purpose of scientific research is permitted under Article VIII of the ICRW.[709] Australia filed a complaint against Japan because it felt Japan's JARPA II scientific programme and the lethal takings permitted under that programme were not justified for the purpose of scientific research under Article VIII of the Convention.

In line with its previous case law, the Court chose not to address the ICRW in the context of the international environmental Treaties raised by Australia (including CITES and the Convention on Biological Diversity) or the underlying purpose of the Treaty. It preferred to focus its judgment on the ICRW and, more specifically, on Article VIII of that Convention. The ICJ stressed the importance of the object and purpose of the Treaty for its interpretation. Nevertheless, it did not decide whether this was conservation, as stated by Australia, or sustainable exploitation, as defended by Japan. Instead, the ICJ found the scientific research requirement of Article VIII to be a goal in itself, and not an exception to the Treaty.[710] Therefore, the *Whaling* judgment is discussed here and not, as would perhaps be expected, under the heading of public interest exceptions.

On the merits, Japan argued that the State should be allowed a certain margin in granting whaling permissions because it is best placed to evaluate the underlying research goals. The ICJ, however, found that an objective standard of review of 'scientific purpose' and 'reasonable application' could be used. Weighing all the scientific evidence, it concluded that although lethal methods were not unreasonable per se, *in casu* the scale of lethal sampling was not reasonable for the stated objectives of JARPA II.[711] Thus, although the ICJ refuses to address the common interest aspect of this case, it does not grant deference to the State and ultimately decides in favour of more strict protection.

The 11 individual opinions attached to the *Whaling* judgment show that this decision is not unproblematic. In the context of this chapter, two issues merit

[708] ICJ, *Case of Whaling in the Antartic (Australia v Japan: New Zealand Intervening), Judgment*, Judgment of 2014.

[709] Article VIII International Convention for the Regulation of Whaling of 2 December 1946, UN Treaty Series, vol. 155, 349.

[710] ICJ, *Case of Whaling in the Antartic (Australia v Japan: New Zealand Intervening), Judgment*, Judgment of 2014, para. 58.

[711] Ibid, paras. 135, 198.

further discussion. First, the ICJ's use of 'reasonableness' as a standard of review to determine whether Japan's whaling activities could be defined as 'for the purposes of scientific research' is not explained. Judge Owada, in his dissenting opinion, traces this standard back to the WTO case of *EC – Hormones*.[712] The main problem with this use of WTO standards is that, unlike the WTO AB, the ICJ does not explain why this standard is used and not, for example, a necessity test.[713] Secondly, Judge Cançado Trindade, in his separate opinion, pointed out that international Treaties could and should be interpreted in a timely manner, as living instruments, especially if they are embedded within a Treaty regime that applies those instruments in the present context.[714] It is therefore regrettable that the ICJ found many of the recommendations made by the Whaling Commission irrelevant for its interpretation of the Treaty.[715]

3.3.2. INTERNATIONAL TRIBUNAL FOR THE LAW OF THE SEA

The UN Convention on the Law of the Sea is progressive in its recognition of the common interest of environmental protection. Article 193 of the Convention provides that 'States have the sovereign right to exploit their natural resources pursuant to their environmental policies and in accordance with their duty to protect and preserve the marine environment'. This provision goes beyond the duty to prevent transboundary harm, which is a reflection of sovereign rights, and recognises environmental protection as a general obligation and an independent objective.[716] The UNCLOS further provides for the protection of the seabed, ocean floor, its subsoil and their resources beyond national jurisdiction. That 'the Area' is approached as a concern of common interest in the UNCLOS is shown in its definition as 'common heritage of mankind'.[717] Because the ITLOS' function is mainly to enforce the UNCLOS, it automatically acts as the protector of the international values that are inherent in the Law of the Sea Convention. Thus, the ITLOS can be seen as an 'organ of the international community with the task of protecting the community's core values and interests'.[718] However, the

712 Ibid, Dissenting Opinion of Judge Owada, paras. 32, 33–36.
713 S. Rolland, 'Whaling in the Antarctic (Australia v. Japan: New Zealand Intervening)' (2014) 108 *American Journal of International Law* 496, 500.
714 ICJ, *Case of Whaling in the Antartic (Australia v Japan: New Zealand Intervening), Judgment*, Judgment of 2014, Separate Opinion of Judge Cançado Trindade, para. 34.
715 Ibid, para. 83.
716 Rashbrooke, above n 402, 519–20.
717 Article 293(1) UNCLOS; von Bogdandy and Venzke, above n 156, 19–24. It is also reflected in the establishment of the Seabed Authority. Articles 137 and 157 UNCLOS; Wolfrum, above n 25, p 1136.
718 von Bogdandy and Venzke, above n 156, 49–72.

UNCLOS also includes many provisions that are purely bilateral.[719] Therefore, it is interesting to examine the balance that the Tribunal strikes between the bilateral and common interest issues recognised in the Convention and by the international community.

In the *Southern Bluefin Tuna* case, the Tribunal decided to suspend the Japanese experimental fishing programmes that allegedly threatened the stock of southern bluefin tuna. The dispute concerned fisheries outside the scope of the Japanese EEZ and therefore fell under Chapter VII of the UNCLOS, which concerns the freedom of fishing in the high seas. Nevertheless, the Tribunal found that the dispute also had to be considered under Chapter XII of the UNCLOS, concerning the preservation and protection of the marine environment.[720] It stated that 'the conservation of the living resources of the sea is an element in the protection and preservation of the marine environment'.[721] The ITLOS thus applied a broad interpretation of this concept by establishing that the duty to preserve is not limited to preventing pollution but includes the conservation of endangered species and ecosystems.[722]

An express recognition of a common interest that is not directly included in the UNCLOS can be found in the *M/V 'SAIGA' (No. 2)* case, in which the Tribunal found that 'stopping and arresting the Saiga Guinea used excessive force contrary to international law and thereby violated the rights of Saint Vincent and the Grenadines'.[723] In its judgment, the Tribunal stated that international law

> requires that the use of force must be avoided as far as possible and, where force is unavoidable, it must not go beyond what is reasonable and necessary in the circumstances. Consideration of humanity must apply in the law of the sea, as they do in other areas of international law.[724]

This interpretation of international law goes beyond that of the International Court of in the 1998 *Fisheries Jurisdiction* case.[725] The ICJ in that case merely

---

719 For example, the right of innocent passage. E. de Wet, 'The International Constitutional Order' (2006) 55 *International and Comparative Law Quarterly* 51, 67.

720 ITLOS, *Southern Bluefin Tuna Case (New Zealand v Japan; Australia v Japan), Provisional Measures*, Judgment of 1999, para. 70. The ITLOS confirmed that the duty to enforce conservation measures is an element of the more general obligation of preventing environmental harm beyond national control (Orellana, above n 243, 48. Cf. the general obligation in ICJ, *Case of Legality of the Threat or Use of Nuclear Weapons, Advisory Opinion*, Judgment of 1996, para. 29).

721 ITLOS, *Southern Bluefin Tuna Case (New Zealand v Japan; Australia v Japan), Provisional Measures*, Judgment of 1999, para. 70.

722 Boyle, above n 122, 373.

723 ITLOS, *The M/V 'Saiga' (No. 2) Case, Judgment*, Judgment of 1999, para. 183(9).

724 Ibid, para. 155.

725 H. Dipla, 'The Role of the International Court of Justice and the International Tribunal for the Law of the Sea in the Progressive Development of the Law of the Sea' in A. Strati, M. Gavouneli and N. Skourtos (eds), *Unresolved Issues and New Challenges to the Law of the Sea: Time Before and Time After*, Martinus Nijhoff Publishers, Leiden 2006, pp 244–45.

declared that enforcing conservation and management measures might imply the use of force.[726]

In the 2002 *'Volga'* case it was shown that common interest issues possibly affect the Tribunal's decision on the reasonableness of a bond asked by the detaining State for the release of a vessel. As stated above, the *'Volga'* case concerned the release of a Russian vessel that was arrested by Australia on the accusation of illegal fishing.[727] The claimant, Russia, found the bond set by Australia for the release of the vessel to be unreasonable in terms of Article 292 of the UNCLOS. In its previous decisions, the Tribunal had stated that the reasonableness of a bond depends on, inter alia, the value of the vessel and the amount of the bond and the possible penalties for the alleged fishing offences.[728] In its defence, Australia argued that the high bond was reasonable considering the gravity of the offences and the international concern over the continued illegal, unregulated and unreported (IUU) fishing in the Southern Ocean.[729] Australia thereby provided evidence of the repeated plundering of the protected resources of the Southern oceans by a fleet of seven vessels, including the *Volga*.[730] The Tribunal answered Australia by stating that the gravity of the offences, as a factor in determining a reasonable bond, refers only to the penalties that may be imposed by the State.[731] Notwithstanding this statement, the ITLOS did state that it 'understands' Australia's concern over the problem of IUU fishing and 'appreciates the objectives behind the measures taken by States'.[732]

After this statement, the Tribunal established that the bond set by Australia consisted of three parts, relating to the release of the vessel, the release of the crew[733] and future behaviour. The Tribunal considered the bond to be unreasonable because of the latter part. This so-called 'good behaviour bond' is a bond aimed at preventing future violations, which is not allowed under the

---

726 ICJ, *Case of Fisheries Jurisdiction (Spain v Canada), Jurisdiction, Judgment*, Judgment of 1998, para. 84.

727 For an overview of the ITLOS case law on reasonable bonds until 2008 see J. Gao, 'Reasonableness of the Bond under Article 292 of the LOS Convention: Practice of the ITLOS' (2008) 7 *Chinese Journal of International Law* 115, 115–42.

728 H. Tuerk, 'The Contribution of the International Tribunal for the Law of the Sea to International Law' (2007) 26 *Penn State International Law Review* 289, 311.

729 ITLOS, *The 'Volga' Case (Russian Federation v Australia), Prompt Release*, Judgment of 2002, para. 67.

730 Oral submissions by David Bennett QC, counsel for Australia, Verbatim Record of Oral Submissions 12.12.2002, 3 pm, available at <www.itlos.org>.

731 ITLOS, *The 'Volga' Case (Russian Federation v Australia), Prompt Release*, Judgment of 2002, para. 69.

732 Ibid, para. 68.

733 Which had become moot because those members of the crew who survived Australia (one member died by accidentally drinking cleaning product) were released and returned home before the Order. Ibid, para. 74.

Convention.[734] However, for the first time in a prompt release case, the Tribunal did not contest the amount set in relation to the release of the vessel and found that the seized catch of tooth fish should not be deducted from the total bond.[735] Accordingly, the Tribunal upheld an important part of Australia's submission.

In conclusion, it can be said that the ITLOS was likely influenced by the environmental concerns involved but had to balance this interest with its limited jurisdiction on the prompt release of vessels, under Article 292 of the UNCLOS. Nevertheless, Judge Cot criticised the ITLOS conclusion in his separate opinion. He noted the imbalance between the coastal State, which enforces the common interest of conservation of marine resources at a high cost, and the flag State, which makes considerable profits from illegal fishing.[736] It can of course be questioned whether the ITLOS adjudication on the prompt release of vessels is the appropriate forum to address such issues.[737]

3.3.3. REGIONAL HUMAN RIGHTS MECHANISMS

3.3.3.1. European Court of Human Rights

An injection of common interest concerns in the ECtHR's adjudication can be found not only in restricting, but also in defending the protection of human rights. When individual rights are balanced against other interests, the considerations made in favour of protecting the individual right are often of a more general nature. An interest that has served both to restrict and to ensure human rights is the common interest of environmental protection. On the one hand, the Court allows this interest to restrict the exercise of some rights, for example the right to property discussed above. On the other hand, the Court finds that protection of some rights requires the safeguarding of an environment of quality.[738] While restrictions on the exercise of rights on the ground of preserving the environment have mainly been considered by the European Court in the context of Protocol No. 1, the preservation of the environment is

734 Ibid, para. 80.

735 Gao therefore suggests that the Tribunal did consider the general issue of illegal fishing in its decision. Gao, above n 727, 134–35.

736 ITLOS, *The 'Volga' Case (Russian Federation v Australia), Prompt Release, Separate Opinion Judge Cot*, Judgment of 2002.

737 D.R. Rothwell and T. Stephens, 'Illegal Southern Ocean Fishing and Prompt Release: Balancing Coastal and Flag State Rights and Interests' [2004] *International & Comparative Law Quarterly* 171, 185.

738 D. García San José, *Environmental Protection and the European Convention on Human Rights*, Human Rights Files, Council of Europe Publications, 2005, available at <www.echr.coe.int>, 8–9.

often seen as an argument in favour of Article 8 of the Convention, the right to private and family life.[739]

The oldest, and perhaps also the best known, of the considered cases on Article 8 ECHR is *Taskin and Others v Turkey*.[740] This case is closely related to *Lemke v Turkey*,[741] a decision concerning the same factual circumstances. The applicants in both cases denounced the lack of enforcement by the Turkish government of a national judicial decision revoking the permit of a gold mine operating in the applicants' vicinity on account of the documented risks to the environment and human health. What is interesting in these decisions is that the ECtHR develops very specific criteria for cases in which the environment is negatively affected.[742] The Court points out that a two-pronged test is required in such cases, including both an assessment of the substantive merits of the national decision and an investigation of the decision-making process of the national authorities, with a focus on the information and procedural safeguards that were offered to the general public.[743]

The Court had already put this two-tiered test forward in the case of *Hatton v the United Kingdom*, where it noted that 'a governmental decision-making process concerning complex issues of environmental and economic policy … must necessarily involve appropriate investigations and studies in order to allow them to strike a fair balance between the various conflicting interests at stake'.[744] In *Taskin* and *Lemke*, the lack of effective procedural safeguards led the Court to conclude that Article 8 was violated in both cases. This procedural focus is considered of significant importance for the advancement of environmental concerns in Europe. After all, it implies that once a State has established a legal framework to protect the environment, it may be forced to implement that framework by the ECtHR.[745]

The same two-tiered, substantive and procedural, test was applied in the case of *Tătar v Romania*. The applicants in this case, father and son Tătar, lived in the vicinity of a mine permitted (since 1998) to extract gold with the use of sodium

739 Ibid, 16.

740 ECtHR 10.11.2004, *Taskin and Others v Turkey*, no. 46117/99.

741 ECtHR 05.06.2007, *Lemke c. Turquie* (only available in French), no. 17381/02.

742 This does not, however, entail that the Court has created a substantive right to or *for* the environment in its case law. That it associates violations of other rights with the public interest of environmental protection is more a 'recognition of the importance of environmental protection in today's political landscape'. O. Pedersen, 'European Environmental Human Rights and Environmental Rights: A Long Time Coming' (2008) 21 *Georgetown International Environmental Law Review* 73, 91–92.

743 ECtHR 10.11.2004, *Taskin and Others v Turkey*, no. 46117/99, para. 115; ECtHR 05.11.2007, *Lemke c. Turquie* (only available in French), no. 17381/02, para. 41.

744 ECtHR 08.07.2003, *Hatton and Others v the United Kingdom*, no. 36022/97, para. 128.

745 This approach is of course limited by the fact that there has to be a victim that can link its harm with non-enforcement.

cyanide. Their main claim was that the health of the son, who suffered from asthma, significantly deteriorated after a massive spill of cyanide-contaminated water in 2000. Furthermore, they denounced the fact that no action was undertaken by the government to prevent further accidents after 2000. While the Court did not find a causal link between the disease of the son and the accident and acknowledged that the government enjoys a wide margin of appreciation to implement its industrial and environmental policy, it found that Article 8 was violated on procedural grounds.[746]

In the first place, the ECtHR established that the government did not abide by its own, national as well as international, legislation in licensing the mine to operate. According to the Court, the applicable legislation provided certain obligations for the government. First, it should have evaluated the risks posed by the mining activities beforehand; secondly, the government should have taken measures to prevent the violation of the rights of those affected; and, thirdly, it should have made public the preliminary environmental impact study, on which the permit was based.[747] In addition to the licensing of the mine, the Court stated that the ECHR was violated by the continued operation of the mine after the accident in 2000. In that context it referred to the State's failure to apply the precautionary principle (as established by the Rio Convention).[748]

3.3.3.2. Inter-American Court of Human Rights

Like the rights discussed in the previous chapter on public interest exceptions, the freedom of expression is not an absolute right in the American Convention and may be restricted, for example, through the imposition of liability in cases of abusive use. However, this restriction 'must be proportionate to the interest that justifies it and closely tailored to accomplishing this legitimate objective, interfering as little as possible with the effective exercise of the right to freedom of expression'.[749] The main difference with the cases studied in the chapter on public interest exceptions, however, is that elements of common interest are also used in strengthening the human rights protection.

The case of *Kawas-Fernández v Honduras* is an excellent example of how the Court assesses the aforementioned criteria. In this case, the Court found the murder by State agents of an environmental activist to constitute a violation of the freedom of association, because the murder was linked to her public opposition

746 ECtHR 27.01.2009, *Tătar c. Roumanie* (only available in French), no. 67021/01, para. 108.
747 Ibid, paras. 112–13.
748 Ibid, para. 120.
749 Inter-American Court of Human Rights, *Case of Ricardo Canese v Paraguay*, Judgment of 31.08.2004, para. 96.

to the illegal exploitation of natural resources.[750] In this context, the Court emphasised the 'undeniable link between the protection of the environment and the enjoyment of other human rights' and the intimidating effect of this event on other environmental activists.[751] Decisive in this case was not so much the importance of the freedom *an sich*, but rather the importance of the freedom of expression and association when they are exercised with regard to issues of common interest.[752] The reasoning in this case law is clearly inspired by the case law of the ECtHR.[753]

Environmental concerns also played a role in the decision of the Inter-American Court to interpret the freedom of expression as a public right to information that is held by the State. The 2006 case of *Claude-Reyes et al. v Chile* concerned the right to obtain information held by the State about a forestry exploitation project with a potentially large environmental impact.[754] In this context, the Inter-American Court found that the requested information was of public interest and, consequently, the failure to provide all the requested information to members of an NGO violated the right to freedom of expression protected under Article 13 of the American Convention.[755] This was the first time that the Court established the right to access to public interest information held by the State as part of the right to freedom of expression. Furthermore, the Inter-American Court clarified that this right is not limited to those that have a direct interest in the information. The right to access can also be exercised by a person without personal interest or an NGO.[756]

Another public interest that is often brought forward by the Court in the context of indigenous property rights is cultural legacy. In the first judgment that recognised land and resource rights of indigenous communities, *Awas Tingni v Nicaragua*, the IACtHR states that the State violated its positive obligation to protect the indigenous property right by granting forest concessions to a timber company on lands that should have been demarcated in favour of the Awas

---

750 Inter-American Court of Human Rights, *Case of Kawas-Fernández v Honduras*, Judgment of 03.04.2009.

751 While the protection of the environment does not fall within the scope of the IACtHR's mandate, it often functions as a background for claims. L. Lixinski, 'Treaty Interpretation by the Inter-American Court of Human Rights: Expansionism at the Service of the Unity of International Law' (2010) 21 *The European Journal of International Law* 585, 596.

752 The 'essential role played by freedom of expression in the consolidation and dynamics of a democratic society' (Inter-American Court of Human Rights, *Case of Ricardo Canese v Paraguay*, Judgment of 31.08.2004, para. 86).

753 References to the European case law in the *Canese* case are abundant.

754 Inter-American Court of Human Rights, *Case of Claude-Reyes et al. v Chile*, Judgment of 19.09.2006.

755 Ibid, paras. 73, 103.

756 Ibid, para. 77.

Tingni Community.[757] It bases the necessity of recognising this 'new' property right on a common interest, namely, the preservation of cultural legacy.[758]

The Court in *Yakye Axa v Paraguay* applied an equally remarkable reasoning. The Paraguayan State in this case asserted that it could not return indigenous lands that had lawfully been transferred to a third party, because this would disregard the latter's right to property.[759] The Court counters this assertion by finding that 'the collective objective of preserving cultural identities ... may constitute a legitimate goal that justifies the restriction of the disputed private property right'. The Court thus suggests the restriction of one right on public interest grounds to enforce another right.[760] While these cases deal with facts that are similar to those introduced under the heading of restrictions to rights, the decisions are older and the Court's decision-making process was not focused on procedural matters yet. In these cases the Court still had to establish the indigenous right to property and did this describing a public interest as an aggregation of individual interests.

3.3.3.3. African Commission on Human and Peoples' Rights

The foregoing chapter on public interest exceptions has clarified that the protection of human rights is not a normative public interest. It is not considered to always be to the net benefit of everyone to protect human rights and derogation is allowed under certain conditions. Nevertheless, it should be noted that the Commission, like the other regional human rights bodies, unconditionally protects the so-called core of each right. As it stated in the case of the *Endorois Welfare Council v Kenya*, 'a limitation may not erode a right such that the right itself becomes illusory. At the point where such a right becomes illusory, the limitation cannot be considered proportionate – the limitation becomes a violation of the right'.[761]

If the right is robbed of its protective effect by the interference, if its central purpose is touched upon, it will always prevail over the public interest. Only if

---

757 For an extensive report of the Awas Tingni proceedings see J. Anaya and C. Grossman, 'The Case of Awas Tingni v. Nicaragua: A New Step in the International Law of Indigenous Peoples' (2002) 19 *Arizona Journal of International and Comparative Law* 1, 1–16.

758 Inter-American Court of Human Rights, *Case of Mayagna (Sumo) Awas Tingni Community v Nicaragua*, Judgment of 31.08.2001, para. 141.

759 Inter-American Court of Human Rights, *Case of Yakye Axa Indigenous Community v Paraguay*, Judgment of 17.06.2005, para. 142.

760 Pasqualucci, above n 661, 84.

761 African Commission on Human and Peoples' Rights November 2009, *Centre for Minority Rights Development (Kenya) and Minority Rights Group International on behalf of Endorois Welfare Council v Kenya*, no. 276/2003, para. 215.

this is not the case may a restriction be permissible. From this, we can conclude that the Commission considers the protection of the core of human rights to be an ethical standard that should not be balanced against other interests.

The same is true for some principles of international law. An example may be found in the only inter-State communication that was decided on by the Commission up to now, *Democratic Republic of Congo/Burundi, Rwanda, Uganda*.[762] The complaint was brought by the DRC on account of the occupation of its territory and the systematic violence and looting of natural resources in the eastern DRC by the armed forces of Burundi, Rwanda and Uganda.[763] In its decision, the Commission notes that the occupation of Congolese territory is impermissible, even if its alleged purpose is to safeguard national safety interests.[764] This position reflects public international law.[765] With regard to the restriction of rights of nationals of other States, the Commission is very clear that this is unacceptable, irrespective of the public interest served.

As discussed in the previous chapters, the interests of a larger public or even the global community are often relied upon to strengthen a decision in favour of an individual human right. The African system is rather peculiar in this respect, because the Banjul Charter itself calls for the protection of certain 'peoples' rights'.[766] In the aftermath of colonialism, these rights were drafted to remind the State parties to rule to the equal benefit of their nationals, not to the benefit of outside powers.[767] One example of the Commission's interpretation of peoples' rights may be found in the case of *SERAC v Nigeria*. In this decision, the military government of Nigeria was found guilty of violating different human rights due to its condoning and facilitating the operations of oil corporations in Ogoni-land. While the Commission 'does not wish to fault governments that are labouring under difficult circumstances to improve the lives of their people',[768] it did not find economic interests to justify the human rights violations that occurred.

---

762 African Commission on Human and Peoples' Rights May 2003, *Democratic Republic of Congo v Burundi, Rwanda, Uganda*, no. 227/99.

763 This case is of particular relevance here because the ICJ judged the same conflict.

764 African Commission on Human and Peoples' Rights May 2003, *Democratic Republic of Congo v Burundi, Rwanda, Uganda*, no. 227/99, para. 76.

765 Ibid, paras. 74–75. The Commission refers to the principle that States shall settle their disputes by peaceful means, as confirmed in Article 33 of the UN Charter and Article III of the OAU Charter.

766 The peoples' rights protected in the African Charter include the right to equality (Article 19), the right to self-determination (Article 20), the right to freely dispose of wealth and national resources (Article 21), the right to development (Article 22), the right to peace and security (Article 23) and 'a generally satisfactory environment' (Article 24).

767 African Commission on Human and Peoples' Rights October 2001, *The Social and Economic Rights Action Center and the Center for Economic and Social Rights v Nigeria*, no. 155/96, para. 56.

768 Ibid, para. 69.

With regard to Articles 16 and 24 of the Charter (right to health and right to a general satisfactory environment), the Commission explains that these rights not only oblige the State to refrain from directly threatening the health and environment of its citizens,[769] They also include the positive obligation to take measures to prevent degradation, including the production of prior environmental and social impact studies, the provision of information to all those concerned and, linked to the latter, the opportunity for local communities to participate in the decision-making process.[770] The Commission expressly states that 'the government of Nigeria ... has the right to produce oil, the income from which will be used to fulfil the economic and social rights of Nigerians'.[771] However, because of the direct threat exercised by the State and the lack of prevention measures, it found a violation of Articles 1 and 24. While it recognises that several public interests are at play in this situation, the pursuit of economic benefits does not justify the flagrant degradation of health and environmental conditions in the Ogoni region. It could be said that the Commission indirectly formulates two demands. On the one hand it demands of the State that it fulfils its positive obligation as far as proportional to the different interests that are involved. On the other hand, it asks the State to fulfil certain procedural requirements to ensure that all sources are consulted to prevent violations by private parties.

3.3.4. SUMMARY: COMMON INTEREST NORMS

The question this chapter raised was whether the judicial bodies studied approach common interests that are explicitly protected by the regime in which they operate differently. The ICJ has set up a special category for some of these interests, namely obligations *jus cogens* and *erga omnes*. It is only recently that these concepts have been given some weight in procedural questions; at the substantive level they do not seem to enjoy priority. The ITLOS case law, as could be expected from a Tribunal whose constitutive Treaty provides for the conservation of the marine environment, attaches great importance to environmental concerns. Nevertheless, the Tribunal cautiously balances its environmental concerns with the other obligations and interests of the parties.[772]

---

769 For a case law review of the Commission's interpretation of social, economic and cultural rights, see M. Ssenyonjo, 'Analysing the Economic, Social and Cultural Rights Jurisprudence of the African Commission: 30 Years Since the Adoption of the African Charter' (2011) 29 *Netherlands Quarterly of Human Rights* 358, 358–97.

770 African Commission on Human and Peoples' Rights October 2001, *The Social and Economic Rights Action Center and the Center for Economic and Social Rights v Nigeria*, no. 155/96, paras. 52–53.

771 Ibid, para. 54.

772 Dipla, above n 725, pp 248–49.

In the regional human rights bodies, common interests are used to give more weight to individual rights. For example, the European Court has interpreted the protection of Article 8 to include the prevention of serious environmental pollution by considering the Convention as 'a living instrument'. Nevertheless, or because of this broad interpretation, the Court is extremely prudent in developing its case law on environmental issues and has mainly focused its review on the procedure that preceded the State's decision, leaving a wide margin of appreciation the State to determine whether measures are necessary.

CHAPTER 4

A COMMON APPROACH TO COMMON INTERESTS

4.1. REASONS FOR (IN)CONSISTENCY IN INTERNATIONAL LITIGATION ON COMMON INTERESTS

4.1.1. INTRODUCTION

The introduction to this book highlighted two important evolutions in international law. The first evolution concerns the purpose of international law. International law was established as a system to protect the sovereign State's rights and interests. In spite of its traditional focus on sovereignty, it evolved into a regime that subjects State measures to judicial scrutiny and aims to preserve and protect what is defined as common interests. These interests, such as human rights protection and environmental preservation, were once considered to fall strictly within the sovereign power of the State but are now explicitly recognised as common interests in international law. A second evolution took place at the level of the international judiciary. The vast proliferation of mainly specialised international judicial bodies has led to concerns about the incoherent application of international law and the possible consequences of inconsistent decision making, such as forum shopping. The latter concern is even more pressing in the context of common interest protection because the proliferation of international judicial bodies is incomplete and not every common interest identified in international law is protected by a specialised international court.

Starting from the observations above, the book examined whether there is inconsistency in the international case law that addresses common interests. It explored how respect for common interests is enforced in the proliferated judicial system that exists today. Both in procedural and substantive decisions, similarities and differences were identified in the methods used by the studied courts and tribunals to deal with such interests. At the procedural level, the decisions of the examined judicial bodies show a clear convergence and, in general, an open attitude to interests that go beyond the case-specific jurisdiction of the mechanism. When considering the merits of the dispute, the studied judicial bodies approve and take account of public interest concerns. Growing judicial integration was found in the interpretation of the so-called public interest exceptions. However, it was also established that each institution makes sure to keep the focus of its decision on the consent of the parties and the values protected in the Treaty that grants jurisdiction. Thus, despite the strong focus of this research, which studied only specific natural resource cases, a consistent approach or 'common law of international adjudication' that is used in all decisions on common interests could not be found.[773]

Nevertheless, this section starts from the hypothesis that to counter concerns about the fragmentation of international law in general, and more specifically the protection of common interests in a fragmented system, the approach to common interests in international litigation should be consistent. This is in line with the traditional understanding of constitutionalism in international law as a way of combating the negative effects of fragmentation.[774] From this perspective a holistic international constitution, which includes at the minimum a set of coordinating mechanisms, is necessary to preserve order, stability and values at the international level.[775] Thus, against the background of global constitutionalism, the chapter examines the potential reasons for convergence in the case law and the factors that restrict a consistent approach. Both the elements that affect the (in)consistency of international litigation in general and the elements that specifically affect common interest litigation are discussed. In the next chapter, the hypothesis of global constitutionalism as a remedy for fragmentation will be questioned, and the reasons for (in)consistency that are discussed here will be used to explore alternative approaches.

4.1.2. REASONS FOR (IN)CONSISTENCY

Before turning to the elements that propel and hinder consistent decision making in the context of common interests, three important remarks have to be made. First, there is no single reason that explains why international litigation on common interest is consistent on certain issues and not on others. A multitude of factors influence the decision making of an international court and it is the

---

773 Concept borrowed from Brown, above n 53. It must be noted that Brown only refers to procedural decisions in his study.

774 See, for example, A. Van Aaken, 'Defragmentation of Public International Law through Interpretation: A Methodological Proposal' (2009) 16 *Indiana Journal of Global Legal Studies* 483, 487.

775 Description by Peters, who is critical of this traditional understanding. Peters prefers to describe global constitutionalism as an 'analytical lens for understanding how international law evolves and works'. A. Peters, *Constitutional Fragments: On the Interaction of Constitutionalization and Fragmentation in International Law*, Working Paper Centre for Global Constitutionalism, no. 2, University of St Andrews, 2015, available at <ssrn.com>, 2.

combination of these different factors that guide its decision-making process. Secondly, not all factors are relevant for each decision. Some factors will be decisive in the interpretation of one issue and will hardly play any role before the same tribunal dealing with a different issue. For example, the permanent nature of a judicial body has been shown to have more influence on the decisions on the merits than it has on the interpretation of procedural rules.[776]

Thirdly, when discussing the factors that affect (in)consistency and the effective protection of common interests it is difficult to stay at the purely doctrinal level. Bodansky states that there are at least four perspectives through which international law can be studied.[777] The doctrinal perspective, which was used in the case law study above, focuses on legal validity and justification. How is international law interpreted in a particular context? Can States use international law to promote common interests? It is the 'insider' perspective of international lawyers. The doctrinal perspective is closely related to, but different from, the explanatory perspective, the instrumental perspective and the normative perspective. The explanatory perspective is that of social science and history, it attempts to determine why law develops in a certain way and what the consequences of its operation are. The instrumental perspective tries to determine how the law can be used most effectively to achieve a certain goal. The normative perspective asks what the law should be, *de lege ferenda*, taking account of policy or morality.

The importance of distinguishing between these different perspectives on international law will be further elaborated in the next chapter. In this chapter, it suffices to say that in the discussion on the (in)consistency of international litigation, both the doctrinal perspective and the explanatory perspective will be used. Therefore, international litigation will not only be studied from a theoretical, more clinical, perspective but also as 'law in action'. However, because this is not (and does not aim to be) a socio-legal study, all explanatory claims will be made with the necessary reservations and purely to provide context and background to the studied decisions. To further streamline the discussion, the factors leading to fragmentation or integration of international litigation on common interests are grouped under two headings: factors that affect the consistency of international litigation in general, irrespective of the topic, and factors that are specifically relevant in common interest cases.

---

776 Compare Webb, who devotes multiple pages to this issue in her study on substantive issues (P. Webb, *International Judicial Integration and Fragmentation*, Oxford University Press, Oxford 2013) with Brown, who hardly mentions the issue of permanence in his study on procedural decisions (Brown, above n 53).

777 D. Bodansky, 'Legal Realism and its Discontents' (2015) 28 *Leiden Journal of International Law* 267.

4.1.2.1. *Factors that Affect the Consistency of International Litigation in General*

4.1.2.1.1. Permanence of the Institution

From the start, this study has suggested that the existence of multiple international courts and tribunals is likely to lead to a fragmented approach to common interests. In the introduction, the proliferation of approaches to common interests was linked to the different objectives of the international courts and tribunals. Apart from the objective of the court, the case law examination showed that the element of time, more specifically the age and permanence of the institution, also plays an important role.

The first element that affects the general consistency of a judicial body's case law is its permanence. In other words, whether its members are appointed for a specific period of time or on a case-by-case basis. The judicial bodies examined in this study can be split into two groups, those that have permanent members and those that are composed ad hoc. Of the dispute settlement bodies discussed in this book only two are composed ad hoc, the investment tribunals established under the ICSID and the WTO panels.[778] In contrast to the international ad hoc criminal tribunals, which are set up for a limited time but include a number of permanent judges, both the ICSID and WTO tribunals do not work within a limited time frame but have judges who are appointed for one specific case only.[779]

The choice of an ad hoc composition can be informed by different reasons: the State parties have more control over the dispute settlement proceedings if they are led by an ad hoc tribunal rather than a permanent body and the appointment of experts on the specific issue of the dispute should lead to more expeditious and efficient dispute settlement.[780] Whatever the reason for its composition, different expectations exist for ad hoc and permanent judicial bodies. The aspiration of establishing a permanent judicial body is to elucidate the law in general through the settlement of specific cases, whereas the ad hoc body is set up to settle one specific (cluster of) dispute(s).

The lifespan of the body has an undeniable effect on its reasoning. The expiry date of permanent bodies is not set in advance. On the one hand, this gives them

778 Under the ICSID, the parties must agree to a method of appointment or follow the method outlined in Article 37 of the ICSID Convention. The WTO panels are constituted ad hoc pursuant to the procedures laid down in Article 8 of the DSU.

779 See, for instance, Article 12 of the ICTY Statute on the appointment of permanent judges and UN Security Council resolutions 1503 and 1534 on the completion strategy for the ICTY.

780 Nevertheless, the average time between the final hearing on the merits and the award in ICSID cases was 425 days in 2009. It is, however, assumed that the arbitrators spend much less than 425 days on writing the awards but struggle to fit this task in their busy schedules as the 'best and the brightest in their field'. A. Sinclair, L. Fisher and S. Macrory, 'ICSID Arbitration: How Long Does it Take?' (2009) 4 *Global Arbitration Law Review* 1, 1–5.

the luxury to clarify or alter their arguments in consecutive decisions. On the other hand, the permanent nature of a body may also encourage it to be more cautious in its reasoning. Precedent does, in theory, not exist in international law and permanent judicial bodies do sometimes deviate from their previous decisions. Nevertheless, the fact that a body can be directly confronted with its previous decisions in future litigation on different facts probably makes it less likely to tackle difficult interpretation issues in a broad, generalised manner.

This may explain why permanent bodies often avoid answering controversial legal questions, including questions on common interest issues, if their answer is not absolutely necessary to solve the dispute at hand. The ICJ, for example, is known to act cautiously and restricts its decision to what is strictly necessary to solve the issue at hand. As a consequence, it has been criticised by one of its judges for 'unduly limiting the scope of its analysis'[781] and exercising 'inappropriate self-restraint'.[782]

Nevertheless, the permanent nature and conservative approach of the Court has led to a relatively stable body of case law. The decisions of the ICJ generally integrate new and previous case law and offer a permanent solution for the specific legal issue that is disputed. To illustrate that permanence and consistency are also linked in newer judicial bodies, it is interesting to look at the case law of the ITLOS.[783] Although the Law of the Sea Tribunal has only issued a couple of dozen decisions, its case law forms one consistent body.[784] This is partially explained by the fact that the Tribunal has framed its decisions in existing international law. In its Advisory Opinion on *Responsibilities and obligations of States sponsoring persons and entities with respect to activities in the Area*, for example, the Tribunal referred to and integrated not only its own case law, but also that of the ICJ to establish the applicability of the precautionary approach as included in Principle 15 of the Rio Declaration.[785]

The ad hoc bodies discussed in this study (the ICSID tribunals and the WTO panels) are dissolved once the specific dispute for which they were constituted is settled.[786] Because different arbitrators are chosen to settle each specific

---

781 ICJ, *Case of Accordance with International Law of the Unilateral Declaration of Independence in respect of Kosovo, Declaration of Judge Simma*, Judgment of 2010, para. 3.

782 ICJ, *Case of Oil Platforms (Islamic Republic of Iran v United States of America), Judgment, Separate Opinion Judge Simma*, Judgment of 2003, para. 6.

783 This tribunal issued its first decisions in 1997 and has a limited list of cases (22 cases at the time of writing).

784 See extensively on the consistency of ITLOS case law, I. Karaman, *Dispute Resolution in the Law of the Sea*, Martinus Nijhoff Publishers, Leiden 2012, p 400.

785 ITLOS Seabed Disputes Chamber, *Case of Responsibilities and obligations of States sponsoring persons and entities with respect to activities in the Area, Advisory Opinion*, paras. 132, 135.

786 This is not always the case. Ad hoc criminal tribunals, such as the ICTY, were established to decide on a number of specified crimes that happened in a certain time and place. They are not established for one or multiple disputes that are identified in advance but work with a completion strategy to deal with specific crimes linked to a specific conflict.

dispute ad hoc, there is less incentive to follow previous decisions of other ad hoc or permanent judicial bodies. On the contrary, the arbitrators are expected to be innovative in their approach and to offer fast and practical answers to difficult legal questions. This logic certainly applies to the ICSID panels, whose main function is to solve a specific dispute in the most efficient manner and not to develop a body of case law. The ad hoc WTO panels, in contrast, have a compelling reason to follow previous case law. Their decisions can be appealed before a permanent court, the WTO AB. To avoid an appeal, they have to align their decisions with the AB's case law.

When comparing the ICSID case law to that of the examined permanent institutions, it is confirmed that ad hoc arbitration is linked to a less uniform body of case law. At times, the case law of the ICSID tribunals is squarely inconsistent. One example of inconsistency that is closely related to the issue of common interests is the ICSID case law on the NT standard.[787] State measures may be exempted from this non-discrimination standard in international investment law if they are based on a public interest. The examination of the NT standard by different ICSID tribunals has revealed major differences in interpretation concerning the required link between the alleged public interest objective and the contested State measure. While one tribunal demanded that a reasonable nexus be established, another found a plausible connection between interest and measure sufficient to conclude that the public interest measure was necessary.[788] This case law example shows that ad hoc tribunals can be rather bold in their interpretation and enjoy great freedom to accept or deny public interest measures in specific circumstances. Thus, the typical characteristics of an ad hoc tribunal may have a negative effect on the consistency of the regime's consideration of common interests.

4.1.2.1.2. Body of Case Law of the Institution

The volume of case law that an institution has produced is another important factor that affects a judicial body's line of reasoning, its tendency to stability and certainty or differentiation and progress. Despite the obvious inconsistencies that were addressed above, the case law of the ICSID tribunals has been shown to evolve into a more consistent body of law with the passing of time. With age comes a more extensive body of case law and, because conflicting decisions are considered to threaten the legitimacy of a dispute settlement regime, a larger body of case law leads to consistency. A 2009 ICSID Tribunal confirmed that 'the harmonious development of investment law' is necessary to 'meet the legitimate expectations of the community of States and investors towards certainty of the

[787] See pp 102ff.
[788] Ibid.

rule of law'.[789] It should be noted that, in this context, it is not the sheer number of decisions but the number of publicly available decisions on different subjects that is important.[790]

The element of time seems to have an important influence on the consistency of decisions within one specific regime, but it is questionable whether the difference between ad hoc and permanent or new and old bodies translates into a less or more consistent approach to common interests. Although permanence and age seem to have a positive influence on the consistency of the case law within the institution, they do not predict a long-term consistent approach to common interests across different regimes.

On the contrary, when a body of case law is long established and highly developed, it could be argued that the judicial body will be less likely to be inspired by the decisions of other judicial bodies. Furthermore, the judicial bodies will have a hard time settling disputes over issues that were not envisaged at their establishment and never considered in previous decisions. In her book on judicial integration and fragmentation, Webb develops the theory that the stage of development of a legal rule is inversely proportional to the leeway for interpretation of the judicial body.[791] To put it simply, when a detailed Treaty provision or extensive jurisprudence already exists on the discussed issue, the court has little space for interpretation. In contrast, the judicial body has more freedom to interpret vague Treaty provisions and customary law that has not yet been the subject of many judicial decisions. Thus, while the case law of new tribunals is sometimes inconsistent but open to change, the case law of more permanent and older institutions is more extensive, detailed and regime specific.

Many of the bodies discussed in this study are relatively new. Aside from the ICJ and the regional human rights bodies, the examined judiciaries have only started truly functioning in the past 20 years.[792] The oldest and most established institution is the ICJ, which is approaching its 70th birthday and has issued more than 100 decisions. Aside from the ICJ, the WTO and the ECtHR have the most developed jurisprudence. This can be illustrated by their case law on public interest exceptions. The WTO interpretation of the General Exceptions Article XX of the GATT has, over time, clarified the scope of that Article in great detail and dictates each step that the WTO panel has to take to determine

789 ICSID, *Saipem S.P.A. Claimant v the People's Republic of Bangladesh, Award*, 30.06.2009, para. 90.

790 ICSID only publishes decisions with the consent of the parties but it now actively seeks this consent, sometimes only for excerpts of the legal reasoning.

791 Webb, above n 776, pp 177–79.

792 Although the first reported ICSID arbitration dates back to 1972, only 29 of the approximately 500 reported ICSID cases were registered before 1994 (<icsid.worldbank.org>, last accessed June 2015).

whether or not a State measure falls within that exception.[793] The same is true for the ECtHR's case law on the public interest exceptions to the right to property. Through a number of decisions that are explicitly linked to each other the Court has developed a set of detailed tests to determine whether a State measure violates the right to property.[794] Although the case law of more permanent bodies does change and evolve over time, the high level of detail within each regime does not to leave much room for integration across regimes.

It can be concluded that the temporal element works on two levels. First, there is a difference between bodies that have a permanent function and tribunals that are established ad hoc. Secondly, there is a difference in dispute settlement between old and new judicial bodies. Because it takes some time to develop a true body of case law and to link the interpretation of different Treaty provisions, the case law of a newer institution is often incoherent. It is only with time that a clear line of reasoning starts to form. This more detailed interpretation often leads to more consistency within a regime. However, it may also make it harder to introduce new elements that are external to the regime, such as common interest concerns, and to accomplish consistency across different regimes.

4.1.2.1.3. Community of International Lawyers

One curious aspect of international litigation is that it involves a relatively small group of individuals. Judges often work across different regimes and lawyers that have made a career within one specific regime have often enjoyed a general international law education. Aside from the actors directly involved in a specific dispute, the individuals and groups that exercise external pressure on different courts and tribunals often also belong to the same small club. Although the identity of the actors involved does not have a theoretical, doctrinal, influence on the decisions of the judicial body, it may provide some insight into the consistency of international litigation in general. As stated above, this explanatory perspective is only explored to provide context and no empirical research has been done on this issue.

The 'global community of courts' that Slaughter described a decade ago was based on the idea that all courts have the same function: they are established to solve disputes on the basis of the rule of law. According to her theory on domestic courts, this element is more crucial for the professional identity of the judges and arbitrators than the law they apply. Because judges of different countries see each other as colleagues, a high level of consistency is developing

---

793 See above, pp 89ff.

794 See above, pp 120ff.

between the jurisprudence of States with different domestic laws.[795] Nevertheless, it is uncertain whether Slaughter's theory applies equally to a functionally fragmented system.

At the global level, different legal regimes can be distinguished on the basis of geography (local, national, regional, international, etc.) and function (trade, human rights, etc.). These international legal regimes can be differentiated on the basis of their common institution (like the WTO), common framework Treaty (such as the UN Charter) or shared ethos (for instance human rights protection).[796] Furthermore, each regime has its own community to which its judges and arbitrators belong. In international relations theory, this community is described as an epistemic community.[797] An epistemic community is a community of experts in a specific field that influences its field because it has an authoritative claim to knowledge within its field.

The members of an epistemic community share an understanding on four elements that are decisive in interpretation. First, they share the same normative beliefs that underpin the interpretation of norms in their regime. Secondly, they identify the same links between actions and outcomes in their regime. Thirdly, they use the same criteria for weighing and validating knowledge in their regime. And lastly, they support a 'common policy enterprise'. In other words, they want to solve the problems, for which their regime was established, in the same way. These shared beliefs lead to a common interpretation of the legal norms that they use.[798]

In tandem with the establishment of a number of functional regimes and accompanying epistemic communities in international law, education as well as scholarly work is increasingly specialising and technocratic expertise of one of the specialised regimes is highly valued. As a consequence, new members are more than ever chosen on the basis of their specialisation. The personnel of different institutions (arbitrators or judges and support staff) increasingly has a different professional background and motivation.[799] Thus, the existence of different epistemic communities is supposedly leading to an increasingly greater divide between different interpretive approaches in international law. This claim can be illustrated by the fact that epistemic communities defend their own interpretation over that of other epistemic communities. For example, in the *US – Shrimp* case, the WTO AB chose to read the GATT 'in light of' the concerns

795 Slaughter, above n 85, 193.

796 M. Waibel, *Interpretive Communities in International Law*, Legal Studies Research Paper Series, no. 62, University of Cambridge, 2014, available at <ssrn.com> (published in *Interpretation in International Law*, Cambridge University Press, Cambridge 2014), 4.

797 Ibid, 5. The role of other interpreters, including national courts and legal advisers, staff of international organisations and different non-state actors is not discussed here.

798 Ibid, 6–7.

799 DiMascio and J. Pauwelyn, above n 535, 59.

expressed in the law of another regime rather than recognising that the law of that regime was *lex specialis*, as the US claimed.[800]

However, it could be argued that most actors are not only part of the specialised epistemic community in which they function at the moment but, by training and background, also belong to the broader community of international lawyers that all have the same goal of solving disputes on the basis of the rule of law.[801] This explains, for example, the overall use of the VCLT interpretation principles that was discussed earlier.[802] As former President of the ICJ Dame Rosalyn Higgins pointed out, the feeling of community between international judges has the consequence that international courts go to great lengths to be consistent with decisions of other international judicial bodies, and to follow the jurisprudence of the ICJ.[803]

The existence of a broader community seems more open ended and less defining for international law than the existence of epistemic communities. Nevertheless, it is a fact that international lawyers constitute a relatively small club of people who frequently move from one dispute settlement mechanism to another. The individuals that have served as judge or counsel before different institutions illustrate that international judges are often experts in different fields of international law. Some renowned judges that have experience as judges in different institutions are Steve Schwebel (ICJ, World Bank and IMF), James Crawford (ICJ, ICSID) and Gerald Fitzmaurice (ICJ, ECtHR). Especially in connected regimes, such as international trade and investment law, there are many lawyers that work in different regimes. Of the 26 WTO AB members that were appointed between 1994 and 2014, at least 10 have also served as arbitrators in international investment disputes.[804]

This transfer of people and knowledge across regimes has a harmonising effect. It is only logical that lawyers refer to all the relevant case law they know, inside or outside of the relevant regime, when building a legal reasoning. Similarly, most international judges consider themselves to be members of the general international judiciary and use their knowledge of different legal regimes when trying to reach a decision. In the ICSID dispute of *Continental Casualty v Argentine Republic*, for instance, the Tribunal had to determine whether the disputed measures were necessary to protect the public interest of Argentina. Instead of following the international customary law interpretation of necessity,

---

800 WTO Appellate Body Report, *United States – Import Prohibition of Certain Shrimp and Shrimp Products*, WT/DS58/AB/R, adopted 12.10.1998, paras. 129–30.

801 As described in Slaughter, above n 85, 193.

802 It specifically explains the use of these principles in the interpretation of Treaties ratified before the VCLT came into force.

803 R. Higgins, 'A Babel of Judicial Voices? Ruminations from the Bench' (2006) 55 *International and Comparative Law Quarterly* 791, 797.

804 J. Pauwelyn, *WTO Panelists Are from Mars, ICSID Arbitrators Are from Venus – Why? And Does It Matter?*, Working Paper, 2015, available at <ssrn.com>, 3.

the test used by the Tribunal to determine necessity was explicitly modelled after the WTO's jurisprudence on necessity under Article XX GATT.[805] This extensive reference to WTO case law can easily be explained by the fact that the Tribunal was led by a former WTO AB judge, Giorgio Sacerdoti.

Although not all judicial bodies are eager to refer to the case law of courts and tribunals operating in different regimes, the membership of judges with different backgrounds leads to consistency in international law. This is especially true when the decision-making process involves most or all members of the Bench. In the ICJ, for instance, all the members are truly involved in each decision and attempt to reach a consensus.[806] While the ICJ generally refuses to explicitly quote other international judicial bodies, the opinions of ICJ judges show how its reasoning is consistent with the case law of other institutions.[807] Although, on the one hand, a setting like the ICJ makes it difficult to come to a decision and references to the case law of other judicial bodies are often avoided in order to reach a decision, on the other hand, the interaction of lawyers with different backgrounds promotes coherence in international litigation.

4.1.2.2. Factors that Are Specifically Relevant for Common Interest Litigation

4.1.2.2.1. Objective of the Institution

Whereas the age and permanence of an institution affect the consistency of its case law in general, the objective of a judicial body has a specific effect on the consideration of common interests across different regimes. In this context, objective refers to the purpose for which the institution was established. Most international judicial bodies are established to enforce the application of one particular Treaty or a set of Treaties on a specific subject, for example the African Charter on Human and Peoples' Rights (ACHPR) or international trade law (WTO DSM). This implies that they have to solve disputes on the basis of the Treaties that they were designed to enforce, even if the dispute covers multiple issues that would be better discussed in different fora. Even the ICJ, which has general jurisdiction, must restrict itself to interpreting one specific Treaty in many instances due to the principle of consensual jurisdiction. When the parties come before the ICJ on the basis of a compulsory clause in a Treaty or on the

805 ICSID, *Continental Casualty Company v the Argentine Republic, Award,* ICSID case no. ARB/03/9, 05.09.2008, paras. 192–95.

806 See Resolution concerning the Internal Judicial Practice of the Court of 12 April 1976, available at <www.icj-cij.org>.

807 See, for example, ICJ, *Case of Gabčíkovo-Nagymaros Project (Hungary/Slovakia), Judgment, Separate Opinion Judge Weeramantry,* Judgment of 1997, para. 140.

basis of an agreement between the parties, the jurisdiction of the ICJ is restricted to interpreting one or multiple specific Treaties.[808] This limitation to the Court's jurisdiction can be illustrated by referring to the *Gabčíkovo* dispute between Hungary and Slovakia.[809] Because the jurisdiction of the Court in this case was based on an agreement between the parties to solve their dispute in light of a bilateral Treaty, the ICJ had to limit itself to the interpretation of that Treaty. Consequently, it refrained from further developing IEL in the *Gabčíkovo* case. Instead, the Court ordered the parties to reinterpret certain provisions included in their bilateral Treaty, taking account of the common interest of environmental protection.[810]

Other than limiting the scope of the decision of the court, the focus of some international judicial bodies on one type of Treaty may also lead to a functional bias. In short, a functional bias means that a court is more likely to come to decisions that enforce the regime for which they were established. This functional bias can be explained from two perspectives. First there is the doctrinal perspective. From this perspective, it can be noted that common interests are often protected by way of exception clauses in Treaties that are not written with the objective of protecting that interest. Because exceptions are generally interpreted restrictively, judicial bodies could have a functional bias because of the way the Treaties they interpret are constructed. The second, explanatory, perspective offers a hypothetical but more plausible explanation of functional bias. It states that a court with specific jurisdiction over one Treaty has to ensure that the relevant Treaty has effect; otherwise it endangers its own relevance for the future. Following this reasoning, the court is likely to enforce the interests protected by its regime over conflicting interests.

A good example of functional bias can be found in the comparison of the case law on property protection before the human rights courts and property protection of individuals who are not investors before the ICSID tribunals. The IACtHR has on multiple occasions favoured the protection of the human rights (of indigenous peoples) over the property rights of investors protected by the State. This was illustrated in the examined cases of *Awas Tingni v Nicaragua, Yakye Axa v Paraguay, Saramaka People v Suriname* and *Sawhoyamaxa Indigenous Community v Paraguay*.[811] The African Commission on Human and Peoples Rights has developed similar case law in the *Endorois* case.[812] In contrast, investment tribunals have shown less intention to protect the human rights of

808 This is different when both parties have recognised the ICJ's compulsory jurisdiction by declaration, but at the moment only 71 States have deposited such a declaration (declarations available at <www.icj-cij.org>).

809 ICJ, *Case of Gabčíkovo-Nagymaros Project (Hungary/Slovakia), Judgment*, Judgment of 1997.

810 See above, pp 132ff.

811 See pp 126ff.

812 See pp 128ff.

non-investors. In *Glamis Gold*, for example, the arbitral Tribunal did not seem to consider the human rights impact of the mining investment on the indigenous community.[813]

As illustrated above, the task and objective of the judicial body impacts its consideration of common interest on two levels. First, many international judicial institutions are established to protect the values of one specific Treaty or regime. As a consequence, the Treaty or agreement that offers jurisdiction to a specialised court often limits the scope of its jurisdiction to one set of Treaties. This limited jurisdiction makes it harder for judicial bodies to justify taking account of common interest rules that are external to their regime. Secondly, there is the element of functional bias. Even if the judicial body states that it will interpret the rules of its own regime in light of international law, it is likely that it will still prefer to protect the objectives of its regime over other objectives. The specific purpose for which most international judicial bodies were established, therefore, hinders the consistent consideration of common interests in the litigation of different regimes.

4.1.2.2.2. Similar Legal Rules

A second important factor that determines the consistency of common interest approaches of different international institutions is the law. When the applicable law of multiple regimes is similar, this may lead to consistent interpretation because, as discussed above, international judicial bodies use the same interpretation techniques and similar provisions promote cross-referencing between regimes. There are several levels of similarity that are relevant here. The first level is the interpretation of identical law. Despite the concerns over overlapping jurisdiction that are sometimes voiced in debates on the dangers of fragmentation in international law, the case law review did not find any examples of natural resource cases in which two international judicial bodies were asked to make a decision on the basis of exactly the same set of legal rules.

The examination of common interest cases did find many examples of international judicial bodies interpreting functionally similar law. This second level of similarity is seen especially in the procedural rules of different regimes. In other words, it is highly relevant for the applicants and *amicus curiae* that aim to introduce common interests in international litigation. The study has shown that there is a high level of consistency in procedural rules.[814] This is not surprising because the provisions included in the constitutive documents of international

[813] Example discussed in E. de Wet and J. Vidmar, *Conflicts between International Paradigms: Hierarchy Versus Systemic Integration*, Pre-publication Paper, 2013, available at <ssrn.com> (published in (2013) 2 *Global Constitutionalism*, 196–217), 17.

[814] See pp 39ff.

courts are often inspired by the procedural rules of older institutions. Many recent procedural rules were based on the tried and tested provisions included in the ICJ Statute. This is most obviously the case in the ITLOS Statute, but the procedural rules included in the ICSID and the Statute of the ECtHR were also inspired by the ICJ Statute.[815] In turn, the original rules of procedure of the IACtHR were modelled after those of the ECtHR.

In the context of substantive provisions, functionally similar rules are often found in Treaties on the same topic applicable in different regions or countries. Examples abound in the regional human rights Treaties and in international investment agreements. It is less common to find exactly the same rights or obligations in international Treaties that cover different topics. Nevertheless, there is a third level of similarity that can be found across regimes. This is what I define as similar constructions. These constructions serve essentially the same purpose. The most relevant example here is the collection of public interest exceptions that can be found in international Treaty law. Public interest provisions determine when State measures may trump the rights or obligations included in the Treaty. They often describe the rule and include an exception for measures that are necessary to protect the public interest in the same provision.

The fact that different regimes include similar legal provisions does not necessitate a consistent interpretation of these provisions across regimes. In the same vein, textual differences in provisions on the same topic do not prevent consistent interpretations. Nevertheless, the similarity of legal provisions is a factor that triggers the consideration of the case law of other regimes, which leads to consistency in international litigation. This is extremely relevant in the context of common interests because, as was argued above, many of the provisions that are used to introduce common interests are similar across regimes.

4.1.2.2.3. Article 31(3)(c) VCLT

All of the examined international judicial bodies use the same general principles of Treaty interpretation. These principles are codified in Articles 31–33 VCLT and are considered to be customary rules of international law.[816] The VCLT provisions cover the general principle of interpretation, the supplementary means of interpretation and the interpretation of Treaties in two or more languages. Reference to the VCLT rules can be found in the case law of each

815 Brown, above n 53, p 226.

816 ICJ, *Case concerning the Territorial Dispute (Libyan Arab Jamahiriya/Chad), Judgment* Judgment of 1994, para. 41.

of the studied bodies.[817] Interpretation principles help to determine which meaning should be given to a legal rule. The VCLT principles determine that a Treaty should be interpreted in light of its context as well as its object and purpose and that any relevant rules of international law applicable between the parties should be taken into account. Especially the latter rule is important in facilitating the consideration of common interests in international litigation. In the *Oil Platforms* case, for example, the ICJ referred to Article 31(3)(c) of the VCLT in its determination of jurisdiction. The jurisdiction of the Court in this case was based on a bilateral Treaty on amity, economic relations and consular rights. The US contented that this Treaty did not offer the Court jurisdiction to decide on the US's use of force in the conflict with Iran. The ICJ, however, judged that in light of the VCLT principles the Treaty could not be seen as independent from the relevant rules of international law. Therefore, it decided that it did have jurisdiction over the issues relating to the use of force between the parties.[818]

Another principle of interpretation that is often used by courts that are willing to bring common interests into the equation and that is subsumed in Article 31(3)(c) VCLT is the principle of evolutionary interpretation.[819] Evolutionary interpretation is prompted by the element of change, which is linked to the growing importance of common interests. Change may act as a catalyst for fragmentation. When judicial bodies struggle to adapt their existing jurisprudence to changing conditions such as globalisation and the increasingly acute urge to protect certain common goods, it is necessary for them to act in a more proactive and creative manner that potentially leads to fragmentation.[820] However, the case law examination has shown that the fact that all bodies have to deal with similar changes may also bring them closer together. The principle of evolutionary interpretation has introduced the same interests in multiple fora. The issue of environmental protection was included in the case law of both the ECtHR and the IACtHR, mainly through an evolutionary interpretation of the

817 A small selection of examined cases that explicitly use Articles 31–33 VCLT include: ICJ, *Case of Pulp Mills on the River Uruguay (Argentina v Uruguay), Judgment*, Judgment of 2010, paras. 64–65; ITLOS Seabed Disputes Chamber, *Case of Responsibilities and obligations of States sponsoring persons and entities with respect to activities in the Area, Advisory Opinion*, para. 57; WTO Appellate Body Report, *United States – Measures concerning the Importation, Marketing and Sale of Tuna and Tuna Products*, WT/DS381/AB/R, adopted 16.05.2012, paras. 212, 371; Inter-American Court of Human Rights, *Case of Yakye Axa Indigenous Community v Paraguay*, Judgment of 17.06.2005, paras. 125–126. The ECtHR has accepted since *Golder* that the Convention should be interpreted using the principles of the VCLT (ECtHR 21.02.1975, *Golder v the United Kingdom*, no. 4451/70, para. 29).

818 ICJ, *Case of Oil Platforms (Islamic Republic of Iran v United States of America), Judgment*, Judgment of 2003, para. 41.

819 G. Marceau, 'WTO Dispute Settlement and Human Rights' (2002) 13 *European Journal of International Law* 753, 784.

820 Webb, above n 776, pp 179–80.

human rights included in the relevant Treaties.[821] Likewise, the WTO AB stated in the *US – Shrimp* case that '[the words of Article XX(g)] must be read by a Treaty interpreter in the light of contemporary concerns of the community of nations about the protection and conservation of the environment'.[822]

However, the VCLT principles are not directives that automatically lead to one result. There exists no step-by-step guide for interpreting international Treaties; instead international judges instinctively use the different interpretation principles included in the VCLT in a flexible way. This 'indeterminate process' of interpretation may lead to inconsistent results.[823] Furthermore, it has been argued that the VCLT principles are often only referred to in order to legitimise the approach of the court or tribunal, without integrating the existing jurisprudence on the VCLT rules.[824] Courts and tribunals are accused of using these widely accepted principles of interpretation to increase their legitimacy, but achieve the outcomes they desire.[825] Thus, like the similarity of the law, the use of the VCLT principles of interpretation does not guarantee more consistency, but at least it promotes the consideration of other relevant law.

4.1.2.2.4. Relationship between Judicial Body and Other Actors

Another element that affects the common interest case law of different judicial bodies is the relationship between the different actors. This relationship is defined by who is allowed to initiate or intervene in the proceedings and who has access to internal or external means of pressure. In domestic systems, the independence and authority of a judicial body is conditioned by a mechanism of State control, a mechanism that prevents abuse of power by the court. However, in international law this mechanism is often ineffective. In contrast to domestic systems, it is very difficult for States to correct judicial decisions by lawmaking at the international level.[826] International politics make international lawmaking a slow and tedious process and only exceptionally a regime, like the

---

821 Although the ACHR includes a right to a healthy environment, this right does not give access to the Commission or the Court to individuals. See R. Pavoni, *Environmental Jurisprudence of the European and Inter-American Courts of Human Rights: Comparative Insights*, Pre-publication Draft, 2013, available at <ssrn.com> (published in *The Environmental Law Dimensions of Human Rights*, Oxford University Press, Oxford 2015).

822 WTO Appellate Body Report, *United States – Import Prohibition of Certain Shrimp and Shrimp Products*, WT/DS58/AB/R, adopted 12.10.1998, para. 129.

823 Van Damme, 'Treaty Interpretation by the WTO Appellate Body', above n 123, 617.

824 See, for example, the divergent use of the VCLT principles by ICSID tribunals, discussed in, above n 114, 301–64.

825 Waibel, above n 796, 33–34.

826 For a detailed explanation of why internal and external controls on international judicial bodies are often ineffective see J. Cogan, 'Competition and Control in International Adjudication' (2008) 48 *Virginia Journal of International Law* 411, 411–450.

NAFTA investment agreement, has a system of interpretative guidelines that is binding.[827] Nevertheless, international judicial bodies are susceptible to (third) party pressure because they need litigants, who keep bringing them cases, and compliance partners, who ensure that their decisions are followed in practice by exercising pressure on the State.[828]

The discussed case law showed that international judicial bodies sometimes change their jurisprudence to please potential litigants as well as other third parties. One well-documented example of an international court that succumbed to State pressure on a procedural issue is the WTO AB. In *EC – Asbestos*, on the French import ban on asbestos and asbestos products, the WTO disseminated procedural rules for *amicus curiae* participation at the start of the proceedings.[829] The WTO members, however, were displeased with this formal recognition of non-State interventions in common interest cases. As a consequence, the panels and AB have since then only explicitly considered those *amicus curiae* interventions that were endorsed by one of the litigating parties. Another example concerning the same procedural issue is the case law of the ICSID tribunals. In the first *Argentina* cases the tribunals did not accept *amicus curiae* decisions. However, after repeated requests for transparency by civil society in cases such as *Aguas del Tunari* and *Aguas Argentinas*, the ICSID tribunals in later cases interpreted Article 44 of the ICSID Convention to allow the tribunal the discretionary power to accept *amicus curiae* submissions.[830] Subsequently, the State parties amended the ICSID Arbitration Rules to explicitly allow third party interventions.[831]

The examples above show that State pressure and public pressure do not necessarily lead to consistent case law. One reason for this is that the actors do not exercise the same amount and type of pressure on different institutions. This is true for both internal and external pressure. States have different institutional powers, in other words means of internal pressure, in different institutions. In some systems more power is given to the States than in others. At the WTO level, for instance, the State parties have the power to reject a panel or AB report

---

827 The Free Trade Commission, composed of representatives of the NAFTA parties, may issue interpretation that or binding for the NAFTA tribunals. North American Free Trade Agreement of 1 January 1994, 32 ILM 289, 605 (1993).

828 On the importance of compliance partners for internationals courts and tribunals see K.J. Alter, *The New Terrain of International Law: Courts, Politics, Rights*, Princeton University Press, Princeton, NJ 2013.

829 WTO Appellate Body Report, *European Communities – Measures affecting Asbestos and Asbestos-containing Products*, WT/DS135/AB/R, adopted 12.03.2001.

830 For instance, ICSID, *Aguas Argentinas, S.A., Suez, Sociedad General de Aguas de Barcelona, S.A. and Vivendi Universal, S.A. v the Argentine Republic, Order in Response to a Petition for Transparency and Participation as Amicus Curiae*, ICSID case no. ARB/03/19, 19.05.2005.

831 Rule 37 Convention on the Settlement of Investment Disputes Between States and Nationals of Other States of 14 October 1966, UN Treaty Series, vol. 575, 159.

by consensus.[832] The level of external pressure that both State and non-State actors can exercise also depends on the institution. External pressure has greater potential when there is direct competition between different institutions. When there is exclusive, compulsory jurisdiction, a strong enforcement mechanism, no reasonable option to withdraw and no lack of litigants, the judicial body will have few incentives to take account of external actors. If only some or none of these conditions are fulfilled, the court or tribunal will automatically be more susceptible to external pressure.

4.2. PROMOTING RESPECT FOR COMMON INTERESTS IN INTERNATIONAL LITIGATION

This chapter started from the hypothesis that a consistent approach to common interest issues in international litigation is preferable to a pluralistic approach. The traditional understanding of global constitutionalism assumes that both the consistency of international law and the protection of common interests would benefit from (at minimum) a set of coordinating mechanisms.[833] This assumption is questioned below. How could such a consistent answer be promoted and is it truly beneficial for the protection of common interests to develop a consistent answer to common interest issues? To answer these questions, the benefits of several promising options for reaching common interest protection as well as consistency will first be examined. The coordination of the case law of various courts and tribunals could be achieved through techniques used in domestic systems or by cross-reference between the judicial bodies.

However, a common approach could also take a different form. It could imply that courts and tribunals use the same decision-making tools, without necessarily coordinating their solutions. One way to achieve this is by systematically bouncing back the compromise of interests to the litigating States by imposing a duty to cooperate in protecting the common interest. Another consistent method of dealing with common interest cases within each regime is reaching a compromise of interests on the basis of proportionality balancing. But (under which circumstances) could the latter options lead to an effective protection of the common interests that are identified under international law? At the end of the chapter, the discussed common approaches will be compared to a pluralistic approach. Is a common approach really preferable or are common interests better protected in a (further) fragmented judicial order?

---

832 Articles 16(4), 17(14) Understanding on Rules and Procedures Governing the Settlement of Disputes, Marrakesh Agreement Establishing the World Trade Organization, Annex 2 of 15 April 1994, UN Treaty Series, vol. 1869, 401.

833 Description by Peters, who is critical of this traditional understanding. PETERS, above n 775, 2.

The latter question will be answered from a normative perspective. In the previous chapter, a distinction was drawn between the different perspectives on international law. Four perspectives were briefly highlighted: the doctrinal perspective that studies how the existing law can justify specific actions; the explanatory perspective that tries to explain why law develops in a certain way; the instrumental perspective that sees the law as a toolbox that may help to reach a desired outcome; and the normative perspective that is used to propose new rules on the basis of policy or morality.[834] It is only possible to have a full understanding of the law by taking account of all four of the perspectives mentioned above. Nevertheless, it is necessary to make a distinction between these perspectives and to clarify what questions are being answered.[835]

In the previous chapter the doctrinal perspective was combined with legal realism, which adopts an explanatory perspective. Although legal realism is highly attractive because it is realistic, it can devolve into an apology for the status quo. Although it is valuable and necessary to examine the law in action, in other words from an explanatory perspective, it is often the expression of ideals that sets the wheels in motion and contributing to an idealistic doctrine in the long run often leads to the realisation of that ideal.

4.2.1. COORDINATION TECHNIQUES

4.2.1.1. Vertical Coordination: Hierarchy

As stated in the introduction, the coordination of the case law of the existing judicial bodies is often suggested to counter the dangers of proliferation of international judicial bodies in general. One practical solution for coordinating international case law is introducing a vertical hierarchy between international judicial bodies. This can be accomplished by introducing a new global review mechanism or by appointing a highest court among the existing courts and tribunals. Several authors have elaborated the latter option with the ICJ, currently the only court with a general competence, at the top of the ladder. Since the end

---

834 Bodansky, above n 777.

835 This is important for two reasons. First, it is important to explicitly identify what perspective is taken to understand that this is not the only possible perspective. Secondly, it avoids the answer to a specific issue being questioned on the basis of observations made under other perspectives. For example, from a doctrinal perspective it could be stated that a court will find a public interest exception to be justified when the disputed measure is legal, in the public interest and proportional to that interest. From an explanatory perspective, however, it could be argued that a court is more likely to grant a public interest exception if the public interest is in line with the personal values of the judges. In this example both observations could be correct. Although the socio-legal observation provides insight into the application of the doctrine, it does not undermine the doctrinal answer.

of the previous century, scholars have suggested that it is necessary to strengthen the ICJ's functions as the central judiciary body of the international community. Proposals have gone from recognising the ICJ as an appellate body to developing a procedure in which the ICJ issues advisory opinions on cases that are pending before other institutions or recognising the ICJ as a *tribunal des conflits*.[836]

However, it is hard to imagine how any of these suggestions could be implemented. First, the contentious jurisdiction of the Court is consensual and limited to States. This is different from many of the institutions that would be lower in hierarchy but do enjoy compulsory jurisdiction and provide access to non-State parties.[837] Secondly, the implementation of any of these suggestions requires an amendment of the ICJ Statute. This requires a two-thirds majority of the UN members, many of them not in favour of expanding the Court's jurisdiction.[838] Thirdly, further expanding the role of the ICJ would either increase its backlog or lower the quality of its decisions and consequently have a negative impact on the length and quality of proceedings before other courts.[839] Besides the issue of feasibility, it is uncertain whether appointing a highest court would have a positive effect on the enforcement of common interests or whether its function, authority and permanence would lead it be extremely prudent and conservative in its decisions.[840]

4.2.1.2. Horizontal Coordination: Procedural and Private International Law Rules

Another approach to dealing with issues that could be brought before multiple international judicial institutions is by using ad hoc horizontal coordination techniques.[841] The main coordination technique that is used at the level of domestic courts is a combination of procedural exceptions (*lis pendens*, *electio fori* and *res judicata*) and private international law. However, domestic coordination

---

836 Referring to the option of the ICJ as a supreme court: Judge Gilbert Guillaume, Speech by the President of the International Court of Justice to the Sixth Committee of the General Assembly of the United Nations 27.10.2000. On the ICJ and advisory opinions: Judge Stephen M. Schwebel, Adress by the President of the International Court of Justice to the Plenary session of the General Assembly of the United Nations, 26.10.1999. On the ICJ as a *tribunal des conflits*: Dupuy, above n 12, 798ff.

837 Webb develops this argument in the context of the relationship between the ICJ and the ad hoc criminal tribunals. Webb, n 776, p 211.

838 Articles 108–09 Charter of the United Nations of 26 June 1945, Treaty Series, 993.

839 Webb argues that this can only be countered by additional staff (and resources), which the Court had not received in previous years (Webb, above n 776, p 212).

840 See p 152.

841 Suggested in J. Vinuales and P.-M. Dupuy, *The Challenge of 'Proliferation': An Anatomy of the Debate*, Working Paper, 2012, available at <ssrn.com> (published in *The Oxford Handbook of International Adjudication*, Oxford University Press, Oxford 2014), 10.

techniques do not work in the international law context because they are not designed to function properly in a fragmented system. Private international law only functions in a system of parallel legal systems that offer solutions for the same legal issues and not in a system of specialised regimes that focus on different legal issues. In the same vein, procedural exceptions can only operate in an integrated legal system where, at minimum, the litigants are the same parties.[842] A second problem with these horizontal coordination techniques is that they offer a binary result. Although multiple Treaties may be relevant for solving the dispute at hand, only one Treaty regime will be considered to be applicable.[843]

4.2.1.3. Coordination through Judicial Dialogue

An alternative solution would be to attribute a more informal guiding role to the ICJ. The ICJ judges themselves could create this leading role by exercising a proactive role in the interpretation of international law. Rather than avoiding difficult legal issues and only focusing on the specific circumstances of the case before them, they could take it upon themselves to clarify the law that is likely to be applied by other international judicial bodies.[844] Furthermore, the ICJ could take the lead in organising inter-judicial dialogue. Informal communication between international judicial bodies through seminars and forwarding relevant case law is probably the easiest method to achieve coherence in international litigation, but it holds no guarantees because it completely relies on the relations between judges. Although in practice there seems to be increasing cross-reference between international courts, it is not clear whether international courts and tribunals would be willing to take part in an inter-judicial dialogue that includes all international courts and tribunals (not only the most prestigious). Furthermore, initial enthusiasm often fades rapidly in an informal cooperation, all the more so when the workload of the different partners is substantial and there is a large physical distance between those involved.

4.2.1.4. Harmonious Interpretation

In light of the latter remark, a more promising concept to guide coordination between international judicial bodies is referring to the case law of other courts

842 Vinuales and Dupuy point out that the identity of subject, cause and object have to be the same for *lis pendens* or res *judicata* to be applicable, which is rarely the case in international law. Ibid.

843 Peters, above n 775, 24–25.

844 Dupuy, above n 12; Dupuy, above n 121.

and tribunals when this case law is relevant for the dispute at hand. Some examples of cross-reference between international judicial bodies have already been given. However, there are no clear guidelines on when and why attention should be given to the case law of other judicial bodies. One option is to use the principle of harmonious interpretation. This principle was developed by the WTO AB. Harmonious interpretation demands that the interpreter keeps in mind the aggregate result of the interpretation and its implications for the future of the Treaty regime and has to uphold the balance between the different rights and obligations negotiated in the regime as far as the Treaty text allows.[845] If applied to international law as a whole, harmonious interpretation implies that, in making its decisions, each judicial body has to take into consideration the effectiveness of all the legal rules applicable between the parties. Van Damme therefore argues that it could operate as 'a force for comity between sub-systems of international law and international courts and tribunals'.[846] In a legal context, the term comity is used to describe the reciprocal relationship between courts that prevents them from demeaning each other's judicial decisions. Although harmonious interpretation is certain to deflate the risk of colliding decisions in international law, it seems less attractive in light of the protection of common interests. As stated before, not all common interests are protected by a strong global judicial regime and, therefore, the reciprocity that forms the cornerstone of harmonious interpretation is lacking.

4.2.1.5. Systemic Interpretation

A more structured approach to cross-reference between Treaty regimes can be found in the principle of systemic interpretation, as captured in the VCLT. In contrast to other coordination techniques, this principle holds potential for the protection of all common interests that are recognised in international Treaty law.[847] In the words of the International Law Commission, the principle of systemic integration shows that

> law is also about protecting rights and enforcing obligations, above all rights and obligations that have a backing in something like a general, public interest. Without the principle of 'systemic integration' it would be impossible to give expression to and to keep alive, any sense of the common good of humankind, not reducible to the good of any particular institution or 'regime'.[848]

[845] Van Damme, *Treaty interpretation by the WTO Appellate Body*, above n 123, 292.
[846] Ibid, 285.
[847] Orellana, above n 243, 3.
[848] ILC 2006, para. 480.

Systemic integration is set out in Article 31(3)(c) VCLT, which states that in the interpretation of a Treaty '[a]ny relevant rules of international law applicable in the relations between the parties' should be considered.[849] This principle requires a form of integration between Treaty regimes. It requires that specific international obligations are interpreted in the wider context of international Treaty law. However, as stated in the previous chapter, it is uncertain whether the application of this principle leads to coherence or a proper protection of common interests.[850] Although Article 31(3)(c) VCLT is widely used and it promotes the consideration of other relevant law, it does not offer any guidelines on *how* judicial bodies should take account of these rules. The VCLT does not clarify how the 'relevant rules' could be identified, whether the considered rules should be applicable to all parties of the discussed Treaty or only to the parties to the disputes, and how to deal with concrete conflicts between Treaties. Thus, the principle of systemic integration does not prevent different judicial bodies assigning a different weight to a common interest or narrowing down the common interest to solve it within the limits of their own regimes.[851]

4.2.1.6. *Interim Conclusion: Coordination to Protect Common Interests*

The coordination techniques presented above do not offer a perfect solution for preventing conflicting interpretations of international law and protecting common interests. Hierarchical and horizontal techniques offer a binary solution, in which only part of the relevant law is applied, judicial dialogue is too non-committal to be considered as a structural solution and the discussed Treaty interpretation techniques lack guidance on *how* the compromise between regime interests and (external) common interests should be made. The principle of systemic integration does, however, offer a promising point of entry for external interests if it is combined with a mechanism that can ensure a proper consideration of common interests. In the next section two decision making methods are studied that could provide such a mechanism.

849 Article 31(3)(c) Vienna Convention on the Law of Treaties of 23 May 1969, UN Treaty Series, vol. 1155, 331.

850 See pp 162ff.

851 An example of this is the integration of environmental interests into human rights Treaties. This integration relies on the assumption that the goal of environmental protection is limited to ensuring human well-being and therefore narrows down the scope of the interests at stake. de Wet and Vidmar, above n 813, 20.

4.2.2. COMMON DECISION-MAKING METHOD

4.2.2.1. Compromise of Interests

Institutions such as the regional human rights bodies and the WTO were explicitly founded to go beyond the compromise between sovereign interests and further develop the rules of their specialised regimes.[852] They use dynamic and functional interpretations to give effect to their regimes' Treaties because their own faith is connected to that of their regimes. Moreover, the use of broad interpretative methods is often advocated in the context of international litigation because the formal amendment of international Treaties is difficult and sometimes near impossible.[853] However, the risk of these broad interpretations is that they progressively extend the authority of the tribunal. As a consequence, the case law of the judicial body no longer reflects the balance of powers between the States and the judicial body.

In contrast to the judicial bodies that use more broad interpretation techniques, the ICJ has the reputation for focusing on finding a compromise between the interests of the different parties above all else. This is rather different from the newer international tribunals, which have not been established with the same preference for public diplomacy. Although the more conservative and more diplomatic approach of the ICJ does not lead to a strong promotion of common interests, it may still offer a valuable alternative to a decision by the judicial body under specific circumstances, for example when there exists no specialised body to protect the affected common interest and thus no body of case law to refer to. In the context of environmental protection, the ICJ has used the duty to cooperate to force the litigating parties to find a compromise between the common interest at stake and their shared interests. Although this approach has its merits in terms of democratic legitimacy and may contribute to the enforcement of common interests, it unfortunately does not offer an effective solution to the legal problem that the litigating parties wish to solve. Moreover, there is no mechanism to supervise the parties' implementation of such a decision and the narrow compromise of interests cannot guide the decisions of other courts and tribunals in future common interest cases.

---

852 See, for example Article 3(2) DSU.

853 J. Arato, *Treaty Interpretation and Constitutional Transformation: Informal Change in International Organizations*, Pre-publication Draft, 2012, available at <ssrn.com> (published in (2013) 38 *Yale Journal of International Law* 289–357), 89.

4.2.2.2. *Balancing*

In the case law study, it was found that all the examined international courts and tribunals (other than the ICJ) have used proportionality balancing to come to a decision in cases with multiple private and public interests. In combination with the principle of systemic integration, proportionality balancing can allow the court to take account of every common interest affected by the case. According to Alexy, balancing is a form of applying principles.[854] It determines what the 'appropriate degree of satisfaction' is of one principle 'relative to the requirements of another principle'.[855] Alexy further argues that balancing, contrary to popular belief, is not an irrational process that depends on the values or the subjectivity of the person that makes the decision.[856] Instead he developed a weight formula that determines the concrete weight of the principle whose violation is examined on the basis of the intensity of the interference, the abstract weight of the principle and the reliability of those factors.[857] Although this formula is interesting in theory and may offer a logical theoretical underpinning for balancing in general, it is somewhat problematic to argue that this formula could offer the basis for a consistent decision-making method in the international context.

The reason for this is that it cannot (and does not claim to) offer guidance in determining the weight of the elements in the formula. When balancing different interests protected in the relevant Treaty regime, the dispute settlement mechanism will determine the intensity of the interference and the abstract weight of the principle on the basis of concepts such as rationality, fairness and reasonableness. However, when the judicial body has to balance a Treaty interest with an interest that typically falls outside of the scope of the relevant regime (common interest or domestic public interest) the court will first have to determine how much leeway it grants to the interpretation and weight given to that interest by the relevant Treaty body or the State. Therefore, the similarities in language that are found when comparing the balancing methods of different international judicial bodies do not necessarily imply a similar technique.[858] There is a real risk that there is consistency in the language used but not in substance. The apparent similarity of the balancing process used by different international courts may hide significant differences in the interpretation of the factors on which that balance is based.

---

854 Alexy argues that proportionality can only be used when constitutional rights are considered to be principles (as he does) and not rules. R. Alexy, 'The Construction of Constitutional Rights' (2010) 4 *Law & Ethics of Human Rights* 19, 24.

855 Ibid, 21.

856 Ibid, 27.

857 Ibid, 29.

858 J. Bomhoff, *Balancing, the Global and the Local: Judicial Balancing as a Problematic Topic in Comparative (Constitutional) Law*, Working Paper, no. 2008/5, Tilburg Institute of Comparative and Transnational Law, 2008, available at <ssrn.com>.

4.2.2.3. *Balancing and the Margin of Deference*

When balancing 'Treaty interests' with external, domestic interests, many international judicial bodies allow a certain margin of deference to the State. This margin is especially relevant in the review of public interest exceptions. In this context, the ECtHR has developed a margin of appreciation doctrine that is based on the idea that judicial organs should show restraint in reviewing domestic public interest decisions because they do not enjoy the same expertise and democratic legitimacy as the State.[859] It reflects the notion that it is in the first place the State that has the task to balance different public and private interests; that it is a shared responsibility of the parties and the Treaty regime to enforce the Treaty. This doctrine has also been applied by other international courts and tribunals, with the exception of the ICJ and the ITLOS, although almost never explicitly. A similar margin of deference could be applied in the context of common interest cases.

Up until this point, the discussion has focused on how balancing is currently used by international courts and tribunals. To discuss the potential of balancing and the margin of deference in common interest cases, a normative perspective is now taken. This perspective starts from the idea that it is morally preferable that common interests are promoted in international litigation. To achieve a better protection of common interests in the international legal system as it exists today, cross-reference between Treaty regimes seems the most promising solution. The problem, as identified in the previous chapter, is that there exists no mechanism to guarantee the consistent consideration of common interests protected in other Treaty regimes. It is argued here that the margin of deference could offer such a mechanism in common interest cases.

Two different scenarios may arise in common interest litigation, either the enforcement of the common interest leads to a violation of the Treaty rule or the violation of the Treaty rule also violates the common interest. In the first scenario, the common interest is invoked as a public interest exception that justifies a differentiation between public interest norms and other norms. In that case, the importance of the public interest is great by definition. The importance of the external interest has a positive effect on the width of the margin of deference, thus when a common interest is at stake there should automatically be a considerable margin. In contrast to the margin of appreciation discussed above, this margin has a double function; it does not only defer discretion to the State. A wide margin of deference would also mean that considerable weight should be given to the interpretation of the common interest as provided by the relevant regime.

---

859 Y. Arai-Takahashi, *The Margin of Appreciation Doctrine and the Principle of Proportionality in the Jurisprudence of the ECHR*, Intersentia, Antwerp 2002, p 154.

In other words, the role of the judicial body would not be to balance the interests at stake but to review whether the State has correctly implemented the principle of systemic integration in its balancing act, whether it has taken account of all the relevant law. By focusing on the procedure that preceded the State's decision it can verify whether the State considered all the relevant Treaties before making its decision, without reviewing the political decision that followed that process. By leaving the decision making, the weighing and balancing of different values to politics and focusing judicial control on procedural testing, it provides a means of managing sensitive legal questions in a political environment. Moreover, this procedural approach offers the State the option to improve its decision-making process and reach a new compromise of interests when the court finds it failed to strike a correct balance.

The combination of balancing and the margin of deference doctrine can be more troubling when the common interest is invoked in support of the violated legal rule – in other words, when the violation of the rule is also damaging to the common interest. In those circumstances, the common interest increases the importance of the legal rule and makes the margin of deference of the State extremely narrow. While in theory this narrow margin of deference should be applauded because it leads to a strong enforcement of the common interest, the problem is that common interests are not always invoked with the best intentions.

Whether consciously or not, the risk exists that international adjudicators use a universally supported common interest to pursue their own interest in having full discretion over a matter. Koskenniemi and Leino have eloquently described this risk:

> The universalist voices of humanitarianism, human rights, trade or the environment should undoubtedly be heard. But they may also echo imperial concerns, and never more so than when they are spoken from high positions in institutions that administer flexible standards that leave the final decision always to those speakers themselves.[860]

Thus, although balancing in combination with a margin of deference may offer a consistent approach to common interest issues and can be rationalised to a certain extent, it is far from a perfect solution and further research is necessary to determine how this margin of deference could be implemented.

860 M. Koskenniemi and P. Leino, 'Fragmentation of International Law? Postmodern Anxieties' (2002) 15 *Leiden Journal of International Law* 553, 578–79.

4.2.2.4. *Interim Solution: Common Decision-Making Method to Protect Common Interests*

Instead of only focusing on a shared and consistent interpretation of the common interests protected in international law, the previous section broadened the search to a shared and consistent decision-making method. Although a common method of decision making cannot always guarantee that different courts and tribunals would reach the same conclusion when dealing with the same facts, it may offer a strong framework for judicial bodies to come to a conclusion in which common interests are accounted for in accordance with the principle of systemic integration. Although susceptible to a functional bias, the combination of a balancing approach with a margin of deference, which includes both the decision of the State and external Treaty regimes, was found to be a good interim solution to allow for the protection of common interests in international litigation.

4.2.3. PLURALISTIC APPROACH

Referring to balancing, corrected by a margin of deference, as an 'interim solution' hinted that there is a better but more drastic option to protect common interests in international litigation. This more idealistic solution is set out here as the pluralistic approach. At the very start of this research project in 2010, the ILC report on fragmentation was only a couple years old and the topic had raised a lot of attention in academic circles.[861] Today, however, the concerns over the increased fragmentation and incoherence of international law have been replaced by a more relaxed attitude. International lawyers seem to have embraced the suggestion to 'keep calm and carry on'.[862] In practice, fragmentation has only led to a few problematic situations and the perception is that in those few instances of overlapping jurisdiction or conflicting case law pragmatic solutions will be available.

Furthermore, there is one considerable advantage to pursuing pluralism. This advantage is related to the objective of the institution and the resulting functional bias towards the values of the court's own regime. In the previous chapter it was found that functional bias threatens consistency in international litigation,

---

861 Difficulties arising from the Diversification and Expansion of International Law, International Law Commission Report of the Study Group on Fragmentation of International Law of 2003 UN Doc. A/CN.4/L.644.

862 A description of Koskeniemmi's attitude toward fragmentation in T. Broude, *Keep Calm and Carry On: Martti Koskenniemi and the Fragmentation of International Law*, ILF Research Paper, no. 10–13, Hebrew University of Jerusalem, 2013, available at <ssrn.com>.

however this does not necessarily mean that functional bias has a negative effect on the enforcement of common interests. On the contrary, the strong promotion of human rights by the regional human rights bodies stems from a functional bias towards human rights protection. Similarly, the sometimes rather bold provisional measures of the ICJ show that, as the main judicial organ of the UN, the Court considers it its task to protect international peace and security.[863] Thus it could be argued that functional bias and the resulting inconsistencies lead to a strong, albeit sometimes conflicting, protection of interests by different international judicial bodies.[864]

Even the above-mentioned possibility of conflicting case law should not be problematic. In a system with some form of free choice of forum, it is very likely that after some contradictory decisions coherence will emerge. Competition between different international judicial bodies is sometimes described as a negative consequence of the proliferation of international litigation. This is based on the assumption that competing courts will decide in a way that attracts new cases. However, such decisions push courts to consider the substantive and procedural decisions of other bodies that receive more claims[865] and thus free choice of forum, for example by explicitly allowing it in Treaties *à la* UNCLOS, would lead to more coherence.[866] Even when there is compulsory jurisdiction, the litigating parties may often choose to reformulate their claim to bring it before a different international dispute settlement mechanism. Thus, even when there is no direct competition, international judicial bodies still have an incentive to align their case law with that of bodies who receive more claims.

Nevertheless, there is one vital problem with pursuing a pluralistic approach in the international system, as it exists today. This problem is that the proliferation of international judicial bodies is not complete; not each common interest regime has a specialised international judicial body to protect that common interest. Both human rights and the environment are not protected by a global specialised court. For these specific interests, promoting proliferation and the resulting functional bias could be detrimental because each specialised institution would prefer the objectives promoted by its own

863 See pp 72ff.

864 As asserted by Charney more than a decade ago: 'the other forums complement the work of the ICJ and strengthen the system of international law, notwithstanding some loss of uniformity'. J. Charney, 'The Impact on the International Legal System of the Growth of International Courts and Tribunals' (1998) 31 *New York University Journal of International Law and Politics* 697, 704.

865 Cogan, above n 826, 442.

866 Article 287(1) United Nations Convention on the Law of the Sea of 10 December 1982, UN Treaty Series, vol. 1833, 3 states that a State may make a declaration choosing one or more dispute settlement mechanisms from the following list: the ITLOS, the ICJ, the ad hoc Annex VII tribunals and the special arbitral tribunals established under Annex VIII.

regime to other objectives. Only a politics of further fragmentation would offer sufficient counterweight to the specialised regimes that exist today and would, in consequence, ensure that functional bias has a positive effect on the respect for all common interests.

Thus, a pluralistic approach can be combined with strong common interest enforcement if the number of specialised international institutions is expanded. Several authors have backed this suggestion with concrete propositions for new international courts and tribunals. In the area of IEL, there has been some discussion on the need for a World Environment Court.[867] This would be a specialised court with jurisdiction over specific or all IEL Treaties.[868] The establishment of a World Environment Court could lead to more legal certainty in IEL and could also allow greater participation of non-State actors.[869] But would such a court attract case law? From 1993 to 2006, the ICJ composed a specialised Chamber for Environmental Matters. The composition of this Chamber was, however, discontinued after it failed to attract a single claim in 13 years. Although this Chamber might receive more claims if it still existed today, there is a risk that a global environmental court would not be very successful, at least as an inter-State mechanism.[870] In the area of human rights, a similar proposal for a global court has been launched in academia. Kozma, Nowak and Scheinin have taken a leading position in this discussion and drafted a Consolidated Statute for a World Court of Human Rights.[871] However, like a global environmental court, a human rights court is unlikely to attract much litigation if it is only accessible to States. This assumption is supported by the fact that the regional human rights courts have received hardly any inter-State claims. The latter remark brings us to the central problem with a further fragmentation of the international judiciary. Building political will to establish a new judicial body with compulsory jurisdiction that is accessible to non-State parties would be an extremely difficult and lengthy process. Thus, although it is advisable to pursue further proliferation in the long run, there is still a need for the more immediate (interim) solution that was presented above.

---

867 Pauwelyn explains in detail what the jurisdiction of this court could be, who its members would be, how it should be financed, etc. J. Pauwelyn, 'Judicial Mechanisms: Is there a Need for a World Environment Court?' [2005] *Reforming International Environmental Governance: From Institutional Limits to Innovative Reforms* 150, 150–77.

868 S.M. Hinde, 'The International Environmental Court: Its Broad Jurisdiction as a Possible Fatal Flaw' (2003) 32 *Hofstra Law Review* 727, 731.

869 Ibid, 738.

870 Guillermo et al., above n 233, 466.

871 J. Kozma, M. Nowak and M. Scheinin, *A World Court of Human Rights: Consolidated Statute and Commentary*, Neuer Wissenschaftlicher Verlag, Vienna 2010.

4.3. CONCLUSION

This chapter started from the hypothesis that a consistent approach is needed to protect common interests in international litigation. Against this background, it examined the elements that affect the consistency of international litigation in general and the factors that contribute to the (in)consistency of common interest litigation specifically. Seven important factors were identified. Three of those factors relate to the establishment and work of the studied judicial bodies. First, the case law study showed that ad hoc tribunals feel less compelled to produce consistent case law, unless they are monitored by a permanent body of appeal. Secondly, the extent of a court's body of case law was found to have a positive effect on its internal consistency, but a (potential) negative effect on its willingness to interact with other regimes and common interests. And thirdly, the specific function or objective of the judicial body also hampers the consideration of common interests. Besides these institutional characteristics, the applicable law and the actors involved in the proceedings are important factors for the consistency of international litigation. Both the similarity of legal provisions and the transfer of people across regimes have a harmonising effect on international litigation. However, the latter factors only trigger the consideration of the rules of other regimes; they do not provide a mechanism to guarantee the consistent consideration of common interests.

Next, the book examined whether this finding is problematic for the protection of common interests. An attempt was made to answer how common interests could be promoted in international litigation. On the basis of the previous findings, it was concluded that the enforcement of common interests would not necessarily benefit from trying to dictate a consistent approach. Coordination techniques such as systemic integration are widely used but offer only a partial solution for the consideration of common interest because they do not offer any guidance as to *how* the compromise between regime interests and (external) common interests should be made. This can be remedied by implementing a common method of decision making such as proportionality balancing. In combination with a developed margin of deference doctrine (that also defers to external Treaty mechanisms), balancing was found to be a good interim solution for considering common interests. Nevertheless, the preferable future for common interest litigation cannot be found in further integration. On the contrary, a stronger fragmentation of international dispute settlement bodies should be pursued. In a completely fragmented system, the competition between different international judicial bodies (and their respective interests) will push courts to consider the substantive and procedural decisions of other bodies. And after some conflicting decisions, coherence is likely to arise in favour of those interests that are truly common.

CHAPTER 5
GENERAL CONCLUSION

The number of cases discussed in this study, which is limited to natural resource exploitation disputes, confirms that common interests are 'marching through the time-honoured institutions of the law of Treaties modelled originally along bilateralist lines'.[872] Step by step, international judicial bodies are adapting their procedural as well as substantive rulings to accommodate the common interests they meet along the way. Not all of them are, however, walking at the same pace and in the same direction. In this book, the case law of the ICJ and six different Treaty regimes was studied to identify how international judicial bodies reconcile common interests with the rules of their specific regimes or the Treaty they have been asked to interpret.

The main questions that this book tried to answer concerned the extent to which (specialised) international judicial bodies engage with common interests and the differences or similarities between the different judicial bodies in this context. It answered these questions on the basis of a case study of natural resource exploitation disputes. In both the procedural and substantive decisions of the selected courts and tribunals, a number of similarities were found. First, at the procedural level, it was examined how common interests affect decisions on jurisdiction, standing, evidence, third party interventions and provisional measures. In the context of establishing jurisdiction, the study found that most of the discussed bodies enjoy compulsory jurisdiction. Therefore, their decisions on jurisdiction are not affected by common interests. The same is true for the ICJ, which holds on to a strict interpretation of consensual jurisdiction that is not broadened to allow common interest cases.

Thus, the fact that common interests are at risk does not make it easier or harder to establish jurisdiction. Establishing standing, however, is easier before most courts and tribunals when common interests can be invoked. Three of the discussed inter-State judicial bodies, the ICJ, the WTO DSM and the ITLOS, (implicitly) consider the common interest obligations that are included in the relevant Treaties *erga omnes partes* obligations and allow standing to all States in cases concerning serious violations of those obligations. The African

872 SIMMA, above n 1, 375.

Commission equally allows an *actio popularis*. Although the other human rights regimes are more conservative and require a direct link between the violation and the claimant, this more strict approach is primarily due to the number of cases they receive. The third procedural issue, evidence, was harder to link to common interest considerations. Only a weak link was found between fact finding by the different courts and tribunals and common interest cases. The decisions on third party interventions that concern common interests showed a much higher level of similarity. All the specialised judicial bodies (not the ICJ) have now formally or informally accepted *amicus curiae* interventions by non-State parties. This is not just a matter of course. The majority of the discussed statutes and procedural rules did not initially provide for *amicus curiae* interventions. These provisions were only included after the court or tribunal had allowed *amicus curiae* briefs in practice. To determine the influence of common interests on decisions on provisional measures, the last procedural element, the decisions of the ICJ and the ITLOS, were studied. It was found that both judicial bodies more easily grant provisional measures in cases that concern a common interest that they explicitly protect. In the studied cases these common interests were peace and security and the protection of the marine environment.

Similarities between the approaches of different courts and tribunals in common interest cases were found not only at the procedural level, but also in the decisions on the merits. To study the substantive decisions of the judicial bodies, a division was made between decisions on public interest exceptions and decisions on common interest norms. When examining public interest exceptions, it became even more obvious that international courts and tribunals are inspired by each other's case law in the context of common interest cases. Two general conclusions can be drawn from the research on public interest exceptions. First, international courts and tribunals are not reluctant to use public interest exceptions and interpret Treaties broadly to include exceptions that allow States to pursue measures in the common interest. For example, the interpretation of the term 'like' by both the WTO DSM and the ICSID tribunals has had the effect of differentiating between measures that pursue a public interest goal and other measures. Thus, both judicial bodies created a de facto public interest exception. Secondly, apart from the ICJ and the ITLOS, the examined judicial bodies all use some form of proportionality balancing to determine whether the alleged inconsistency is justified on the basis of a public interest exception. Thus, although they tend to stay as close as possible to the text they are asked to interpret, the methods used by international judicial bodies to allow common interests to justify inconsistencies with their Treaty regimes are clearly similar.

Lastly, the book focused on decisions on common interest norms, in other words decisions in which the relevant Treaty explicitly protects or is interpreted to protect the invoked common interest. In this context it was found, again, that proportionality balancing is used by tribunals other than the ICJ and the ITLOS to balance common interest norms with other Treaty norms. However, it was also established that proportionality balancing is used differently by different bodies. Especially the use of a margin of deference in proportionality balancing is different; this is the leeway that is given to the State to decide on the balance of different interests. While some bodies explicitly allow deference to the State for common interest decisions (for example the ECtHR), others do not allow deference (for example the WTO DSM) or do not allow it on the basis of a predictable standard (for example the ICSID tribunals).

The next section of the book determined the reasons for both the similarities and differences in the decisions of the international courts and tribunals. Several key elements were extracted from the case study. First, there are some reasons for (in)consistency that affect international litigation in general. These are the permanence of the different judicial bodies, their body of case law and the community of international lawyers. The case study showed that the latter element has a positive effect on the consistency of international litigation in general. In contrast, both the permanence and more elaborated case law of an institution make it less likely to adapt its decisions to decisions or norms of other regimes and, therefore, lead to inconsistency. Secondly, some elements were identified that have a specific effect on the consistency of common interest decisions. These are the objective of the institution, the similarity between legal rules, the use of Article 31(3)(c) VCLT and the relationship of the judicial body with other actors. It was established that the different objectives and relationships of judicial institutions lead to inconsistencies in their decisions. Furthermore, the interpretation principles in the VCLT do not offer very specific guidelines of interpretation. Thus, only the similarity between legal rules was demonstrated to have a positive effect on the consistency of decisions. This conclusion could also be deduced from the case study on natural resource disputes. In combination with the conclusion that judicial bodies are increasingly considering (the same) common interests, the discussion on similarities and differences raised a question that was, more briefly, discussed. Could the use of similar decision-making techniques prevent inconsistencies and, as a consequence, lead to a better protection of common interests?

From the case study on natural resource disputes it can be concluded that the glass is half full, not half empty, for the consideration of common interests in international litigation. Looking at the case law of the selected bodies, there is reason to be optimistic. Judicial bodies are increasingly taking into account common interests in both their procedural and substantive decisions. Furthermore, in many procedural decisions judicial bodies apply a similar interpretation of the procedural rules; and in many substantive decisions they use a similar method of deciding between common interests and other interests. Nevertheless, the case study also showed that in substantive decisions the widespread use of proportionality balancing does not guarantee consistent approaches and does not guarantee that sufficient weight is given to the common interest. This is the most problematic aspect of the consideration of common interests in the proliferated international judicial system that exists today. While many common interests are protected by Treaties, they are often not protected by global judicial bodies. As a result, the competition between different interests is unfair in the context of litigation. A stronger protection of common interests could be reached in a completely fragmented system, where each common interest is protected by a specialised global judicial body and competition between courts and tribunals leads to unity in the long run. However, because further proliferation of judicial bodies is not likely to happen in the short term, it is necessary that judicial bodies develop a system to deal with common interests at the substantive level. Therefore, it was argued that implementing a common method of decision making across all judicial bodies could offer a solution, for now. On the basis of the case study, it was suggested that proportionality balancing is a suitable method to consider common interests if it is combined with a strongly developed margin of deference doctrine. This doctrine would allow the State to protect common interests while, at the same time, it would allow the judicial body to protect the values of its Treaty regime. In my opinion, the case study confirmed that judicial bodies are open to the consideration of common interests and would be able to further define a margin of deference that takes account of such considerations.

Both the suggested solutions and the case study are of course limited in several ways. As already stated at the start of the book, only some of the disputes in this area are settled by publicly available litigation, the case law research focuses only on a limited group of disputes and the suggested solutions are conceptual, not elaborated in detail. However, these limitations can also be seen as strengths. Publicly available litigation may not be the biggest source of dispute settlement in common interest or natural resource cases, but it is a very influential source. The narrow focus of the case study research limits the conclusion to certain disputes on natural resource exploitation, but it has also made it possible to study the case law of seven different institutions at both the procedural and substantive level within a limited period of time. And lastly, the conceptual nature of the proposed solutions gives me the opportunity to suggest that further research on the combination of proportionality balancing and the margin of deference in common interest cases is needed, because research that crosses the boundaries of different regimes and takes account of common interests requires a collective effort, but benefits the community as a whole.

BIBLIOGRAPHY

Alexandrov, S.A., 'The Compulsory Jurisdiction of the International Court of Justice: How Compulsory Is It?' (2006) 5 *Chinese Journal of International Law* 29.

Alexy, R., 'The Construction of Constitutional Rights' (2010) 4 *Law & Ethics of Human Rights* 19.

Allen, D., *'This Business Will Never Hold Water' International Investment Arbitration on Public-Private Water Service Provision – A Comment on Biwater Gauff (Tanzania) Limited v. United Republic of Tanzania*, Working Paper, 2010, available at <ssrn.com>.

Alter, K.J., *The New Terrain of International Law: Courts, Politics, Rights*, Princeton University Press, Princeton, NJ 2013.

Alvarez, J. and Khamsi, K., 'Argentine Crisis and Foreign Investors: A Glimpse into the Heart of the Investment Regime', *Yearbook on International Investment Law and Policy* 2008–2009, 379.

Alvarez-Jimenez, A., 'The WTO Appellate Body's Decision-Making Process: A Perfect Model For International Adjudication?' (2009) 12 *Journal of International Economic Law* 289.

Anaya, J. and Grossman, C., 'The Case of Awas Tingni v. Nicaragua: A New Step in the International Law of Indigenous Peoples' (2002) 19 *Arizona Journal of International and Comparative Law* 1.

Andenas, M. and Zleptnig, S., 'Proportionality and Balancing in WTO Law: A Comparative Perspective' (2007) 20 *Cambridge Review of International Affairs* 71.

Anghie, A., *Imperialism, Sovereignty and the Making of International Law*, Cambridge University Press, Cambridge 2007.

Anton, D., Makgill, R. and Payne, C., *Advisory Opinion on Responsibility and Liability for International Seabed Mining (ITLOS Case No. 17): International Environmental Law in the Seabed Disputes Chamber*, Research Paper, no. 11–06, Australian National University, ANU College of Law, 2011, available at <ssrn.com>.

Aquinas, T. with Gilby, T., *Summa theologiae – Law and Political Theory*, Cambridge University Press, Cambridge 2006.

Arai-Takahashi, Y., *The Margin of Appreciation Doctrine and the Principle of Proportionality in the Jurisprudence of the ECHR*, Intersentia, Antwerp 2002.

Arato, J., *Treaty Interpretation and Constitutional Transformation: Informal Change in International Organizations*, pre-publication draft, 2012, available at <ssrn.com> (published in (2013) 38 *Yale Journal of International Law* 289–357).

Aristotle with Newman, W., *The Politics of Aristotle*, Arno, New York 1973.

Arnardóttir, O.M., *Non-discrimination Under Article 14 ECHR: The Burden of Proof*, Scandinavian Studies in Law, 1999–2012, available at <ssrn.com>.

Ascensio, H., 'L'*amicus curiae* devant les juridictions internationales' (2001) 105 *Revue Générale de Droit International Public* 897.

Ayres, G. and Mitchell, A., *General and Security Exceptions under the GATT and GATS*, pre-publication draft, 2012, available at <ssrn.com> (published in *International Trade Law and WTO*, Federation Press, 2012).

Bankes, N., 'International Human Rights Law and Natural Resources Projects Within the Traditional Territories of Indigenous Peoples' (2010) 47 *Alberta Law Review* 457.

Bartels, L., *The Chapeau of Article XX GATT: A New Interpretation*, University of Cambridge Faculty of Law Research Paper, 2014, available at <ssrn.com>.

Bekker, P., 'Gabcikovo-Nagymaros Project (Hungary/Slovakia), Judgment International Court of Justice' (1998) 92 *American Journal of International Law* 273.

Benzing, M., 'Community Interests in the Procedure of International Courts and Tribunals' (2006) 5 *The Law and Practice of International Courts and Tribunals* 369.

Bernasconi-Osterwalder, N., Magraw, D.B., Oliva, M.J., Orellana, M. and Tuerk, E., *Environment and Trade: A Guide to WTO Jurisprudence*, Earthscan, London, Sterling, VA 2006.

Bodansky, D., 'Legal Realism and its Discontents' (2015) 28 *Leiden Journal of International Law* 267.

Bomhoff, J., *Balancing the Global and the Local: Judicial Balancing as a Problematic Topic in Comparative (Constitutional) Law*, Working Paper, no. 2008/5, Tilburg Institute of Comparative and Transnational Law, 2008, available at <ssrn.com>.

Bown, C.P., *Self-Enforcing Trade: Developing Countries and WTO Dispute Settlement*, Brookings Institution Press, Washington, DC 2009.

Boyle, A., 'The Environmental Jurisprudence of the International Tribunal for the Law of the Sea' (2007) 22 *The International Journal of Marine and Coastal Law* 369.

Bozeman, B., *Public Values and Public Interest: Counterbalancing Economic Individualism*, Georgetown University Press, Washington, DC 2007.

Broude, T., *Keep Calm and Carry On: Martti Koskenniemi and the Fragmentation of International Law*, ILF Research Paper, no. 10-13, Hebrew University of Jerusalem, 2013, available at <ssrn.com>.

Brower, C. and Schill, S., 'Is Arbitration a Threat or a Boon to the Legitimacy of International Investment Law' (2008–2009) 9 *Chicago Journal of International Law* 471.

Brown, C., 'Provisional Measures Before the ITLOS: The MOX Plant Case' (2002) 17 *International Journal of Marine and Coastal Law* 267.

—— *A Common Law of International Adjudication*, Oxford University Press, Oxford 2007.

Buergenthal, T., 'The Advisory Practice of the Inter-American Human Rights Court' (1985) 79 *American Journal of International Law* 1.

—— 'Remembering the Early Years of the Inter-American Court of Human Rights' (2004) 37 *New York University Journal of International Law and Politics* 259.

Burbano Herrera, C., *Provisional Measures in the Case Law of the Inter-American Court of Human Rights*, Intersentia, Antwerp 2010.

Burgorgue-Larsen, L. and Úbeda de Torres, A., *The Inter-American Court of Human Rights Case Law and Commentary*, Oxford University Press, Oxford 2011.

Burke-White, W. and Von Staden, A., *Investment Protection in Extraordinary Times: The Interpretation and Application of Non-Precluded Measures Provisions in Bilateral Investment Treaties*, Scholarship at Penn Law, Paper 152, 2007, available at <lsr.nellco.org> (published in (2008) 48 *Virginia Journal of International Law* 307).

—— and von Staden, A., 'Private Litigation in a Public Sphere: The Standard of Review in Investor-State Arbitrations' (2010) 35 *Yale Journal of International Law* 283.

Cass, D.Z., *The Constitutionalization of the World Trade Organization: Legitimacy, Democracy, and Community in the International Trading System*, Oxford University Press, Oxford 2005.

Cassese, A., *International Law*, Oxford University Press, Oxford 2001.

—— *International Law*, Oxford University Press, Oxford 2005.

Cavallaro, J. and Brewer, S., *Reevaluating Regional Human Rights Litigation in the Twenty-First Century: The Case of the Inter-American Court*, Public Law & Legal Theory Working Paper Series, no. 09-31, Harvard Law School, 2008, available at <ssrn.com>.

Cerone, J., 'Introductory Note to African Commission on Human and Peoples' Rights: Centre for Minority Rights Development (Kenya) & Minority Rights Group International on Behalf of Endorois Welfare Council v. Kenya' (2010) 49 *International Legal Materials* 858.

Charney, J., 'The Impact on the International Legal System of the Growth of International Courts and Tribunals' (1998) 31 *New York University Journal of International Law and Politics* 697.

Chinkin, C., 'Articles 62–63' in A. Zimmermann, C. Tomuschat and K. Oellers-Frahm (eds), *The Statute of the International Court of Justice: A Commentary*, Oxford University Press, Oxford 2006, 1331–92.

Choudhury, B., 'Recapturing Public Power: Is Investment Arbitration's Engagement of the Public Interest Contributing to the Democratic Deficit' (2008) 41 *Vanderbilt Journal of Transnational Law* 775.

Christoffersen, J., *Fair Balance – A Study of Proportionality, Subsidiarity and Primarity in the European Convention on Human Rights*, Dissertation, University of Copenhagen, Faculty of Law, 2008, available at <www.humanrights.dk>.

Cochran, C., 'Political Science and "The Public Interest"' (1974) 36 *The Journal of Politics* 327.

Cogan, J., 'Competition and Control in International Adjudication' (2008) 48 *Virginia Journal of International Law* 411.

—— 'The 2010 Judicial Activity of the International Court of Justice' (2011) 105 *American Journal of International Law* 477.

d'Aspremont, J., *Contemporary International Rulemaking and the Public Character of International Law*, International Law and Justice Working Papers, no. 2006/12, New York University School of Law 2006, available at <www.iilj.org>.

De Brabandere, E., 'NGOs and the "Public Interest": The Legality and Rationale of Amicus Curiae Interventions in International Economic and Investment Disputes' (2011) 12 *Chicago Journal of International Law* 85.

—— 'Non-State Actors and the Proliferation and Individualization of International Dispute Settlement' in B. Reinalda (ed), *The Ashgate Research Companion to Non-State Actors*, Routledge, Ebook, 2016.

De Feyter, K., *Globalization and Shared Responsibilities of States*, Ashgate, London 2012

de Wet, E., 'The International Constitutional Order' (2006) 55 *International and Comparative Law Quarterly* 51.

—— and Vidmar, J., *Conflicts between International Paradigms: Hierarchy Versus Systemic Integration*, pre-publication paper, 2013, available at <ssrn.com> (published in (2013) 2 *Global Constitutionalism* 196–217).

Diggs, B., 'The Common Good as Reason for Political Action' (1973) 83 *Ethics* 283.

DiMascio, N. and Pauwelyn, J., 'Nondiscrimination in Trade and Investment Treaties: Worlds Apart or Two Sides of the Same Coin?' [2008] *American Journal of International Law* 48.

Dipla, H., 'The Role of the International Court of Justice and the International Tribunal for the Law of the Sea in the Progressive Development of the Law of the Sea' in A. Strati, M. Gavouneli and N. Skourtos (eds), *Unresolved Issues and New Challenges to the Law of the Sea: Time Before and Time After*, Leiden, Martinus Nijhoff Publishers 2006, 235–50.

Dolidze, A., 'The Arctic Sunrise and NGOs in International Judicial Proceedings' (2014) 18 *Asil Insights* 1.

Dolzer, R. and Schreuer, C., *Principles of International Investment Law*, Oxford University Press, Oxford 2012.

Du, M., *'Treatment No Less Favorable' and the Future of National Treatment Obligation in GATT Article III: 4 after EC–Seal Products*, 2015, available at <ssrn.com> (later published in (2016) 1 *World Trade Review* 139).

Dupuy, P.-M., 'The Danger of Fragmentation or Unification of the International Legal System and the International Court of Justice' (1999) 31 *International Law and Politics* 791.

—— 'Article 34' in A. Zimmermann, C. Tomuschat and K. Oellers-Frahm (eds), *The Statute of the International Court of Justice: a Commentary*, Oxford University Press, Oxford 2006, 545–63.

—— 'Competition among International Tribunals and the Authority of the International Court of Justice' in U. Fastenrath, R. Geiger, D.-E. Khan, A. Paulus, S. von Schorlemer and C. Vedder (eds), *From Bilateralism to Community Interest – Essays in Honour of Judge Bruno Simma*, Oxford University Press, Oxford 2011, 862–76.

Ebobrah, S., 'The Admissibility of Cases before the African Court on Human and Peoples' Rights: Who Should Do What?' (2009) 3 *Malawi Law Journal* 87.

Evans, M., 'Case Concerning the Gabcikovo-Nagymaros Project (Hungary v. Slovakia)' (1998) 47 *International & Comparative Law Quarterly* 688.

—— and Murray, R., *The African Charter on Human and Peoples' Rights: The System in Practice, 1986–2006*, Cambridge University Press, Cambridge, New York 2008.

Fastenrath, U., Geiger, R., Khan, D.E., von Schorlemer, S. and Vedder, C., *From Bilateralism to Community Interest – Essays in Honour of Judge Bruno Simma*, Oxford University Press, Oxford 2011.

Fauchald, O.K., 'The Legal Reasoning of ICSID Tribunals – An Empirical Analysis' (2008) 19 *European Journal of International Law* 301.

Fishman, J.P., 'Locating the International Interest in Intranational Cultural Property Disputes' (2009) 35 *Yale Journal of International Law* 347.

Fitzmaurice, M., 'International Protection of the Environment' (2001) 293 *Recueil des Cours (Collected Courses of the Hague Academy of International Law)* 9.

—— 'The International Court of Justice and the Environment' (2004) 4 *Non-State Actors and International Law* 173.

Francioni, F., 'Beyond State Sovereignty: The Protection of Cultural Heritage as a Shared Interest of Humanity' (2004) 25 *Michigan Journal of International Law* 1209.

—— 'Access to Justice, Denial of Justice, and International Investment Law' in P.M. Dupuy, F. Francioni and E.U. Petersmann (eds), *Human Rights in International Investment Law and Arbitration*, Oxford University Press, Oxford 2009, 63–81.

Friedmann, W., *The Changing Structure of International Law*, Columbia University Press, New York 1964.

Gao, J., 'Reasonableness of the Bond under Article 292 of the LOS Convention: Practice of the ITLOS' (2008) 7 *Chinese Journal of International Law* 115.

García San José, D., *Environmental Protection and the European Convention on Human Rights*, Human Rights Files, Council of Europe Publications, 2005, available at <www.echr.coe.int>.

Gautier, P., 'NGOs and Law of the Sea Disputes' in T. Treves (ed), *Civil Society, International Courts and Compliance Bodies*, Cambridge University Press, Cambridge 2005, 233–42.

Gavouneli, M., 'From Uniformity to Fragmentation? The Ability of the UN Convention on the Law of the Sea to Accommodate New Uses and Challenges' in A. Strati, M. Gavouneli and N. Skourtos (eds), *Unresolved Issues and New Challenges to the Law of the Sea: Time Before and Time After*, Martinus Nijhoff Publishers, Leiden 2006, 205–34.

Gerards, J. and Senden, H., 'The Structure of Fundamental Rights and the European Court of Human Rights' (2009) 7 *International Journal of Constitutional Law* 619.

Greer, S., '"Balancing" and the European Court of Human Rights: A Contribution to the Habermas-Alexy Debate' (2004) 63 *Cambridge Law Journal* 412.

—— *The European Convention on Human Rights: Achievements, Problems and Prospects*, Cambridge University Press, Cambridge 2008.

Grossman, C., 'The Inter-American System of Human Rights: Challenges for the Future' (2008) 83 *Indiana Law Journal* 1267.

Guillermo, J., Coustasse, S. and Sweeney, E., 'Adjudicating Conflicts Over Resources: The ICJ's Treatment of Technical Evidence in the Pulp Mills Case' (2011) 3 *Goettingen Journal of International Law* 447.

Hafner, G., 'Pros and Cons Ensuing from Fragmentation of International Law' (2004) 25 *Michigan Journal of International Law* 849.

Hammer, D., 'Allowing Genocide?: An Analysis of Armed Activities on the Territory of the Congo, Jurisdictional Reservations, and the Legitimacy of the International Court of Justice' (2007) 16 *Minnesota Journal of International Law* 495.

Harris, D.J., Warbrick, C. and O'Boyle, M., *Law of the European Convention on Human Rights*, Oxford University Press, Oxford 2009.

Held, V., *The Public Interest and Individual Interests*, Basic Books, New York 1970.

Henckels, C., 'Indirect Expropriation and the Right to Regulate: Revisiting Proportionality Analysis and the Standard of Review in Investor-State Arbitration' (2012) 15 *Journal of International Economic Law* 223.

Hennebel, L., 'The Inter-American System for Human Rights: Operation and Achievements' in F. Gómez Isa and K. De Feyter (eds), *International Human Rights Law in a Global Context*, University of Deusto, Bilbao 2009, 805–51.

Hernandez, G., *The International Court of Justice and the Judicial Function*, Oxford University Press, Oxford 2013.

Hestermeyer, H., 'Article III GATT' in R. Wolfrum, P.-T. Stoll and H. Hestermeyer (eds), *WTO – Trade in Goods*, Martinus Nijhoff Publishers, Leiden/Boston 2011, 1225.

Hey, E., 'International Water Law Placed in a Contemporary Environmental Context: the Gabcikovo-Nagymaros Case' (2000) 25 *Physics and Chemistry of the Earth* 303.

—— 'Global Environmental Law: Common Interests and the (Re)Constitution of Public Space' (2009) 1 *Iustum Aequum Salutare* 41.

HEYNS, C., 'The African Regional Human Rights System: The African Charter' [2004] *Penn State Law Review* 108.

HIGGINS, R., 'A Babel of Judicial Voices? Ruminations from the Bench' (2006) 55 *International and Comparative Law Quarterly* 791.

HINDE, S.M., 'The International Environmental Court: Its Broad Jurisdiction as a Possible Fatal Flaw' (2003) 32 *Hofstra Law Review* 727.

HOWSE, R., LANGILLE, J. and SYKES, K., 'Sealing the Deal: The WTO's Appellate Body Report in EC – Seal Products' [2014] *Asil Insights* 18.

JANSEN CALAMITA, N., *International Human Rights and the Interpretation of International Investment Treaties – Constitutional Considerations*, pre-publication draft, 2013, available at <ssrn.com> (published in *The Interaction of International Investment Law with Other Fields of Public International Law*, Cambridge University Press, Cambridge 2013).

JOHNSON, L. and TUERK, E., 'CIEL's Experience in WTO Dispute Settlement: Challenges and Complexities from a Practical Point of View' in T. TREVES (ed), *Civil Society, International Courts and Compliance Bodies*, Cambridge University Press, Cambridge 2005, 243–60.

JOHNSTON, R., *The Dictionary of Human Geography*, Blackwell Publishers, Oxford 2000.

JUMA, D., 'Provisional Measures under the African Human Rights System: The African Court's Order against Libya' (2012) 30 *Wisconsin International Law Journal* 344.

KARAMAN, I., *Dispute Resolution in the Law of the Sea*, Martinus Nijhoff Publishers, Leiden 2012.

KAWHARU, A., 'International Law's Protection of Foreign-Owned Property against Uncompensated Expropriation: Preserving Host State Regulatory Freedom' in D. GRINLINTON and P. TAYLOR (eds), *Property Rights and Sustainability: The Evolution of Property Rights to Meet Ecological Challenges*, Martinus Nijhoff Publishers, Leiden 2011, 341–64.

KELLY, J.P., 'The Seduction of the Appellate Body: Shrimp/Turtle I and II and the Proper Role of States in WTO Governance' (2005) 38 *Cornell International Law Journal* 459.

KINGSBURY, B. and SCHILL, S., *Investor-state Arbitration as Governance: Fair and Equitable Treatment, Proportionality and the Emerging Global Administrative Law*, Public Law and Legal Theory Working Papers, Paper 146, New York University, 2009, available at <ssrn.com>.

KINSCH, P., 'On the Uncertainties Surrounding the Standard of Proof in Proceedings Before International Courts and Tribunals' [2009] *Individual Rights and International Justice* 427.

KOLB, R., *The International Court of Justice*, Hart Publishing, Oxford 2013.

KOSKENNIEMI, M. and LEINO, P., 'Fragmentation of International Law? Postmodern Anxieties' (2002) 15 *Leiden Journal of International Law* 553.

KOZMA, J., NOWAK, M. and SCHEININ, M., *A World Court of Human Rights: Consolidated Statute and Commentary*, Neuer Wissenschaftlicher Verlag, Vienna 2010.

KRATOCHVÍL, J., 'The Inflation of the Margin of Appreciation by the European Court of Human Rights' (2011) 29 *Netherlands Quarterly of Human Rights* 324.

KRIEBAUM, U., REINISCH, A., SCHREUER, C. and BINDER, C., *International Investment Law for the 21st Century: Essays in Honour of Christoph Schreuer*, Oxford University Press, Oxford 2009.

KWIATKOWSKA, B., 'Southern Bluefin Tuna (New Zealand v. Japan; Australia v. Japan), Order on Provisional Measures (ITLOS Cases Nos. 3 and 4)' (2000) 94 *American Journal of International Law* 150.

LANCE, B., 'The Amicus Curiae before International Courts and Tribunals' (2005) 5 *Non-State Actors and International Law* 209.

LAVRANOS, N., 'The Epilogue in the MOX Plant Dispute: An End Without Findings' [2009] *European Energy and Environmental Law Review* 180.

LEACH, P., *Taking a Case to the European Court of Human Rights*, Oxford University Press, Oxford 2012.

——, PARASKEVA, C. and UZELAC, G., *International Human Rights & Fact-Finding: An Analysis of the Fact-finding Missions Conducted by the European Commission and Court of Human Rights*, Report, Human Rights and Social Justice Research Institute, London Metropolitan University, 2009, available at <www.londonmet.ac.uk>.

LETSAS, G., 'Two Concepts of the Margin of Appreciation' (2006) 26 *Oxford Journal of Legal Studies* 705.

LEVINE, E., 'Amicus Curiae in International Investment Arbitration: The Implications of an Increase in Third-Party Participation' (2011) 29 *Berkeley Journal of International Law* 200.

LIPPMANN, W., *The Public Philosophy*, Transaction Publisher, New Brunswick 2006.

LIXINSKI, L., 'Treaty Interpretation by the Inter-American Court of Human Rights: Expansionism at the Service of the Unity of International Law' (2010) 21 *The European Journal of International Law* 585.

LOCKE, J. with PEARDON, T., *The Second Treatise of Government*, Liberal Arts Press, New York, 1952.

LOWENFELD, A., 'The ICSID Convention: Origins and Transformation' (2009) 38 *Georgia Journal of International and Comparative Law* 47.

MACKENZIE, R., ROMANO, C.P., SHANY, Y. and SANDS, P., *Manual on International Courts and Tribunals*, Oxford University Press Oxford, Oxford 2010.

MAHINGA, J.-G., *Le Tribunal du droit de la mer: Organisation, compétence et procédure*, Larcier, Brussels 2013.

MARCEAU, G., 'WTO Dispute Settlement and Human Rights' (2002) 1 *European Journal of International Law* 753.

MARTIN, M., *WTO Dispute Settlement Understanding and Development*, Martinus Nijhoff Publishers, Leiden 2013.

MATSUSHITA, M., 'The Dispute Settlement Mechanism at the WTO: the Appellate Body – Assessment and Problems' in A. NARLIKAR, M. DAUNTON and R. STERN (eds), *The Oxford Handbook on the World Trade Organization*, Oxford University Press, Oxford 2012, 507–34.

——, SCHOENBAUM, T. and MAVROIDIS, P., *The World Trade Organization: Law, Practice and Policy*, Oxford University Press, Oxford 2006.

MBELLE, N., 'The Role of Non-governmental Organisations and National Human Rights Institutions at the African Commission' in M.D. EVANS and R. MURRAY (eds), *The African Charter on Human and Peoples' Rights: The System in Practice, 1986–2000*, Cambridge University Press, Cambridge 2008, 289–315.

MCHARG, A., 'Reconciling Human Rights and the Public Interest: Conceptual Problems and Doctrinal Uncertainty in the Jurisprudence of the European Court of Human Rights' (1999) 62 *Modern Law Review* 671.

MENSAH, T., 'The Tribunal and the Prompt Release of Vessels' (2007) 22 *The International Journal of Marine and Coastal Law* 425.

MERRILLS, J., 'The Means of Dispute Settlement' in M. EVANS (ed), *International Law*, Oxford University Press, Oxford 2006, 533–60.

MITCHELL, A., *Legal Principles in WTO Disputes*, Cambridge University Press, Cambridge, New York 2008.

—— and HENCKELS, C., *Variations on a Theme: Comparing the Concept of 'Necessity' in International Investment Law and WTO Law*, pre-publication paper, 2012, available at <ssrn.com> (published in [2014] *Chicago Journal of International Law* 93).

MOWBRAY, A., 'A Study of the Principle of Fair Balance in the Jurisprudence of the European Court of Human Rights' (2010) 10 *Human Rights Law Review* 289.

—— *Cases, Materials, and Commentary on the European Convention on Human Rights*, Oxford University Press, Oxford 2012.

NARLIKAR, A., DAUNTON, M. and STERN, R.M., *The Oxford Handbook on the World Trade Organization*, Oxford University Press, Oxford 2012.

NEFF, S., *A Short History of International Law*, pre-publication draft, 2003, available at <www.oup.com> (published in *International Law*, Oxford University Press, Oxford 2003, 31–58).

NELSON, L., 'The Jurisprudence of the International Tribunal for the Law of the Sea: Some Observations' in T.A. MENSAH, T.M. NDIAYE, R. WOLFRUM and C. KOJIMA (eds), *Law of the Sea, Environmental Law and Settlement of Disputes: Liber Amicorum Judge Thomas A. Mensah*, Martinus Nijhoff Publishers, Leiden 2007, 967–88.

NOLLKAEMPER, A., *International Adjudication of Global Public Goods: The Intersection of Substance and Procedure*, SHARES Research Paper 09 (2012), ACIL 2012-08, Amsterdam Center for International Law, 2012, available at <sharesproject.nl>.

OELLERS-FRAHM, K., 'Article 41' in A. ZIMMERMANN, C. TOMUSCHAT and K. OELLERS-FRAHM (eds), *The Statute of the International Court of Justice: A Commentary*, Oxford University Press, Oxford 2006, 923–66.

—— 'Expanding the Competence to Issue Provisional Measures – Strengthening the International Judicial Function' (2011) 12 *German Law Journal* 1279.

ORAKHELASHVILI, A., 'Case concerning Armed Activities on the Territory of the Congo (Democratic Republic of the Congo v. Rwanda), Jurisdiction and Admissibility, Judgment of 3 February 2006' (2006) 55 *International & Comparative Law Quarterly* 753.

ORELLANA, M., 'The Law on Highly Migratory Fish Stocks: ITLOS Jurisprudence in Context' (2004) 34 *Golden Gate University Law Review* 459.

—— 'Investment Agreements & Sustainable Development: The Non-Discrimination Standards' (2012) 11 *Sustainable Development Law & Policy* 3.

—— 'The Swordfish Dispute between the EU and Chile at the ITLOS and the WTO' (2002) 71 *Nordic Journal of International Law* 55.

ORREGO VICUNA, F., 'The International Tribunal for the Law of the Sea and Provisional Measures: Settled Issues and Pending Problems' (2007) 22 *The International Journal of Marine and Coastal Law* 451.

ORTINO, F., 'Non-Discriminatory Treatment in Investment Disputes' in P.-M. DUPUY, F. FRANCIONI and E.U. PETERSMANN (eds), *Human Rights in International Investment Law and Arbitration*, Oxford University Press, Oxford 2009, 344–66.

Oxman, B. and Bantz, V., 'The M/V 'Saiga' (No. 2) (Saint Vincent and the Grenadines v. Guinea), Judgment (ITLOS Case No. 2)' (2000) 94 *American Journal of International Law* 140.

Padideh, A.I., 'Judicial Lobbying at the WTO: The Debate over the Use of Amicus Curiae Briefs and the U.S. Experience' (2000) 24 *Fordham International Law Journal* 62.

Palchetti, P., 'Opening the International Court of Justice to Third States: Intervention and Beyond' (2002) 6 *Max Planck Yearbook of UN Law* 139.

Parkin, M., *Economics*, Pearson, Boston, MA 2008.

Pasqualucci, J., *The Practice and Procedure of the Inter-American Court of Human Rights*, Cambridge University Press, Cambridge 2003.

—— 'International Indigenous Land Rights: A Critique of the Jurisprudence of the Inter-American Court of Human Rights in Light of the United Nations Declaration on the Rights of Indigenous Peoples' (2009) 27 *Wisconsin International Law Journal* 51.

—— *The Practice and Procedure of the Inter-American Court of Human Rights*, Cambridge University Press, Cambridge 2013.

Paulus, A., *From Territoriality to Functionality? Towards a Legal Methodology of Globalization*, pre-publication draft, 2004, available at <www.cpogg.org> (published in *Governance and International Legal Theory*, Martinus Nijhoff, Leiden 2004, 59–95).

—— 'Reciprocity Revisited' in U. Fastenrath, R. Geiger, D.-E. Khan, A. Paulus, S. von Schorlemer and C. Vedder (eds), *From Bilateralism to Community Interest – Essays in Honour of Judge Bruno Simma*, Oxford University Press, Oxford 2011, 113–37.

Pauwelyn, J., 'Judicial Mechanisms: Is there a Need for a World Environment Court?' [2005] *Reforming International Environmental Governance: From Institutional Limits to Innovative Reforms* 150.

—— *Conflict of Norms in Public International Law: How WTO Law Relates to Other Rules of International Law*, Cambridge University Press, Cambridge 2008.

—— *WTO Panelists are from Mars, ICSID Arbitrators are from Venus – Why? And Does It Matter?*, Working Paper, 2015, available at <ssrn.com>.

Pavoni, R., 'Environmental Rights, Sustainable Development, and Investor-State Case Law: A Critical Appraisal' in P.-M. Dupuy, F. Francioni and E.U. Petersmann (eds), *Human Rights in International Investment Law and Arbitration*, Oxford University Press, Oxford 2009, 525–56.

—— *Environmental Jurisprudence of the European and Inter-American Courts of Human Rights: Comparative Insights*, pre-publication draft, 2013, available at <ssrn.com> (published in *The Environmental Law Dimensions of Human Rights*, Oxford University Press, Oxford 2015).

Payne, C.R., 'Pulp Mills on the River Uruguay (Argentina v. Uruguay), International Court of Justice' (2012) 105 *American Journal of International Law* 94.

Pedersen, M.P., 'Standing and the African Commission on Human and Peoples' Rights' (2006) 6 *African Human Rights Law Journal* 407.

Pedersen, O., 'European Environmental Human Rights and Environmental Rights: A Long Time Coming' (2008) 21 *Georgetown International Environmental Law Review* 73.

Pelc, K., *Does the International Investment Regime Induce Frivolous Litigation?*, paper, 2016, available at <ssrn.com>.

PETERS, A., *Constitutional Fragments: On the Interaction of Constitutionalization and Fragmentation in International Law*, Working Paper Centre for Global Constitutionalism, no. 2, University of St Andrews, 2015, available at <ssrn.com>.

PINTO, M., 'NGOs and the Inter-American Court of Human Rights' in T. TREVES (ed), *Civil Society, International Courts and Compliance Bodies*, Cambridge University Press, Cambridge 2005, 47–56.

POSNER, E. and DE FIGUEIREDO, M., *Is the International Court of Justice Biased?*, John M. Olin Program in Law and Economics Working Paper, no. 234, University of Chicago Law School, 2004, available at <chicagobound.uchicago.edu>.

PREISS, E., 'The International Obligation to Conduct an Environmental Impact Assessment: the ICJ Case concerning the Gabcikovo-Nagymaros Project' (1999) 7 *New York University Environmental Law Journal* 307.

PRÉVOST, D., 'Services and Public Policy Regulation in WTO Law: The Example of the US-Gambling case' in J. VAN DE GRONDEN (ed), *The EU and WTO Law on Services: Limits to the Realisation of General Interest Policies within the Services Markets?*, Kluwer Law International, Alphen aan den Rijn 2009, 215–45.

QIN, J., *Accommodating Divergent Policy Objectives under WTO Law: Reflections on EC—Seal Products*, AJIL Unbound, 2015, available at <asil.org>.

RADI, Y., 'Realizing Human Rights in Investment Treaty Arbitration: A Perspective from within the International Investment Law Toolbox' (2012) 37 *North Carolina Journal of International Law and Commercial Regulation* 1107.

RAO, P.C. and GAUTIER, P., *The Rules of the International Tribunal for the Law of the Sea: A Commentary*, Nijhoff, Leiden 2006.

RASHBROOKE, G., 'The International Tribunal for the Law of the Sea: A Forum for the Development of Principles of International Environmental Law?' (2004) 19 *International Journal of Marine and Coastal Law* 515.

RASK MADSEN, M., 'Judicial Globalization: The Proliferation of International Courts' in S. CASSESE (ed), *Research Handbook on Global Administrative Law*, Edward Elgar, Cheltenham 2016, 595.

REGAN, D., 'The Meaning of "Necessary" in GATT Article XX and GATS Article XIV: The Myth of Cost–Benefit Balancing' (2007) 6 *World Trade Review* 851.

—— *Measures with Multiple Purposes: Puzzles from EC-Seal Products*, AJIL Unbound, 2015, available at <asil.org>.

REITZ, J., 'How To Do Comparative Law' (1998) 46 *American Journal of Comparative Law* 617.

RIDDELL, A. and PLANT, B., *Evidence before the International Court of Justice*, British Institute of International and Comparative Law, London 2009.

ROLLAND, S., 'Whaling in the Antarctic (Australia v. Japan: New Zealand Intervening)' (2014) 108 *American Journal of International Law* 496.

ROMANO, C., 'The Southern Bluefin Tuna Dispute: Hints of a World to Come ... Like It or Not' (2001) 32 *Ocean Development & International Law* (313).

ROSENNE, S. and RONEN, Y., *The Law and Practice of the International Court, 1920–2005*, Brill/Nijhoff, Leiden 2006.

ROTHWELL, D.R. and STEPHENS, T., 'Illegal Southern Ocean Fishing and Prompt Release: Balancing Coastal and Flag State Rights and Interests' [2004] *International & Comparative Law Quarterly* 171.

SANDS, P. and PEEL, J., *Principles of International Environmental Law*, Cambridge University Press, Cambridge 2012.

SCHADENDORF, S., 'Human Rights Arguments in Amicus Curiae Submissions: Analysis of ICSID and NAFTA Investor-State Arbitrations' (2013) 10 *Transnational Dispute Management*, available at <ssrn.com>.

SCHALL, C., 'Public Interest Litigation Concerning Environmental Matters before Human Rights Courts: A Promising Future Concept' (2008) 20 *Journal of Environmental Law* 417.

SCHILL, S., *The Multilateralization of International Investment Law*, Cambridge University Press, Cambridge 2009.

SCHREUER, C., *The ICSID Convention: A Commentary*, Cambridge University Press, Cambridge 2009.

—— 'From ICSID Annulment to Appeal Half Way Down the Slippery Slope' (2011) 10 *The Law and Practice of International Courts and Tribunals* 211.

——, ORTINO, F. and MUCHLINSKI, P., *The Oxford Handbook of International Investment Law*, Oxford University Press, Oxford 2008.

SCHRIJVER, N., *Sovereignty over Natural Resources: Balancing Rights and Duties*, Cambridge University Press, Cambridge 2008.

SCHULTE, C., *Compliance with Decisions of the International Court of Justice*, Oxford University Press, Oxford 2004.

SEPULVEDA, M., VAN BANNING, T., GUDMUNDSDOTTIR, G.D. and CHAMOUN, C., *Universal and Regional Human Rights Protection: Cases and Commentaries*, University for Peace, Ciudad Colon 2004.

SHAFFER, G. and TRACHTMAN, J., 'WTO Judicial Interpretation' in A. NARLIKAR, M. DAUNTON and R.M. STERN (eds), *The Oxford Handbook on the World Trade Organization*, Oxford University Press, Oxford 2012, 535–60.

SHAFFER, G.C., *Defending Interests: Public-private Partnerships in WTO Litigation*, Brookings Institution Press, Washington, DC 2003.

SHANY, Y., 'Toward a General Margin of Appreciation Doctrine in International Law?' (2005) 16 *European Journal of International Law* 907.

SHAW, M., *International Law*, Cambridge University Press, Cambridge 2003.

SHELTON, D., 'The Participation of Nongovernmental Organizations in International Judicial Proceedings' (1994) 88 *American Journal of International Law* 611.

—— 'Common Concern of Humanity' (2009) 1 *Iustum Aequum Salutare* 33.

SIMMA, B., 'From Bilateralism to Community Interest in International Law' (1994) 250 *Recueil des Cours (Collected Courses of the Hague Academy of International Law)* 217.

SINCLAIR, A., FISHER, L. and MACRORY, S., 'ICSID Arbitration: How Long Does it Take?' (2009) 4 *Global Arbitration Law Review* 1.

SLAUGHTER, A.-M., 'A Global Community of Courts' (2003) 44 *Harvard International Law Journal* 191.

SORAUF, F., 'The Public Interest Reconsidered' (1957) 19 *The Journal of Politics* 616.

SSENYONJO, M., 'Analysing the Economic, Social and Cultural Rights Jurisprudence of the African Commission: 30 Years Since the Adoption of the African Charter' (2011) 29 *Netherlands Quarterly of Human Rights* 358.

—— *The African Regional Human Rights System: 30 Years After the African Charter on Human and Peoples' Rights*, Martinus Nijhoff Publishers, Leiden, Boston 2011.

Stec, S., 'Humanitarian Limits to Sovereignty: Common Concern and Common Heritage Approaches to Natural Resources and Environment' (2010) 12 *International Community Law Review* 361.

Stephen, M., 'The 2006 Judicial Activity of the International Court of Justice' (2007) 101 *American Journal of International Law* 602.

Stone Sweet, A., 'Investor-State Arbitration: Proportionality's New Frontier' (2010) 4 *Law & Ethics of Human Rights* 46.

Tams, C., 'Individual States as Guardians of Community Interests' in U. Fastenrath, R. Geiger, D.-E. Khan, A. Paulus, S. von Schorlemer and C. Vedder (eds), *From Bilateralism to Community Interest – Essays in Honour of Judge Bruno Simma*, Oxford University Press, Oxford 2011, 379–405.

—— and Sloan, J., *The Development of International Law by the International Court of Justice*, Oxford University Press, Oxford 2013.

Tan, M., 'Upholding Human Rights in the Hemisphere: Casting Down Impunity Through the Inter-American Court of Human Rights' (2008) 43 *Texas International Law Journal* 243.

Teitel, R. and Howse, R., 'Cross-Judging: Tribunalization in a Fragmented but Interconnected Global Order' (2009) 41 *New York University Journal of International Law and Politics* 959.

The Encyclopedia Americana: International Edition, Grolier, Danbury 1986.

Thirlway, H., 'The International Court of Justice' in M. Evans (ed), *International Law*, Oxford University Press, Oxford 2006, 561–88.

Tomka, P. and Wordsworth, S., 'The First Site Visit of the International Court of Justice' (1998) 92 *American Journal of International Law* 133.

Trachtman, J., *The WTO Seal Products Case: Doctrinal and Normative Confusion*, AJIL Unbound, 2015, available at <www.asil.org>.

Trujillo, E., 'The WTO Appellate Body Knocks Down U.S. "Dolphin-Safe" Tuna Labels But Leaves a Crack for PPMs' (2012) 16 *Asil Insights* 1.

Tuerk, H., 'The Contribution of the International Tribunal for the Law of the Sea to International Law' (2007) 26 *Penn State International Law Review* 289.

Van Aaken, A., 'Defragmentation of Public International Law through Interpretation: A Methodological Proposal' (2009) 16 *Indiana Journal of Global Legal Studies* 483.

Van Damme, I., *Treaty Interpretation by the WTO Appellate Body*, Oxford Scholarship Online, 2009, available at <www.oxfordscholarship.com>.

—— 'Treaty Interpretation by the WTO Appellate Body' (2010) 21 *European Journal of International Law* 605.

Van Dijk, P., van Hoof, F., van Rijn, A. and Zwaak, L., *Theory and Practice of the European Convention on Human Rights*, Intersentia, Antwerp 2006.

Van Harten, G., *Investment Treaty Arbitration and Public Law*, Oxford University Press, Oxford 2007.

Vande Lanotte, J. and Haeck, Y., *Handboek EVRM: algemene beginselen*, Intersentia, Antwerp 2005.

Viljoen, F., 'State Compliance with the Recommendations of the African Commission on Human and Peoples' Rights, 1994–2004' (2007) 101 *The American Journal of International Law* 1.

—— *International Human Rights Law in Africa*, Oxford University Press, Oxford 2012.

Villalpando, S., 'The Legal Dimension of the International Community: How Community Interests Are Protected in International Law' (2010) 21 *European Journal of International Law* 387.

Vinuales, J. and Dupuy, P.-M., *The Challenge of 'Proliferation': An Anatomy of the Debate*, Working Paper, 2012, available at <ssrn.com> (published in *The Oxford Handbook of International Adjudication*, Oxford University Press, Oxford 2014).

Vinuales, J.E., *Foreign Investment and the Environment in International Law: An Ambiguous Relationship*, Research Paper, no. 02, Centre for International Environmental Studies, 2010, available at <ssrn.com> (published in (2009) 80 *British Yearbook of International Law* 244–332).

Voeten, E., 'The Impartiality of International Judges: Evidence from the European Court of Human Rights' (2008) 102 *American Political Science Review* 417.

von Bogdandy, A. and Venzke, I., *On the Functions of International Courts: An Appraisal in Light of Their Burgeoning Public Authority*, ACIL Research Paper, no. 2012-10, Amsterdam Center for International Law, 2012, available at ssrn.com (published in (2013) 26 *Leiden Journal of International Law* 49–72).

Waibel, M., *Interpretive Communities in International Law*, Legal Studies Research Paper Series, no. 62, University of Cambridge, 2014, available at <ssrn.com> (published in *Interpretation in International Law*, Cambridge University Press, Cambridge 2014).

Waincymer, J., 'Balancing Property Rights and Human Rights in Expropriation' in P.-M. Dupuy, F. Francioni and E.U. Petersmann (eds), *Human Rights in International Investment Law and Arbitration*, Oxford University Press, Oxford 2009, 275–309.

Wallace, R. and Martin-Ortega, O., *International Law*, Sweet & Maxwell, London 2009.

Webb, P., *International Judicial Integration and Fragmentation*, Oxford University Press, Oxford 2013.

White, R., Jacobs, F. and Ovey, C., *The European Convention on Human Rights*, Oxford University Press, Oxford 2010.

Wieland, P., 'Why the Amicus Curia Institution is Ill-Suited to Address Indigenous Peoples' Rights before Investor-State Arbitration Tribunals: Glamis Gold and the Right of Intervention' (2011) 3 *Trade Law & Development* 334.

Wilson, B., 'Compliance by WTO Members with Adverse WTO Dispute Settlement Rulings: The Record to Date' (2007) 10 *Journal of International Economic Law* 397.

Wirth, D., 'European Communities – Measures Affecting Asbestos and Asbestos-Containing Products' (2002) 96 *American Journal of International Law* 435.

Wolfrum, R., 'Article XI GATT' in R. Wolfrum, P.-T. Stoll and H. Hestermeyer (eds), *WTO – Trade in Goods*, Martinus Nijhoff Publisher, Leiden, Boston 2011, 1225.

—— 'Enforcing Community Interests through International Dispute Settlement: Reality or Utopia?' in U. Fastenrath, R. Geiger, D.-E. Khan, A. Paulus, S. von Schorlemer and C. Vedder (eds), *From Bilateralism to Community Interest – Essays in Honour of Judge Bruno Simma*, Oxford University Press, Oxford 2011, 1132–45.

Wood, M., 'The International Tribunal for the Law of the Sea and General International Law' (2007) 22 *International Journal of Marine and Coastal Law* 351.

Zimmermann, A., Oellers-Frahm, K., Tomuschat, C. and Tams, C., *The Statute of the International Court of Justice: A Commentary*, Oxford University Press, Oxford 2012.

INDEX

Law and Cosmopolitan Values

In this series, the editors envisage monographs and collections of essays that address fundamental topics in law and globalisation, which range over doctrinal as well as normative questions of International and European law, human rights, justice and democracy. A main purpose of the series is to encourage scholarship that explores and transcends the categories and assumptions on which contemporary debates on globalization are conducted, and to stimulate reflection upon questions concerning the interplay between law, policy and principle. Recognizing that there is no occasion to distinguish sharply between theoretical and systematic work in the field from an analysis of law in context, the editors welcome studies from a wide variety of methodological traditions. Contributions to the series, inevitably crossing disciplinary lines, will be of interest to students, researchers and professionals in public law, international law, human rights law, political science, legal and political philosophy. Submissions of manuscripts by anyone who is working in the field are strongly encouraged.

Instructions to authors

Manuscripts can be forwarded to any member of the editorial board at any time.

If the entire manuscript or a minimum of 2 chapters are available then the author is required to submit a detailed table of contents and brief proposal (up to 3 pages) outlining methodology, likely public, and the contribution the book is or is likely to make. If no manuscript is available, then the proposal should, in addition to the above, contain summaries of all chapters (no longer than 10 pages).

Every contribution should be accompanied by a statement that it is the author's own original work, that it is not being considered for publication elsewhere, and that it does not constitute a substantial repetition of work published or to be published elsewhere.

Manuscripts that are deemed worthy of further consideration will be forwarded by the editors to a member of the advisory board or an external expert for a second review. Peer review reports are signed and should be detailed, describing and commenting on content, methodology, likely public, and the contribution the book makes or is likely to make. In case of disagreement between first and second reviews, the editorial board will ask a third reviewer for a further opinion.

It is expected that the reviewing process will not exceed 2 months in each case.

Related link:
http://lcv.intersentia.com

www.ingramcontent.com/pod-product-compliance
Ingram Content Group UK Ltd.
Pitfield, Milton Keynes, MK11 3LW, UK
UKHW051847100926
8556IPUK00005B/498

9 781780 684468